TEOTWAWKI

The End Of The World As We Know It

Everything's Gonna Be Okay

Thomas Moore

NEWMAN SPRINGS PUBLISHING
320 Broad Street
Red Bank, NJ 07701

First originally published by Newman Springs Publishing 2020

ISBN 978-1-63692-024-5 (Paperback)
ISBN 978-1-63692-025-2 (Digital)

Printed in the United States of America

For My Four Sons
And…
To all the Haters who doubted me,
You were right.

Contents

What Is TEOTWAWKI?

The world we live in today is a deception, a sham, a house of cards that is bound to fall. It simply cannot last. Even if it is not *designed* to fail (as I highly suspect it *is*), it is at least *destined* to. If not from its own weight, then either because of natural disaster or if you're a hardcore conspiracy theorist, because the government decides to do something drastic.

In any event, TEOTWAWKI is **The End Of The World As We Know It**. One sidenote here, if you will indulge me. I am <u>not</u> a "Conspiracy Theorist." I am a conspiracy *realist*. Due to some of the things that I have done, places where I have worked or been, I have had access to information denied to others, information that confirms as TRUE many of those "theories" that so many people laugh at.

But what does it all mean, this "The End Of The World" thing? It means you are looking at the wrong end of the horse. The important part is that "*As We Know It*" bit. We are all accustomed to living our useless little lives in this greed-driven, alcohol-fueled, medication-soothed, drug-enhanced, always connected theme park that we have designed for ourselves. It is so far removed from the life that MY generation grew up with that it is almost like Fantasyland. It is so far from the lives of my grandparents that it might as well be another planet entirely.

The year was 1966. I was fourteen years old. I had built my first band, and the keyboard player was the son of a successful insurance salesman. I went over to Jack's house one day and found his whole family gathered in the living room watching television. They were watching a show that had aired the night before!

There was *no* cable TV at that time. It was all broadcast TV. I think we had like five channels and they all went off the air at midnight. Jack's dad had just bought a video recording system from a TV station that was remodeling. It was as large as a coffee table and used a tape cassette that was about six-by-fourteen inches with two-inch tape inside. It would hold one hour's worth of programming. I had just seen my first VCR, and it cost him a whopping $4,000! <u>*USED!*</u> At a time, when you could buy a brand-new CAR for $3,000! Today, you can record thirty movies on a piece of plastic that is one-inch square, one-eighth inch thick, and costs thirty bucks.

In 1966, you would call someone on the ROTARY DIAL telephone, and if there was no answer, you tried again a couple of hours later. You couldn't even leave a message on a tape machine. There were none available on the consumer market. You just kept trying until you connected. Or you went over and waited on their porch.

Today? We pick up a cell phone to call someone, and if we do not hear their voice in forty-five seconds, we explode in rage. The world has become one where we expect, no, DEMAND instant gratification. This need to have everything we want *when* we want it and *how* we want it is one of the bigger contributing factors to mass shootings, road rage, school bullying, you name it.

It has instilled in this younger generation a sense of entitlement. "I want it now, and if I can't get it, I'm going to do something bad until I DO get it." Bad parenting has let this happen. It is the main reason that society is becoming more and more like a jungle.

Get the point? We live in a world where we have available everything we could possibly want. Being able to BUY it might be another story. But it IS out there. Food? Run to the grocery. Thirsty? Drop into the convenience store. Need to travel a hundred miles? Hit the gas station and fill up your car. Don't <u>even</u> think about the fact that just one hundred years ago that one-hundred-mile journey might take you three DAYS with a horse and buggy. TWO days if you rode a fast horse.

How many people do you know who _really_ understand the implications of the statement that there are only THREE DAYS' worth of groceries on the shelves at your local supermarket at any point in time? Thank the idiot who invented just-in-time inventory control for that one, folks. Not that it will make a hill of beans when TSHTF.

Think about what those shelves look like just four hours after the announcement of an impending snowstorm. Almost empty. What do you think they would be like if everyone heard that the US banking system was in crisis and about to be shut down? Or if there were a _really_ big terrorist attack on our soil? Yeah, bigger than 9/11. What about if the entire nationwide power grid was to be suddenly disabled? I have heard there are nine points in the US where the grid can be taken completely down by disabling just one of the nine nodes. I do not know _that_ for a fact, but I do believe it to be true.

Think about that statement. If we lost power _everywhere_, what would the effect be? How could you survive? Feed and protect your family? What happens when our lives are thrown into turmoil because we can no longer run to the store or the café? These are the things that we will discuss in this book.

Wait. Wait. Before you continue on into the gist of this biscuit, I gotta warn you. I write like I talk. I don't MEAN for it to sound totally "out there," but it probably does. That is just the net result of sixty-eight years of country living combined with some _very_ unusual life experiences. (Don't ask. You wouldn't believe it.)

There is one more caveat that I must put in here. In this book, I speak on many things, some at length, some in depth, but in order to _really_ understand any issue, you need to _do your own research_. While you have the chance. As complex and numerous as these issues are, you should consider spreading the load. Assign certain areas of research to others in your family or pack. See the more detailed description of _pack_ or _tribe_ in the chapters on Data Banking and Mi Familia. MY purpose is to tell you what you can expect and what you should be on the lookout for. NOT to give you all the answers. Maybe in book 2! (IhopeIhopeIhope)

You can be absolutely sure of one thing, and that is you are certain to find people and books out there that disagree with me. Some of them absolutely refute me, and some will even make me sound like an idiot. Which I am, of course. But that one psychological exam and two court orders notwithstanding, these dissenting opinions are to be expected when dealing with *any* subject.

So don't be despaired. Just pick one. Seriously. Believe me or believe them. I do not care. This is YOUR life, your family, your decision. YOU decide who is spreading the manure too thin to grow corn and who is trying to give you enough information to keep you alive.

AND…there are a few places where I sound like I hate cops. Don't trust cops. Ain't true, Lou. I am a 100 percent dyed-in-the-wool patriot. I support our veterans, our military, the law enforcement community and in fact, ALL first responders. I AM a first responder. I have an ingrown respect, no, love for law enforcement.

My great-grandfather was the county sheriff in the 1930s. My great-uncle held that very same office for twenty years in the 1990s and 2000s. One cousin retired a major on the sheriff department, two more as captains. And a first cousin who was permanently disabled "on the job" thirty years ago.

My family owned four restaurants in my hometown. I worked in them from the time I was nine years old. My biggest takeaway from those times was this: "Honor your protective services and they will honor you." For over twenty years, no cop or fireman EVER paid for a meal while on duty when they ate at our restaurants. And on Sunday, their whole family ate for free. And if the whole damned department showed up, fine. We fed 'em.

So, no, I do NOT have an agenda against law enforcement, but I DO know that these days, there are many more cops who have lower standards than there should be. And bad attitudes. THAT is the group I rail against. And that is because of my family members who were on the force and told me about how much they despised working with bigoted, hot-tempered jackasses. *I am only writing about those LEOs who will take advantage of the situation.* After The Fall, YOU will know, deep in your gut, if your situation, or any of your actions would warrant a visit from the police. And you will act accordingly.

So if YOU are in law enforcement and are offended by those passages, please keep in mind that I KNOW that most cops are truly good people, white hat and all. But YOU know that there are lots of people on the job who are NOT. If you're a good cop, those words were not aimed at you.

Now. Back to that "As We Know It" bit. Like I said, it will NOT be life as we know it now, but my purpose here is to give you enough information that, if you follow it, if you do your homework, if you are diligent, and if you choose your partners well, it will not matter what type of disaster befalls us. YOU will survive and thrive. Buckle your seat belt, Charlie. You may be in for a rough ride and a rude awakening.

1

Things That Could Go Wrong To Cause It

What could go wrong to end our peaceful little paradise? Darn near anything. Here, in the United States, we are especially vulnerable to minor upsets in our carefully tuned, finely honed system. Europe is not quite so exposed. Great Britain is in about the same boat as we are, but large portions of Europe could still produce food and heat and protect themselves for the most part except the big cities. China would be okay except for those cities where Westernization has taken over. Most third world countries would do just fine. But US? We are sunk. In fact, anywhere in this whole world where there are large numbers of people congregated into a small land area, they're gonna die.

My list has six scenarios that could take us down in a hot New York minute:

- Nuclear strike
- Terrorist attack
- Failure of the electrical grid
- Biological/chemical attack or "natural" pandemic
- Natural disaster, like asteroid strike or hurricane
- Economic fiasco—natural or man-made

Nuclear Strike

In what the military calls a "limited engagement," the immediate effects from the blasts would eliminate somewhere around 10–20 percent of our population due to the concentration of people in major cities. Current estimates run from 40 to 90 percent population losses in various cities. The difference being the number and type of target facilities in and around that city. Like Atlanta is expected to be hit with EIGHT warheads. Think about that. About 12 to 20 percent of our population will be lost in the first strike.

Then you have the delayed effects. Radiation poisoning and fallout will take months to work its magic, but it will get another 15 to 40 percent quickly. And it will poison the water and crops for a large area around each blast. I have heard it said that only ten nuclear bombs could take us back to the Stone Age here. And how many do YOU think would be thrown at us in that event? Fifty? A hundred? A thousand? Sure, we would strike back, but what good would THAT do us? None. And if it happened to us, do you really think there would be anyone left to HELP us? Guess again. If WE get hit, E-V-E-RY-body is going to get hit in some form. So there ain't no help a-coming, folks. It will be every country for itself.

And remember, those estimates are for a "limited" engagement. Wonder what a few days run would cost us?

Terrorist Attack

A terrorist strike on American soil? Not only possible but almost guaranteed. I know it is conspiracy theory stuff, and I cannot prove it to YOU, even though I have proven it to myself, but there <u>are</u> *terrorist training camps* located right here in America. The rumors say they are in almost every state. Like the five in Georgia and three in Tennessee that I am <u>*personally*</u> aware of.

The story has it that these camps were set up and are funded by a secret arm of the CIA. I believe *that* also! Muslim extremists, living and training right down the road. Supported and protected by your Imperial Federal Government. Did you ask "Why"?

The tale that you hear goes something like this:

At some opportune moment, in the not-so-distant future, those jihadists will be told (by someone) to go forth and be fruitful. Which means…kill everything that is not like them. They will swoop down from the hills and start wiping out everyone and everything they see. If we assume only <u>one</u> camp per state and one thousand men trained in each camp (and then returned to their lives in our communities), that's about forty-eight thousand armed and angry religious fanatics raping and pillaging their way throughout the countryside.

And that is exactly what they will do. Now look at the two states where I personally *know* there exist *three* (or more) camps each. In those areas, at least, you have three to nine thousand angry fanatics running loose in the land of their dreams, an entire nation full of infidels (that means <u>*US*</u>!) just ripe to be robbed, raped, and rendered room temp. And the authorities will do nothing to stop them. Why? Becaaauuuse…

That gives whoever is president at the time the authority to impose martial law. THAT gets him (or her) around the restrictions of *The Posse Comitatus Act*, which is a law preventing the use of American armed forces against American citizens on American soil. Do away with posse comitatus and he (or she) can turn the army, air force, marines, coast guard, Boy Scouts, Red Hat League, hotel doormen, and just about everybody else in a uniform loose on the countryside, with only the requirement to *"restore order by any means necessary"* as their guide.

There you have the makings of a massacre upon the American people. The jihadists are killing *us*, the military is killing "them," and WE are caught in the middle! "Collateral damage," some will call the decimation of American civilians. Some estimate that by the time this phase of the plan is finished, we will be left with somewhere between 10 and 25 percent of our population. Thirty to seventy million people out of the current 328 million.

Failure Of The Electrical Grid

Electromagnetic Pulse. It's a really nasty side effect of a nuclear bomb, by the way, but also achievable several other ways. Electricity and magnetism are two sides of the same coin. Where there is one, there is the other. Generate a huge electrical surge with a huge electrical voltage, and you get a huge magnetic pulse.

This magnetic pulse spreads out and affects anything electrical it may cross. Like a power line or transformer. That is where it creates overloads that burn things out. And more. If that huge magnetic pulse crosses a wire inside your car, it generates an electrical pulse that fries your car computer. No more car.

The upshot is that they intend to take down our power grid. And it really IS a grid, interconnected in so many intricate ways it is like a spider web. It was built that way on purpose, you understand.

If Arkansas is producing more power than it is using, the excess production can be instantly routed to New York or Los Angeles or Missouri. If something happened to say 25 percent of our generating capacity by a few well-placed EMPs, who do you think is going to get the juice? Wyoming? Nope. The big cities will get first call, leaving the rest of us in the dark.

I've heard lots of people say "Aw, come on, we're America! We'll rebuild it in no time. Why, I bet we'll have that ole grid back up and humming within two weeks." Apparently, these people have no clue. Did you ever drive by an electrical substation? Did you look at those huge transformers in there? Sure, you did. But I bet you never thought for one minute about how they build them. Or how long it takes. Did you?

One of those twelve feet tall, eighty-thousand-pound behemoths can take up to *two years* to manufacture! And there is almost NO backstock on those things. Almost every one of them is custom-built due to too many factors to list. But every one of those factors affects things like the size of the wire used inside and how many turns of wire to use where. There are too many reasons to list, but that grid will NOT be coming back up in a few weeks. Or a few months. Probably not within a few years, even. I have heard estimates of up to ten years to fully restore power. Bad, bad news. Really. *Very* bad news.

Biological/Chemical Strike

I suppose you could count this as a subset of terrorist attack, but I like to think of it separately since it would be a different method. And, really, any of the things listed here except for natural disaster could be instigated by either terrorists wanting to attack us, or as a false flag attack by your Imperial Federal Government. The result is the same.

Think simultaneous release of anthrax in all the major cities. Or typhoid or whatever. Or hantavirus if you want to get really creative. Maybe some VX nerve gas coming out of those chem-trailing airliners? Mass confusion, dead bodies lying in the streets for months. Uugghh. Any way you cut it, you could have literally *millions* of dead Americans within ninety-six hours. What would that do our economy? Now, do that in three or four or ten or a hundred different places at the same time. See that picture?

While we're *here*, what about the new coronavirus that's been going wild all over the world? As of this writing, _COVID-19_ has killed 96,691 people, with over 1,600,000 confirmed infections. It is popping up in some weird places. Almost as if it were being carried there and intentionally released! (Wink, wink.)

And you don't believe that your United States Imperial Federal Government is capable of doing something like that on purpose? I have four words for you. Blankets for the Indians. A well-documented historical fact. The government ordered blankets that were infected with smallpox to be passed out to an Indian tribe that refused to move. They all died. Every one of them.

As I finish this final draft, we have just entered the first stages of the 2020 coronavirus pandemic of COVID-19. By the time this book hits the shelves, we will likely be in some deep kimchi. And it's going to get much worse before it gets better. Look at what it's doing to our economy right *now.*

But I believe it *will* get better. I believe we *still* have time to prepare. Properly. So get busy. Stock up as soon as possible.

Natural Disaster

What about a series of major earthquakes shaking our cities to the ground? Dropping huge portions of our coastline into the sea? Or rising sea levels from melting ice? A large portion of our population is concentrated along the coastlines. Not because we like going to the beach on vacation, but because that is where we first set up housekeeping when we got here 250 years ago. Then, when we got to the west coast, we had to have shipping, so we started building up along THAT coast also. There is a reason there is always a concentration of cities, industry, and people around water. Shipping.

Or how about fifty tornadoes ripping through the Midwest? Throw in five or ten hurricanes bearing down on our seacoasts? Have you heard of HAARP? That's a government "weather research" program with huge multi-megawatt transmitters scattered around the globe.

Word has it that the heating or vibratory effect that this system can produce in a localized bit of atmosphere can create any of those scenarios, including earthquakes. There are many instances of mysterious large-scale deaths of birds and sea creatures that are blamed on HAARP. As an engineer, I find the concept feasible myself.

The deal is this: Any natural disaster of sufficient magnitude can greatly disrupt this country's economy. And if there were a "perfect storm" of say, multiple hurricanes hitting at once, coupled with several major earthquakes or electrical grid disruption, then we would be in a mess. Not as bad as some of the *other* messes we're talking about, but bad enough.

While I'm on natural disaster, let's talk a minute about the fragility of our climate. THE major influence on our weather here is the North Atlantic Current. That is a huge "river" of warm water flowing from the equator northward, bringing heat along with it to keep us, here in America, nice and warm. Okay, mostly.

While that warm water is flowing at or just below the surface of the Atlantic, cool water is moving southward underneath it to replace the warm water going north. And this circulation system depends on the salinity of those two streams. If too much fresh water from melting icebergs enters the North Atlantic, that will upset the salt content of the water and *BAM!* The circulation stops, the temperature *drops*.

Temperatures across North America and Northern Europe will drop rapidly. Wicked wild weather. Watch *The Day After Tomorrow* for an idea of just <u>how</u> wicked. Again, think HAARP as a possible culprit. Seriously, watch that movie if you have not already seen it. Hey, watch it again.

While we might recover from most natural disasters, the possibility is very real that we could encounter that perfect storm of issues that bring us to our knees. The powers that be <u>*could*</u> just be waiting for the right level of disaster before dumping something else on us.

While we're talking about things like climate change, natural disaster, bad coleslaw, and the like, let's take a quick look at what those things could cause. About the simplest way to do that is to check out the work done by Gordon-Michael Scallion. He has written several books and has some *really* neat maps about what he thinks the world will look like after the sea levels rise. I highly recommend looking into his work.

How about an asteroid strike? I hesitate to even bring this one up, and it is not included in the following discussions of preparation due to one especially important reason. That reason is that the odds of ANY of us surviving a major asteroid strike is so close to nil as to make no difference at all. Statistically we are about due for one. The last major strike to hit our continent was about thirty-five to forty thousand years ago.

Smaller meteors, such as the ones that created any of the sixty craters in the United States, MIGHT be survivable if you have a year or two of food and fuel stocked up already. It will be nigh akin to a nuclear winter. No sunlight, plants dying, animal life dying off, no more Major League Baseball, things like that. More ice than ANY respectable margarita would ever need. Chances of survival? Twenty percent tops. But a major asteroid strike like Tunguska? Probably less than 1 percent. So we're not going dwell on those at all.

But while I am here, I probably should say a word about things like polar shift, planetary misalignment, and the possible ramifications of all that.

IF an asteroid strikes the earth a glancing blow at the right spot, close to one of the poles, there is a very real danger that it will actually *roll* the planet onto its side, throwing our entire ecosystem into chaos from which there is no recovery. Death will be certain. It is easy to see why, in my opinion (and that of many major scientists as well) an asteroid strike will probably be an **Extinction Level Event (ELE)**.

There is also a real possibility of our magnetic poles shifting, or flipping, exchanging positions. North becomes south, south becomes north. It DOES mean that your compass will no longer accurately report the direction of what we have come to think of as "north." Maps will be useless without some idea of where North SHOULD be. It means that the GPS satellites that guide everything from taxis to Terex earth movers and airplanes to communications satellites will suddenly not know where they are. Now, for the _bad_ news. The magnetic poles have been slowly moving for decades. And they *could* suddenly reach a point where they simply *flip*. Oh yeah, there is some *proof* that this has happened several times already, historically. In the far past.

Economic Disaster

Of all the scenarios we could face, this one is my second least favorite. Meaning I do NOT like the odds of us surviving it. The downfall of the US economy is so extremely easy for someone, like our government (*or* another one!) to engineer.

I'm no economist myself, but I know a few, and they all sing the same song. It would be easy to do, and the results would be catastrophic for the entire world. World? Did he say WORLD? Yes. World. The entire world is tucked into <u>our</u> economy so tightly that if WE fall, THEY fall.

I still remember learning about pre-war Germany where people were carrying wheelbarrow loads of money to buy one loaf of bread. You think inflation is bad NOW? Give 'em a chance, and the Big Wheels can starve us out almost overnight. If it happens, it will not matter how much you have in the bank, you won't be able to get to it. It won't matter how much you have hidden in your mattress; it won't be worth squat. Nobody will be accepting our fiat currency anymore. You had best be ready.

I mean, look at where we are right now! This is about my nineteenth time through this writing and editing process, and it now has me doing the final edit before this book goes to press. And right now, we are at the bleeding edge of the COVID-19 outbreak.

Hand sanitizer selling online for $70 a bottle. Toilet paper being hawked on street corners at a hundred bucks for a pack of twelve rolls. Grocery shelves everywhere are empty. There are already restrictions on travel in some areas, and there is talk of a nationwide ban on interstate travel. Where will it end?

After The Fall

Out of all the ways that we could get our collective hats handed to us, the REAL issue is what happens *after* whatever happens, happens! There is a <u>Presidential Directive</u>, #13603 by name, signed by President Obama, that gives the government, in the event of martial law, the power to confiscate EVERYTHING you have that could help you survive. Fuel, food, medicine, tools, transportation, and weapons. *<u>ALL</u>* of it! *<u>READ THAT AGAIN.</u>* Then, **READ THAT AGAIN!**

I didn't believe it either when I first heard about it. And being the skeptical, untrusting rascal that I am, I went straight to the horse's mouth, so to speak. (Or jackass, as the case may be. It WAS done by Democrats.)

I went to the Library of Congress. You can too! Get online and go to ***www.loc.gov*** and search for Executive Order 13603. Download it and read the whole thing. You will find that it is true. ALL of it.

Does THAT scare you enough to make you want to bug out right now? More on this later.

Now, I would like to spitball for a minute. There are rumors out there about things like "Agenda 2100," "Agenda 2010," etc. There are more numbers than you can name. And the end game of ALL of those things is this: somebody "out there" wants to reduce the world population to almost nothing. Why?

Because THEY own the armies and the manufacturing and the banks. Very literally. The upshot is that fewer people are easier to control. And SOMEbody has to grow the corn, pick the cotton, build them yachts, and roll them SEE-gars. Guess who that will be? Those few of us who are left. Those who survive. Those that they can FIND, that is. Those they canNOT find will be the nexus of the next revolution.

I'm not talking about the Georgia Guidestones either. The instructions contained there are really just good, common sense advice actually. You see, people…well, people are like a virus in a lot of ways.

<u>Every</u>. <u>Other</u>. <u>Organism</u>. on this planet will grow and expand into its environment without overrunning it. A herd of deer will only expand as much as the available food supply and the presence of predators will allow. Man? Man will just keep on expanding and expanding, using up everything in his path. When it is all used up, we just move on to the next piece of land. Available or not. Look what we did to the American Indians.

If this world held only fifty million people, think what a Utopia it would be. With the technology we have today, ten farms could produce all the wheat the world needs. One manufacturing plant could produce all the vehicles we need. NEED. Not *WANT*. *Need* should drive our production. Not salesmanship or profit.

That is the biggest reason I believe we are destined to fall. To fail. And it *IS* coming.

2

What Will Happen WHEN It Happens

Okay. You are here. It has happened. The excrement has impacted upon the oscillating rotational air moving device. TSHTF. What next? What do I do? Surely the police will help us! The army? Grandma? Do not count on ANY of that, bucko.

Just like it used to be way back when, it is YOUR responsibility to protect and defend you and yours. Time to man up and grow a pair. YOU are the provider, not Uncle Sam. Despite our tendency to believe in their "cradle-to-grave" care system, it just ain't true. Especially if you find yourself riding the first wave of TEOTWAWKI.

So what should you expect? The answer to that question will depend on the severity of the disaster that has befallen us all. Look at what happens: anywhere, anytime, there is a disaster. Like a hurricane. I was sitting here typing the first draft and watching coverage of Hurricane Florence, watching the looters just walking around with armloads of stuff. From weapons to televisions, food to futons. Yeah, the cops were doing their best, but they already had their hands full trying to rescue people who were stranded in cars or attics or on roofs. When lives are at stake, property is a distant third.

So where does that leave YOU? At best, we have had a natural disaster of some sort and you have decided that this is a short-term problem. Everything will be pretty much back to normal in a week or two post-event. "So we'll just wait it out right here, honey. Right here in our eighth floor apartment. With no power, no water, no heat." Well, it CAN be done. If you've properly prepared and the problem does not last more than a month or so. But if you are like 90 percent of the sheeple out there, you are NOT prepared for something like this.

For instance, protection. Sometimes it amazes me that *anybody* in this country still has a firearm at home, what with all this hoopla about gun control, etc. But if YOU do not have one, what are you going to do when the gangs get to YOUR house? Hide in the closet? You need a weapon and training, and you need it now. We will talk about how to "hunker down in place" later.

You have seen how opportunistic some people will get if given the chance. And the worse the conditions get, the longer it is likely to last, and the worse things will become. Now let's look at what will happen when the worst happens. Let us say we have been hit by an EMP attack. What do you think will be the result? Well, you will lose your electricity, of course. And you're thinking "Hey! We're okay! I have a generator and lots of gas!" Fine. That takes care of YOU. For a while. What else will you lose? Ready? *EVERYTHING*.

Without electricity, our world stops. Literally. Electricity even runs the pumps that provides your water. I had someone argue with me about this one once. He said, "You're an idiot. The water is in those big tall tanks. It's the height of the tank that provides the pressure, you dolt." I let him smirk for a full minute while I just smiled. (Real rocket scientist, that boy.) Then I said, "And just how do you think the water got IN those big tall tanks? Magic? No. It was PUMPED up there. With electricity powering the pump." Even if your water utility has backup generators, it will be a short-lived reprieve.

No electricity nationwide also means no power to run the gasoline and diesel pumps at the gas stations that fill our fuel tanks. So the big tanker trucks that bring us fuel to run those backup generators will not have fuel themselves. That's the *good* news. Remember when I said there were only three days' worth of groceries on the store shelves at any point in time? Guess what. No big trucks running…no more food coming into the stores.

The store shelves will be stripped bare in a matter of hours. And not just by criminals either. Honest, law-abiding citizens will be grabbing everything they can to prolong their own survival by a few days or weeks. What happens when THAT runs out? Everybody will turn into animals. Absolute animals. When backed into a corner, our primal instincts kick in. Survival. Food. I need food. Where is food? AHA! That old couple down the street! THEY will have some set back in the pantry! They're old. They won't need it all.

Your neighbor is hungry. He's angry because they don't want to share. The next thing you know, he has struck the old man and taken a box full of groceries from them. That is not the worst that will happen, folks. The REAL criminals out there will not only be stealing food, they will turn VERY vicious and SUPER savage. They will not stop with stealing your food when they get to your house. They will torture you and your family. They will rape you, your wife, <u>and</u> your children. Maybe the dog, too.

And when they are through having fun with you and eating your food and stealing anything they can find, they will kill you. Brutally. And just for fun, Daddy, they'll save you for last. Just so you can watch your family be raped again, maybe skinned alive and *then* killed. If you are very lucky, they will kill you before they leave. They might just leave you there, gagged and bound, to slowly starve to death. These are some <u>*evil*</u> bastards after all. Then they will go on to the next house or the next block or the next town.

While they are roaming about, stealing, killing, and creating mayhem, they will accumulate stragglers, hangers-on, sycophants, food, weapons, etc. Their ranks will grow exponentially, with one leader per pack, one *absolutely ruthless* individual who has no regard for person or property. YOU, my friend, are now at the bottom of the food chain.

The rule of law has likely gone out the window. If you see a cop on the street, it is very possible that the only thing you can count on is for him or her to try to exercise their supposed authority (which by now may be nonexistent) over you and force you to turn over your weapons, your food, your medicines, whatever. Remember this: At this point, YOU CANNOT AUTOMATICALLY TRUST

ANYONE that you do not have a preexisting relationship with. (Maybe not even *then!* You would be surprised how quickly people will change when it's their skin on the line!) More on that later.

Neighbors you have known for twenty years, coworkers, cops, people wearing what appears to be military garb, EVERYone you meet is suspect and not to be trusted out of hand. You must really grab hold of this idea…it is now every man for himself. If you are not ruthless, you are FOOD! I will repeat that. You need to HEAR it!

If *you* are not <u>ruthless</u>, you are FOOD!

At the very least, you are someone to be robbed, used, abused, and discarded or killed. It is them or you. I know, I know. It sounds harsh. It IS harsh. We are not conditioned to be harsh. We have been trained all our lives to "help thy neighbor," right? But at this point, your very survival will depend on your ability to put that behind you and get your family to safety as quickly as possible.

Okay. Let's say you are ready. You have followed this book to the T. What now? Well, while you and your family and your pack of friends who have thrown in with you to build your escape compound are busy settling in and starting up your survival camp, the rest of the world is going to hell. Those roving gangs are still roving. Still stealing, still killing. And still raping dogs. After they have taken all that they can from the immediate area in and around whatever city they are from, the gangs will start moving outward.

Take a typical big city like Atlanta, Georgia. While the city proper has a population of only 475,000, the Greater Metropolitan Area, which encompasses five very large counties, is home to almost SIX MILLION people. ALL those people are now in for the fight of their lives.

From within this area, you can expect about two to five hundred *packs* of roving killers, each containing thirty to five hundred troops, looking for food, supplies, fresh women, weapons, even children that they can grab and force to do everything from washing their clothes to performing sexual acts. And these bastards are ruthless enough to do it. The children are expendable, too. If they are not strong enough, willing enough, or just get sick, *BANG!* They are DRT. Dead. Right. There. One less mouth to feed.

Two hundred to five hundred packs of probably an average of one or two hundred people banded together. One hundred thousand killers are now at large and winding their way through the rest of the populace like a cloud of locusts. Sure, they will all encounter some resistance. Some of the gangs will be killed by decent folk trying to defend their families. Mostly unsuccessfully.

Imagine you are a man with a wife and three kids living in a nice home in the suburbs when suddenly a gang of two hundred armed thugs turn the corner. You and your wife are both excellent shots, well-practiced, and you start blowing them out of the water. Maybe.

MOST people cannot come to grips with the concept that TARGET proficiency with a weapon does not in any way translate to COMBAT proficiency. Adrenaline pumps, you hit "fight, flight, or freeze." And 90 percent of you will freeze. For those who do not, you will be successful, for a while. Until they get forty of them coming in through the back doors and windows while you're shooting at the frontal attack. You will last ten minutes. Twenty, tops. And then you get to watch your wife and kids get the treatment. You die last.

Oh, your neighbors are shooting at them too? So that's four or ten or thirty people trying to hold off two hundred. Feel any safer? I wouldn't. I would not want to be within a hundred miles of that kind of carnage. The numbers just don't support the likely survival of the average Joe. The odds are weighted too heavily in favor of the savages.

They are of a different mind-set altogether. No morals, no compassion, no scruples, no mercy. No hope. YOU would not shoot a child or an old woman, would you? Those are the people that _they_ will put out in front of their shooters as cover, human shields. You are dealing with a rabid dog here, people.

Now we are a year down the road. The gangs are still moving. These people are too lazy to try to provide for themselves. They only think about their next meal, their next high, their next sex. They know there is still plenty of all that out there for the taking. Because there are plenty of country folk out there who grow their own food, their own weed, brew their own beer, etc. All they have to do is keep moving, knocking over families and farms along the way.

These old country folks will band together ferociously. I know. I am one of them. And I have set up several community associations for mutual protection. I know some people who have plans to blow the large bridges that connect their mountain to the next. Isolation beats death, they say. But that will only slow the raiders down for a little while. I can't seem to convince them of that fact.

I think we can expect these roaming gangs to continue to hunt for maybe three to five years before they either (a) get killed off in raids or internecine fighting or (b) decide to settle down and form their own survival community. Some of the raiders will drag behind the group, hoping to find someone who will take them in, let them quit the raider life.

Personally, I would have a real hard time trusting someone who was ever a part of a raider group. Even if they were coerced into it. You _must_ remember, the raiders will NOT be above sending a kid, a sick old lady, or a scantily clad teenaged girl out to try to suck you in (pun intended). The gang will be hiding in the woods waiting for you to take their confederate in. Then an hour, a day, or a week later, they strike. Don't fall for it. You are fighting for the survival of your family.

3

How Long Do I Have?

Well, *there's* a big question, isn't it? To tell the truth, I don't have a clue. I don't believe that anyone does. Too many things to consider, and too many unknowns. The best we can hope for is to have enough time to prepare if we start getting ready. Now.

Face it. We've had a good, long run here in these United States, but I think we all know that it cannot last. Plato hit the nail right between the eyes when he said, "A democracy will last only until the people learn that they can vote themselves money from the treasury." Guess where we are right now?

Yeah, yeah, yeah, I know, this is NOT a "democracy." It's a "representative republic." BFD. A distinction without a difference. Guess what? People in this country have been voting themselves money from the treasury ever since LBJ started the Great Society in 1965, creating the current welfare state. Things have been headed downhill ever since. People have figured out that the government will pay them to stay home and have children. The more children you have, the more money you get.

I know it is not a lot of money, but if you drive through some of the neighborhoods that are populated predominately by welfare recipients, I guarantee you will see a LOT of cars nicer than mine! Understand, this is NOT a racist comment, no matter what anyone says. The welfare society is a truly classless phenomenon. White, black, red, brown, about the only color missing is GREEN. It is a mind-set only. An attitude.

The point is that we are literally on the precipice, ready to topple whichever direction the wind blows us. And we are doing this to ourselves on a daily basis. Take the gun control issue. The reason it _is_ an issue is because the only people being really vocal about it are on the wrong side of the equation. The naysayers.

Every large change in our society in the last sixty years has been because a bunch of bleeding hearts and bleating mouths started crying on television about this or that. Want to know how they think? It was summed up very nicely by a sign I saw on television during a protest where a white cop had shot a black kid who had robbed a store. A woman was holding a sign that said, "No mother should have to fear for her son's life every time he robs a store." A real Einstein, that one. But THAT, my friend, is really how these people think.

My personal belief is that we MUST hold on to our firearms. For two reasons. Number one, the Constitution allows it (so far, that is.) Two, our forefathers TOLD us that we should be ready to retake our government from time to time by means of the same force that they used to relieve themselves of the tyranny of King George. And for the same reasons. Or, in the current vernacular, "government and diapers should both be changed frequently. And for the same reason." And, finally, door number THREE, how else will you protect yourself and your family? Rubber bands with paperclip bullets?

The _problem_ with guns is not with the guns. It is with the people, with our society in general. And, in my humble opinion, with this "participation trophy" mentality crap. This junk about letting bullying continue in our schools. _That_ is one of the major factors in mass shootings.

THINK about it! A kid gets picked on his entire life, he has no strong father figure in his life, and he is left alone to THINK too much! He sees that NO one will protect him, so he takes matters into his own hands. It might be thirty years later before he acts, but that rage _WILL_ come out eventually.

STOP the bullying. Let kids WIN or LOSE. It develops character. For the love of Mike, WAKE _UP_. DON'T let the school suspend your kid for protecting himself in a fight against a bully. Make them stop. SUE them if necessary. And if THAT doesn't work, I'll back your play if you want to just go down to the school and have a "Come-To-Jesus" meeting with the principal. Be prepared for a visit from the local constabulary.

Those are just a few of the reasons that I think that the Big Fall will bring about a total collapse of the American economy. While it might take another ten years for it to all fall in place and finally crumble, it seriously could happen at any moment. It could come next week.

Be ready. You can have your bug-out bag (BoB) ready to go in a day or so. A week at the most. You can get armed within the next few days if your record is clean enough. You can have your house or apartment ready for HDIP (hunker down in place) within the week if you apply yourself. You could have a bug-out location (BoL) ready for you to skate into within the next year. All it takes is some thought and elbow grease. Well, SOME money must change hands, sure. But frankly, it can be done on a small budget if you are willing to make some adjustments, change a few priorities.

I know guys that spend $60 or $100 a week on _beer_ for crying out loud. Add another two or three hundred a month for smokes. Seven hundred bucks a month will buy you eight to twenty guns this year. You can find the land you need for a hundred-dollar-a-month payment. Remember this: when TSHTF, there will NOT be anybody knocking on your door wanting the payment for your BoL. Or your car. Or your bug-out truck or whatever.

Personally, I think maybe five years is what we've got. Of course, a natural disaster could strike YOU at any time, no matter where you live. And we have not even discussed _personal_ tragedy. What if you are sitting in a restaurant somewhere when you see a guy walking across the parking lot with a weapon in his hand? Do you think he's coming inside to meet someone who wants to buy his gun?

Not likely. If I'm in there and see that, I am going out the door, my handgun at High Ready, and I am headed straight AT this clown. If his weapon so much as shakes in his hand, I will personally introduce him to the Most High God. I will not stand by and let some idiot hurt me or anyone near me. I must be ready to act on that conviction. For <u>that</u> situation, I am already OUT of time. I must be ready when I leave the house in the morning.

For the HDIP scenario, you probably have at least a year to prepare, but you might get caught short, betting on that, so the sooner the better, Buck-o.

It takes a bit more planning, preparation, and execution to get a BoL up and running. Like I said, you *might* have five years to do it in. But the keywords are <u>*always*</u> *probably* or *maybe*. My preference would be to get the property and start caching supplies in the ground all around the edges of the property as you go. See what happened? Adjust your priorities and planning to fit your situation. Always stay flexible.

Short answer? One to ten years. Shoot for five.

Be ready in two. Start today.

4

First Steps—Weapons

We need to take a bit here and look at the things you really should get started on immediately. Like even before you finish this book. Such as procuring things that could disappear quite suddenly. Given today's antigun climate, it could easily happen at any time, even overnight, and it will definitely be without warning. You will wake up one morning and find that all the gun stores are closed. No more ammunition either. You will probably still be able to get hunting bows and knives, but there is the real possibility that guns will soon disappear from our lives. It is even possible that the government will go door-to-door *confiscating* weapons!

Until they <u>do</u> get around to that, I suggest you start at once getting concealed weapons carry permits for all adults in the family. Yes, of *course*, the list of persons with a CWC will be the first thing the cops look at when deciding where to confiscate weapons. And every time you buy a weapon or some ammo, you leave a trail of blood for them to follow.

I had a friend suggest to me that I create a paper trail relieving me of those weapons, just in case. If you want to do that, I will not argue with you. Make bills of sale showing where you sold this gun and that gun to Mr. Jones or Mr. Blalock on such and such a date, showing model and serial of each one. With differing buyer's signatures if you please.

This means that if you are working on supplying your bug-out location also, you should take those extra weapons there and cache

33

them as soon as you have them tested, cleaned, oiled, and properly packed. See the section about long-term storage later on. You are keeping a few weapons in your house, so if they come gun grabbing, give the cops a 22 rifle and a .380 ACP. Show bills of sale where you sold everything else and you should be golden. Meanwhile, there are two AR15s and four 9mm ACPs inside a compartment in a mattress. Close to the *middle* of the mattress. Or better yet, built into a false wall inside a closet. Do a good job of this, so they can't tell it. Don't forget to adequately oil and seal the muzzle and breech of the weapons to keep insects and foreign debris out while they are stored.

While we're on that tack, I would also like to recommend that for each and every weapon and piece of equipment that you buy, you take a picture of the item in multiple views, including a clear, readable picture of its serial number and the receipt. Put these on your computer and onto the external hard drive you will learn about later. File the receipt with a hard copy of the pictures and those fake bills of sale so you can "prove" chain of custody. These things will go into the safe pack of documents you will carry with you if you bug out.

If the cops come a-hunting for the guns and you hand them bills of sale for twenty weapons you allegedly no longer possess, what are you going to tell them when they ask why you bought so many weapons last year but have sold them all? Are you dealing weapons to criminals as a sideline, Mr. Smith? Plan your response so it seems reasonable and provable. (My favorite is, "Well, you know, I was trying them out to see what I liked.")

Remember, DO NOT "volunteer" any information. If the cops ask you about a Glock 17 G2 that you bought, make them give you the serial number. Then pull only THAT receipt to show them. WHY, you ask? Well, if you bought three Glock 17s last year and the cop only knows about ONE, then if you just reach in and grab a receipt and BOS and it happens to not match the one he's looking for, you are probably going to have a little chat with their baton.

You need to decide what weapons you want and how many of each. This is something you can tackle in steps, but the sooner it is started, the better off you are. I started with the idea that I would eventually bug out for good to a location where my family and a few others would dig in and stay out of harm's way. That is based on a total collapse of society and government. Therefore, my weaponry needs were predicated on the knowledge that I would NEVER be able to buy another gun or more ammunition.

If my family will live there forever, I need ammunition for thirty or fifty years. And trust me, I did NOT buy that all at once! Just to be safe, I have also bought reloading equipment and supplies for all my guns.

Your first order of business in the weapons department is for immediate survival and protection. Something you can keep in the house and car, for the moment when they become necessary. I firmly believe that every person in the family over twelve years should be trained and practiced in gun safety and marksmanship.

I understand that a large portion of the females in the country and even some males are thoroughly against firearms and most of those are just absolutely adamant about never allowing a gun in the house. That is a question for your conscience and your divorce attorney. Not me.

I believe in concealed carry. So, if you live in a state where it is legal to open carry or carry concealed with a permit, carry a weapon at all times. Get comfortable with both it and the opposition you will likely get from antigun folks.

Whenever someone asks me why I wear (carry) a weapon, I reply, "Because you do not and if something bad happens while I'm here, your wife and children can stand behind me." Every person I have said this to has come back with "My wife and kids? What about ME?" And I reply, "You don't need a gun, remember?" Then I turn and walk away.

While there are some issues with keeping weapons secured in the home, it really is easily doable. And one of the biggest issues there is training. If you have male children, they will typically love having something "adult" that they can do with dad. And the girls will often take the same attitude. But that will depend a lot on how you prepare your family for what is coming. Keep all weapons except the ones you are wearing locked in a good, secure place. And if the cops come, they will want to SEE that gun safe where you are supposed to store your weapons. It had better be almost empty. MY weapon is on my side 24-7. I come home it goes on the table next to my chair. When I go to bed, it is on my nightstand. If the cops show up, that weapon had better be ON YOUR SIDE or IN YOUR HAND, not lying on a table where the kids can get to it. Because that is the law, even in open carry states.

Children, even older teenagers, typically do not have a clue about what is going on in the world around them. They are too absorbed in social media. If you are reading this book, it's a pretty safe bet you and your partner have already discussed the possibility of the "Big Fall" or catastrophic natural disaster. If not, you need to get busy on that. And I would suggest you plan that conversation before you have it. This is not a fight you want to lose.

One of the biggest problems with the kids is that kids love to talk and brag about whatever they think is cool. Like "Hey, me and my sister? We're taking GUN lessons!" Or "Sorry, guys, I can't go. We have family target practice at the gun range." Somehow, you have got to convince them to NOT do that. One thing that will help, I think, is to assure them FOR CERTAIN that you are not planning to just up and move to the mountains next summer. If one of your kids slips up and does break the silence protocol, don't punish them for it. Take the opportunity to practice forgiveness and love. Otherwise it will leave a bad taste in the kid's mouth that may backfire on you.

Stress that all this training and preparation is just in case the country falls apart or there is a big war or something. (Another thing they should not talk about but SHOULD learn about.) Be sure to check their social media for signs that they cheated on this rule. If so, relieve them of their access. And their cell phone if necessary. Get 'em a flip phone.

Just a precaution, but there IS a possibility of things going wrong, and you want to be able to keep them alive and safe. If the country holds together, nothing in their lives will change except they will have some new skills. Kids usually hate change.

Okay, so you and your family are now committed to this course, so let's choose some weaponry. One of your first considerations is personal defense. And for that, a handgun is always best, in my opinion. Yes, I have shotguns and long guns galore, but my first purchase was the 9mm ACP that I still wear today. In fact, it is sitting on the table beside me as I type this.

I know that there are literally TONS of people out there who will argue this point, but I am pretty convinced on my choice of weapons here. Ninety percent of personal defense firefights take place within about thirty feet. And at ANY distance, the keyword is gun control. That means hit what you aim at.

I once read about a cop and perpetrator in some big city that exchanged over sixty rounds while just twenty-five feet apart on exterior fire escapes. No one was hurt. At thirty feet, a 9mm is almost as deadly as the much lauded .40 and .45 cal. But the bullet must actually *hit* something.

There are naturally some differences between the choices of caliber. With larger calibers, you can pack more punch into each round. More powder to push more bullet. And you canNOT get around the fact that it can make a difference. But in my eyes, those gains are overcome by the deficits.

For the most part (there ARE some exceptions), a 9mm ACP is much lighter than, say, a .45-caliber 1911 Colt action. Combine lower weight with the slightly lesser power, and there is less "kick" when firing it. Less kick translates to less "climb" and therefore less time needed to reacquire the target and squeeze off another round, although practice can overcome that. I am comfortable with a 9mm, and I will always use it.

In that vein, I just learned that in 2016 the FBI switched BACK from .40-cal S&W to 9mm ACP. That is significant. For me, I do not expect to run into a raider who is wearing body armor. THAT would be when I would need a .40 or .45 cal. Or a hand grenade. You can find a local gun range that will rent you a variety of weapons to try out. My local indoor range and gun shop is always willing to help a newbie pick the best weapon for them.

Okay, I just mentioned body armor, so let's talk about that for a minute. Most of it is bulky and heavy, even though today's improved versions are lighter and more flexible. And I don't know if you have heard about the new FeatherLite armor, but it is truly amazing stuff.

About as thick as your average small-town newspaper but with the stopping power of steel plate. But it is not even out to the cops yet, only the military has it.

So whatever anyone else has will be a bit restrictive and will slow their response time and mobility somewhat. But, still and all, they will be armored from toes to nose. If you are ever in a situation where you must shoot at someone in body armor, go for the throat. It's a hard shot, but the best shot. The second-best choice is the side of the knee or hip. A crippling shot, not a kill shot. But it *will* take them out of the game.

The one main thing you need to consider has nothing to do with caliber, it's about brands. I'm not here to push any one brand over another. That's between you and your wallet. The point that I have to make is this: Pick a model and stick with it. Why? Inter. Change. Ability. If everybody in your pack is carrying a 9mm Taurus Millennium G2 and one of them runs out of ammo at a critical moment, then ANYbody can toss them a magazine and it will fit.

I don't care if you decide on Taurus, SCCY, Browning, Colt, Kimber, or whatever. Get what you want. But stick with what you get. One more word, though? You should try all the frame sizes to see which one fits you *all* best. You have basically three size choices: full, compact, and subcompact. But consider that if you have three sizes of guns to work with, you have three sizes of magazines, too. My 9mms are all compact frame, and the .380s are subcompact. The kids can start out with the .380 in a subcompact, then GROW into the 9mm compact version.

A .380 ACP can be carried in your pocket, purse, glove box or briefcase. Three-eighty is basically a "9mm short." True! Do the math. Point 380 inches is equal to 9mm. It has enough punch and enough heft to the bullet to be effective as a backup weapon. Basically, it is less punch due to less powder.

I usually wear mine in an ankle holster. It is also good in a pocket or purse. And again, pick what you want but stick with what you pick. For everyone. And think "capacity." A subcompact will usually hold five to seven rounds. Some compacts (like my Taurus

G2) hold twelve rounds. Some full-size guns can carry up to fifteen bullets. And please, carry extra magazines.

Now for the long guns. I like to plan to include all possibilities. If I am building supplies to hunker down in place, I am selecting items that will also work for a bug-out. I am going to assume that if I am in an HDIP situation, I am NOT going to be outdoors hunting.

But I MIGHT be in my living room hunting or out in the backyard hunting. Thieves, looters, and killers, I would be hunting. So, for maximum effect in those scenarios, I want a shotgun. Something without too much kick, I think.

My go-to gun for that type of hunting is the .410-gauge autoloader. And once I get it home, I saw it off. I know, I know. That's illegal. And if they catch you with it, they WILL take it away from you, and they just might take you away from your wife for a while.

The best idea is just don't get caught with it. The reason I like to saw my 410 off is swinging radius. If I'm in the living room or hallway, there is not much room to swing a long rifle. We all have this tendency to get distracted, right?

So you're in a dark room at night, looking for invaders because you heard a noise. You swing to the left and fire, swing to the right and CRASH, there goes a lamp and every mother loving son on this rock will hesitate after knocking over that lamp. There you have it. You are DRT. Dead. Right. There. But I'm a criminal for sawing off a shotgun. I wouldn't have it any other way.

At the bug-out location, the sawed off is a good choice to sling on your side while you work on the site. If a killer or predator were to step out from behind a tree and draw down on you, you immediately start falling backward, out of his original sight line. Just swing that sawed off .410 up in his general direction and pull the trigger. You WILL hit him. If it's an autoloader like I recommend, you just keep firing. I also have several .410s at the BoL that are not shortened. And various loads of shells, from bird shot to slugs.

Okay, so we have got the close-quarter personal defense firefights covered. What about long range? You've battened down the hatches and hunkered down in place. Ten days later, you hear gunfire outside. You look out your window and see a gang of thugs coming your way, shooting anyone they see, breaking into houses, and taking whatever they want. What do you do?

If your IQ is above room temperature, you have already grabbed an AR-15 out of the closet false wall, and when they come within thirty yards of your home, you start picking them off. Because you have SEEN them shooting innocent people, right?

The ARs that you can buy from a gun shop are all single shot only. They're still great, but you can also find some gun nut somewhere who can convert it to either automatic or three-shot burst. I personally think that single shot is great. One, it forces you to think about your shot and get it right. Two, it conserves ammunition. In three shot (or "burst") mode, one trigger pull sends three bullets downrange. Not as bad as full auto but still wasteful in my opinion.

Those crooks in your yard will also have ARs or AK-47s. You need to be a good shot. You will want a green dot laser sight or similar. Those are sights that project a dot onto the sight glass only, so it does not alert your target that they ARE a target. Sometimes a real laser sight can be handy, also. Especially at night. But remember that a laser sight leads your adversary right back to you.

Make sure the walls beside the doors and underneath the windows are well protected. You want some serious wood under and beside those windows and doors for you to hide behind.

So now you've got your handguns picked out along with a scatter gun (shotgun) and an assault rifle. Now if you're ready to continue building your arsenal for your bug-out location, there's only a few more considerations. You need a big game rifle and a varmint plinker, plus some bow and arrow sets and a crossbow or two.

The big game rifle will also be used for defense of your bug-out location. Most people seem to find the 30-30 (thirty-thirty) or 30-06 (thirty aught six) to be the best choices. Almost the same thing, both guns shoot a 30 caliber (.308) cartridge. The "06" in the name simply means that the chambering and firing mechanism was designed in 1906 by Springfield Armory. The 30-30 Winchester designation is just a little different from the aught six.

The Springfield 30-06 is a higher velocity round, by a goodly margin. But some folks find the lesser kick of the Winchester 30-30 to be a plus. A high-power, high-quality scope is always a good investment for this gun.

For a varmint plinker, I like a .22 long rifle with autoload. Just pick a brand. Use this rifle for hunting squirrel and rabbit. Also great for shooting crows attacking your corn field. A scope is also nice on this one. Of course, no bug-out location is complete without a few shotguns for hunting and defense. The big debate is between 12 and 20 ga.

Remember that when you deal with gauges in ANYthing, smaller numbers mean bigger whatever. So the 20 ga is actually a smaller diameter shell. The 20 also has less recoil. The downside is that it is also less powerful.

You need to weigh having different guns with slightly different uses against interchangeability of ammo. Remember, you can kill a bear with a 22 pistol! Shoot him in the eye and that bullet will rattle around in his brain pan till it is scrambled eggs in there. But you have to be a _real_ good shot.

I also suggest that you get several sets of bow and arrow gear for your bug-out location. I personally like a recurve bow for small game and protection. A compound bow is great for large game and protection purposes. Whether you're talking about guns or bows, the key element is practice. LOTS of practice.

You've seen movies where the hero fires his gun at the bad guy almost without looking and hits his mark, right? That's not just movie magic, that's possible. All you need is practice. Practice and lots and lots of shafts and tips and bullets. I plan to do the majority of our food hunting with bow and arrow to conserve ammunition that I might need later. For protection.

When I was fourteen, I started taking classes in taekwondo. I absolutely _hated_ those hours and hours spent stomping up and down the room in a horse stance throwing punches or kicks. It was two years before an instructor explained it to me. It is "muscle memory." If you practice any movement enough times, it becomes an unconscious act to repeat it. Accurately. The same thing applies to hand–eye coordination. If you practice shooting enough, you get to a place where it is just point your finger (the gun) and pull the trigger.

Now let's talk ammo for a minute. For the most part, you just want the standard FMJ bullets for your handguns. That's full metal jacket. A lead bullet in a copper jacket in a brass shell. By ALL means, do NOT get STEEL CASE bullets OR aluminum. You want BRASS shells ONLY. Steel will develop small, invisible rust on the shell case that will cause jams. Brass will not.

While you might want to have a supply of specialty bullets like rippers or talons on hand (and probably loaded into several magazines that are marked to indicate a different load), the vast majority of your shooting will be with FMJ, simply because of the price. Talk to your local gun shop. They know everything that you don't.

Ammo. Quantity. MASS quantities. I own five AR-15s and ten thousand rounds of ammo *for each*. We have eight 9mm ACPs and twenty thousand rounds for each of those. I have been gathering ammo for a long time, folks. For my shotguns, five thousand shells each. The vast majority of my ammo is nitro-packed into Ziploc bags, then sealed in ammo cans that are nitro-packed and cached around my BoL. I have two thousand rounds of 9mm, one thousand rounds of .380, and two thousand rounds of .223 for the AR-15 that I keep around the house. Speaking of the AR, I have five magazines of fifty round capacity for each weapon, loaded and ready. You should also have about five to ten extra magazines for *each* handgun. Loaded. In some sort of canvas or leather bag that is easy to grab and run with.

I have also invested in a supply of replacement parts for my guns. Particularly magazine springs, main slide springs, trigger springs, and firing pins. That way I can keep those guns shooting for years. You also need to invest in several cleaning kits for each weapon. If you have four handguns, get four cleaning kits and like twenty extra bottles of cleaner and oil and patches for each kit. Cleaning your weapon is essential. Clean it often. Particularly after firing it for any reason. A gun has only two enemies—rust and politicians. And remember, you are buying enough supplies to last thirty years. You will need it. Nitro-Pak ALL supplies for longevity.

Here's a partial list of parts you should have for various weapons:

For Semi-Auto Handguns

Recoil spring	Extractor and spring	Hammer
Firing pin and spring	Sear	Mainspring
Ejector and spring	Trigger spring	

For Rifles

Firing pins	Firing pin springs	Sear
Extractor pin	Extractor	Hammer
Trigger spring	Extractor spring	

For Shotguns

Extractor and spring	Firing pin and spring	Hammer
Trigger	Sear	Spring

Revolvers:

Cylinder pin spring	Cylinder latch spring	Cylinder release spring
Ejector rod	Mainspring	Ejector rod spring
Hammer	Sear	Trigger spring

The bow and arrow is also a formidable weapon, and it has several advantages over guns. Namely, it is quiet. But it does require a bit of practice to become proficient in its use. Personally, I like the recurve bow. It's just a regular old long bow with the tips curved forward. That gives you a little bit more oomph to your shaft.

Of course, most hunters these days prefer the compound bow. The pulleys give the arrow a much higher speed, and higher speed means more penetrating power and greater range and accuracy. Whichever bow you choose, be sure to get *lots* of extra strings, lots of different tips, and plenty of shafts and fletching and other repair parts as needed. Take courses from your outdoor shop in maintenance, safety, and shooting. Remember, after The Fall, you will never see another outdoor shop. So get all the supplies and training you can.

One good thing about arrows is you can usually retrieve them after they are shot. Unlike bullets! So you get to reuse them again and again.

A shooting instructor once told me that you can take a bullet— that's just the lead part, not the entire cartridge, mind you—hold it out at arm's length and shoulder height and drop it. When it hits the ground, that's the same time a bullet leaving your rifle would hit the ground. That's why you have to elevate your muzzle when firing long distance, to account for the falling of the bullet. I've never heard otherwise, and I have not tested the theory, but it makes sense to me. And you can probably assume that an arrow does likewise.

But really? Your bullet leaves the muzzle at something like 900 to 1,500 FEET PER SECOND (in most cases). That's a quarter of a mile! If you're shooting at something a hundred yards away, that's three hundred feet, so maybe one-fifth the distance the bullet travels in one full second. So, if your test shows the bullet will hit the ground in 4/100ths of a second, then the distance it falls in three hundred feet is just an inch or so. But that is a significant distance, and it *will* cause you to miss your target.

Whether you're talking about guns, bow and arrow, boomerangs, or water balloons, the only way to get proficient is to practice. Every member of the pack should practice several times a week if possible until they can hit the bull's-eye nine out of ten times at twenty-five feet, eight out of ten at fifty with a handgun *or* bow and arrow, and at least six of ten at one hundred yards with a long rifle in quick-fire. And by bull's-eye, I mean the four-inch circle in the very center. All other shots should be in the eight-inch circle.

Let us also keep in mind that target proficiency DOES NOT equate to combat proficiency. It is a science unto itself to explain why. Just expect it to happen. Here's a few tips:

(1) Practice drawing your weapon from many positions.
(2) Each time you draw your weapon, also draw a spare magazine, and hold it oriented correctly to slam into the gun. Understand that when push comes to shove in a firefight, your adrenaline becomes the boss, and the first thing he

has you do is FORGET everything you have ever learned or practiced.

When you make trips to the BoL to work, try to include everyone. They can all be useful in some manner. And get in some practice. Make some man-sized targets to place in various locations throughout the woods. Make sure everyone knows to NOT shoot toward the central compound at any time. Practice, practice, practice. Until it becomes automatic for everyone to draw, fire, and hit their target and reload their weapon.

Teach everyone how to "circle the wagons." If you are attacked, it is a sure bet that the brunt of the attack will come from one direction, but it is just as likely that smaller forces will be circling around to flank you. You should have at least one person facing the areas that are not the main attack. Everyone is to continually scan the area in front of them only and to shoot approaching enemy ONLY in THEIR area of responsibility. If they try to help the person to their left, they are lowering their guard on THEIR area, and that is when it all goes south. Don't do it, unless it is MOST dire.

Think of your circle like a clockface. The main attack is coming in at twelve o'clock, directly ahead. <u>You</u> are protecting from eleven o'clock to one o'clock. You might want two or more people aiming in that direction with you. You also want one person facing two o'clock, and they are scanning from one to three. Another person faces four o'clock and scans and protects from three to five.

Continue like this around the clock. Get everyone used to thinking and talking in terms of the clockface. Directly ahead is twelve o'clock, directly behind is six, the sides are three and nine. So if someone says, "Deer at five o'clock," we all know where to look.

Knives, you will need knives. Not just for close quarters combat, you will also have to clean and skin animals, from squirrels and rabbits to deer and bears. A ten-inch Bowie is a rather good choice for a knife to carry on your belt. Big enough to kill things or cut small trees. But it *is* a little unwieldy for skinning rabbits. Remember that outdoor shop? Talk with the knife salesman. He'll know what to recommend.

I *would* like to suggest that you get a set of throwing knives also. And practice with them. You will never know how handy that skill can be. It is even possible to hunt for small game with throwing knives once you get good at it! But the big deal is that you can kill a man silently from twenty to forty feet away.

A flensing knife, and a standard 3½" blade lockback knife should round out your knives unless you or your outdoor shop expert can think of something I have missed. And sharpening equipment. Manual or auto. Whetstone or motorized sharpener. Or all of them. Everyone should carry a pocket stone or steel on their person at all times. You never know when you will need to touch up your edge.

Be sure to get plenty of extra shafts and tips for the arrows, and reloading gear for the guns. When I target practice at the farm, I spread a tarp where the brass is destined to land and just collect it all up when we're done. Brass is hard to find in the grass. And impossible to buy after The Fall.

You will obviously want multiple copies of everything, even gun cleaning kits. Keep one out for use and put the rest in storage. Nitro-packed in a good tight ammo case. Plastic cases are fine for everything but electronics. Those must be in metal cans and nitro-packed. Grease the can gasket with Vaseline and cover the hinge and the metal lock bar with it also. Also, it wouldn't hurt to tightly wrap the ammo can thoroughly in multiple layers of plastic cling wrap, just for added protection.

5

Get Tough

In today's world of comfort and convenience, people are turning soft. Some folks manage to make it to the gym, most do not. I must admit that even *I* did not go to the gym yesterday. That makes six years in a row now. But the real tragedy is that this translates into one fact: I dare say not one in five thousand regular people can hold their own in hand-to-hand combat with your average street tough. Now, *that* is a crying shame.

But do you know what the biggest difference is between the average Joe and your common street thug? Scruples. *They* have none. They have an overinflated sense of self-worth coupled with zero regard for others, multiplied by a huge sense of entitlement and that equals no scruples. The only thing that matters to these people is what they can get for themselves with zero to low effort. In other words, they care only for themselves. The property, well-being, even the *lives* of others is of no consequence to them.

That is how they manage to feel that they can rob without regret, mug with malice and kill with no conscious. And because of the fact that *they* live in a world where those things are the norm, a place where you must fight every day to keep what little you have, they are so much more prepared to enter into a fight with confidence. Most "normal" folks do not have that drive to survive like that. That "will" that says they will drive a truck over a child if it means _they_ get to survive one more day. No compassion.

The *second* most important difference between they and you is ferocity. Which translates as "He who hesitates is lost." I have taught many seminars on "Self-Defense for Women" over the years, and the one concept that is the hardest to get across to women is *DO NOT WAIT.* If you are confronted, your opponent will often dance around you, literally and figuratively—just to "play" with you. It has several effects. One, it is unnerving. It makes you scared. And two, it gives them time to work up a good "mad." Both of those are huge advantages to them, but number one is the worst. If you are scared, you can_not_ fight well.

So the primary rule in fighting is **_JUMP!_** Do not wait. The moment something does not look right or feel right. STRIKE. _HARD_. And relentlessly. You see it all the time in the movies. There's the big fight scene when bad guy gets the hero knocked down, they dance around or step back to admire their work. That is their mistake.

Because THAT'S when the hero gets back up and kills him. If you GET them down, KEEP them down. You are fighting for your life and the lives of your loved ones. DO NOT BACK UP. KEEP POUNDING UNTIL THEY ARE DEAD! It is you—or them, pal. A kick to the throat is worth twelve to the gut. FALL on their throat OR HEART with your knee and they will not get back up. Period.

I know what you're saying…you're asking, "Do I really need to think like that to survive?" No. We all know better. But you DO need to think that way to survive against *them*! So the answer is really, yes. How does all that relate to the title of this chapter? It is because that "I don't care about anything or anyone" attitude permeates their entire existence.

Nowhere is it more visible than in a fight or some other act of violence. That is where you really see this attitude pay off for them. If you don't care about anyone other than yourself, you pull no punches. You do not hesitate. *That* is their secret. But you can ACT that way when needed and still be a loving, caring person.

It took me a long time to realize that truth. I had been picked on most of my life, and at the age of fourteen, I signed up for karate classes. I figured I _had_ to learn how to fight. I learned much later that it was not _how_ to fight that I needed, it was the *confidence* to walk into a fight, unafraid, that I lacked. That confidence is automatic when you have nothing to care about, like a thug does. But for caring, thinking people like you and I, it impedes our ability to be effective fighters.

Great. Now I'll get a million letters from ex-military saying, "I know how to fight, and I care about people!" Yeah, but when you go into the military, the first thing they do is tear you down mentally and rebuild you. That's what basic training is all about. Make you a new person in their image. So *you* are a total anomaly in this discussion. Get over it. Also, thank you for your service.

The point of all this falderal is this: YOU need to get tough. Well, you and all your tribe, actually. Are you *all* tough enough to make a three-week hike under super-stressful conditions? If you get jumped by a thug or a wild dog (like there's a difference), can you muster the grit to be fierce enough to prevail? That is what you must develop in yourself. The attitude, the toughness, the WILL to win. Coupled with the skills necessary. I mean, all the attitude in the world won't help you if you can't make a fist or throw a punch or *block* a punch, will it? But, yeah, you gotta lose the *fear*, mainly. Develop the *fierceness*.

There are tons of disciplines out there that can teach you to defend yourself. My personal favorite is taekwondo. I'm also very fond of Krav Maga. If karate is your thang, find a dojo with a sensei who is tough yet compassionate, hard but fair, driving and driven. Learn to defend yourself correctly. You need to toughen your body all over, increase your stamina, your resistance to pain. But mostly, you need to develop an intense mental attitude. One of concentration and focus. A will that cannot be broken cannot be denied.

If it's Krav Maga you krave (sic), get yourself an Israeli ex-pat, any high-level CIA covert operative (I think there are like 214 of them left), select First Recon guys, or Lrrr, ruler of the planet Omicron Persei 8. If you convince one of these to teach you, you will be the most awesome force on the planet.

And if or, rather, *when* that "golden moment" arrives where you find yourself in that fight for your life, there is one thing to remember. In any physical confrontation, "He Who Hesitates Is Lost" is more than just an old saying. It is your mantra. If someone jumps out from behind a bush and sticks a gun in your face, you have two choices. ONE: You hesitate. You freeze. For one tenth of a second, you do nothing. And you lose. Maybe your life.

Or TWO: You spin into the arm with the weapon, grab the hand, pushing it up, twisting the palm UP then jerk the back of his elbow down across your shoulder with all of your strength and will, breaking the elbow. Grab his gun and kill him. Because you do NOT want this, this ANIMAL to ever do that again. To *any*one. I don't care if he was your neighbor yesterday. Don't forget to riffle his wallet.

THAT is the difference between you and him, your mugger. He does not care if you live. He is willing to kill you for your money, your gun, or your kids. YOU must be willing to disable or kill him in exchange for your life. These mad dogs who have no regard for others *never* hesitate. They charge in swinging as if it is their birthright. And in order for you to win, you must be able to do the same.

A few quick tips: Gouge the eyes. Don't be afraid to damage them. HE wouldn't. If grabbed from behind, rake the outside of your foot against his shin from the knee down. HARD. Ladies, grab him by the ear and twist it hard while taking him to the ground. On the way down, bring your near knee up into his nose HARD. Throw sand in his eyes. Clap both hands over his ears VERY hard. Breaks eardrums. Very painful. Stick an ink pen into his nostril and push it up hard. Or jab it in an ear. DEEP. Remember, you are fighting <u>for your</u> life. NOT just trying to discourage an attacker. THIS IS YOUR LIFE AT STAKE!

6

Meet BoB

Your pal, your buddy, your lifeline. BoB. Your bug-out bag. In the event that you and yours must leave your home for good and head to your bug-out location (BoL), this bag is your lifeline. It must contain everything that you need to survive in the wild until you reach your BoL.

It doesn't really matter if you will be able to drive out or if you have to walk out, your BoB will save your life. IF you have put enough thought and effort into its preparation. BoB can also save your life should you get stuck out on the highway in a snowstorm, flood, or behind a huge wreck that blocks everything up for a few days.

Consider this: The balloon goes up, meaning The End has come. Time to leave. You and yours are driving to your BoL, five hundred miles away. About halfway there, you encounter a group of raiders who are the Bad Boys of Baden County. And they want your stuff. You manage to fight them off, but they killed your car. A bullet in the radiator. What will you do? You will walk if you can't find a car to steal AND have the know-how to steal it. (But there IS an emergency repair for a *small* leak in the radiator that involves a common condiment!)

There are many things to consider when assembling this vital piece of your overall strategy. It must be multipurpose and able to adapt to your immediate need. You will probably not have enough time to repack it if the situation changes, so do it right the first time.

Let us take a few minutes to talk about what you will *likely* need. Your individual needs might dictate changes to my recommendations, and that is fine. The important thing I want to accomplish here is to get you to *thinking* about the process of putting it together for YOU!

First off, there is the issue of clothing. No matter where you are headed or how, you will need to change clothes occasionally to keep yourself comfortable and alert along the way. If you get filthy dirty, you will feel awful, and with today's mind-set about cleanliness, it will start to nag at your mind until it is all you can think about. And then you are no longer alert enough to help guide and protect those with you.

Of course, there are some adjustments, some compromises that must be made. You cannot possibly carry enough clothing to let you change every day or twice a day or whatever you normally do now. You'll have to settle for changing every two or three days. And you will have to wash some, too. But that extra clothing in your BoB will come in handy if you're caught out in an emergency situation that will last a day or twelve.

Your choice of clothing for this journey must by necessity be geared toward utility and durability. You need dungarees, not do-dads. No fancy shoes or pretty blouses. If your wife or daughter wears a pretty blouse while trekking through the woods and it gets snagged on a branch and tears, leaving a shred behind, then anyone following you _knows_ that you have a beautiful lady with you. And that is probably JUST what he wants. Also, by wearing a durable work-type shirt, a female can more easily pass as a man if she puts her hair up under a hat. A scarf is also a dead giveaway. And no jewelry, please.

I have never been a fan of camo pants and shirts in the civilian world, I think it looks tacky. But when you are in this situation, you need to be unseen as much as possible. So I really recommend that all your wearables be camo.

No matter how long the journey, each person should carry no more than three changes of clothing, plus the one they wear makes four. Five extra changes of underwear, five changes of socks, and maybe two extra pair for warmth. You might consider reducing that to two full clothing changes and three of underwear. You choose. But that's about two or three pounds less that you will have to carry.

You are wearing one pair of boots and maybe carrying an extra. You should also carry tennis shoes and a light, airy shoe like you would wear to the beach or lake. This is to slip on quickly for those late-night runs to the local log to answer a call of nature. But I said *shoes*, not flip-flops.

If you are out in the woods at night going "toity" and you miss, they get soiled. Your next day's travel is not delayed or uncomfortable if you are wearing those light shoes instead of your boots or tennis shoes. And you can wear them to go into the creek to wash clothes without ruining your main boots. Also, be sure to carry waterproofing for your boots and keep it applied frequently. If the ground is soft and damp, you don't want it seeping into your footwear if you can avoid it.

Also pack two sets of boot laces and one spare for the tennis shoes. Toiletries, like toothbrush, toothpaste, a bar of bath soap (that can also be used to wash clothing), towel, and face cloth. By the way, bar soap will be best for washing clothes in the wild. It does not suds up so much and the suds will dissipate quickly, leaving a much smaller indication downstream for someone to follow.

You will want everyone in your tribe to carry one of those little "Clicker" child's toys that makes a distinctive clicking noise when pressed. They are great for almost silent, nonverbal communication. Make up a code and practice it. Keep it in your pocket.

Two tee shirts. At *least* one set of long underwear. You never know what time of year you'll be going, plus it could be a "day after tomorrow"-type scenario where the weather is really screwed up. Be prepared. You will also need some leather gloves for heavy work, a pair of decent cold weather gloves and a lightweight glove to wear as you walk. These should be light enough that you can carry two or three pair without knowing it. And maybe ten pairs of nitrile surgical gloves. And hand sanitizer. Disease is everywhere. All types.

This is not an advert or endorsement, but I like Gorilla Grip gloves myself. They are stretchy with a rubberized palm, offering a great grip that is very comfortable, and they shed water well. And you would be surprised how much that comfort can mean during a long day's journey through the woods. Round out your clothing set with a light jacket, preferably water resistant if not waterproof, plus a heavier jacket, just in case. OH! OH! A poncho!

And don't forget hats or caps. I keep a knit cap (watch cap) and full face knit (ski) mask for blizzard conditions. I find a brim hat is indispensable and more versatile than a bill cap. But it is *your* choice. Remember, this stuff is just for travel. You should have plenty of clothing already stashed away at the BoL.

Everyone in the pack should carry his or her own medicines and sanitary products, including toilet paper, cloths, towels, and, yes, menstrual supplies. As for TOOLS, each person should carry a folding multipurpose entrenching tool. You might ALL have to dig and dig fast. A hatchet, and/or machete, twelve- to sixteen-inch folding saw, flashlight, spare batteries, small camp light, and a headlamp. And a lot of spare batteries. At least two changes for each lamp. Did I mention spare batteries?

I have several bags that easily attach to my MOLLE backpack for things like batteries and toilet paper. Things I might need to access in a hurry.

Possibly one of those three function LED headlamps that will also produce green and red lights. Green is really great for walking in the woods at night. It is hard to see from a distance, and it lights your way really well. The red setting would be used inside a structure, tent, or cave. And don't forget spare batteries. Everyone should have a good belt knife, like an eight- or ten-inch Bowie.

And you will need extra ammunition for your sidearm and/or rifle *on your person, not inside your bag*. A good walking staff can be useful during a hike like this, and it also can be used as a weapon. Get a book or take a course in quarterstaff combat. And practice. A lot. Practice quarterstaff against opponents who are unarmed, and those who are armed with a rifle or staff or even a handgun. Maybe attach a knife blade to the top end of your staff.

Each person should have a bedroll or sleeping bag and a tarp or eight-by-twelve-foot piece of heavy plastic. Maybe two. Everyone should carry four to six pieces of quarter-inch poly braid rope about twenty-five feet long and a fifty or hundred feet length of ½" poly core braided utility rope along with about eight carabiners. Not the el cheap-o ones you get at Ace or Wal-Mart. You want _good_ carabiners. Maybe not the premium titanium for mountain climbing, but at least guaranteed to support 300# or so. Carry your own mess kit, water bottle, water filtration straws, a fire starter, and personal field rations.

If the carabiners and/or mess kit are attached to the outside of your pack, be sure to muffle them to keep them quiet. You do not want some clanking pot to attract predators, either two- or four-legged.

There should be a few fishing kits and filet knives among your troop. And everyone should carry their personal one gallon of water for the first day. Carry your own compass and a copy of the map to the BoL. And a small brush or something to clean your own mess kit. Like a nylon scrub pad.

Let's not forget that your clothing choices must be tailored to fit seasonal and regional differences also. If you live up north, you need everything heavier. Also consider battery heated socks. They rock.

You can divvy out the "one-off" items that must accompany you. Like a sewing kit, first aid kit, SUTURE KIT, cooking grate, cooking supplies, and utensils. Folded-up aluminum foil is a must-have. Someone must carry the axe, the bow saw (with blade guards, mind you). The leader MUST carry a lensatic compass, map, and binoculars, but it would be prudent if everyone had their own compass, at least.

If you can possibly do it, I would also highly recommend that you get maybe two sets of night vision goggles. They can be invaluable for traveling or tracking at night. But be warned, if someone (like a raider) shines a flashlight at you, you will not be able to see for fifteen to thirty minutes.

If one or two people want to carry a two- or four-man tent, okay, but I don't recommend it. I would prefer to spread one of the eight-by-twelve sheets on the ground and cover the area using the other plastic sheets supported by the small ropes. A tent can be too much trouble to take down and pack in a hurry. It's hard to think about, but you might have to bug out while you are bugging out.

I would rather see you take the time to put together a lean-to shelter than pitch a tent. You can run away from a lean-to and never miss it. Not so much with a $400 tent. But if you DO make a lean-to shelter, be sure to scatter its components when you leave, if you have time. Tents can make you _too_ comfortable. Wherever and however you bed down, don't forget to trench around the bed area for water runoff in case of rain. Don't forget to make a two-foot-deep latrine about thirty feet away from the bed. When you leave, cover the latrine and scatter any debris, track, or remnant of your presence. Trash should be fifty feet from camp.

<u>RECAP LIST</u>

Individual BoB

Personal identification
Two or three changes clothing
Four or five changes underwear
Four or five changes socks
Two extra tee shirts
Long underwear
Extra boots with two sets extra laces (extra boots are optional)
Tennis shoes with extra laces
Lightweight water shoes
Leather work gloves
Lightweight general duty gloves—two or three pairs
Cold weather gloves
Watch cap
Ski mask
Light, waterproof jacket
Heavy coat
Rain poncho
Bill cap or brim hat

Personal medicine and sanitary needs
Toiletries—toothbrush, toothpaste, bath soap, towel, facecloth, face
    towel, toilet paper
Folding multipurpose entrenching tool
Folding saw
Camp light
Headlamp—three functions include green/red light
Four sets spare batteries for each light
Bedroll or sleeping bag
Eight-by-twelve feet tarp or heavy plastic, like 9-mil polyethylene
Four pieces 25' × ¼" polybraid nylon rope
One-hundred-foot coil of one-half-inch poly core nylon-braided
    utility rope
Eight carabiners (wrapped in towels for soundproofing)
Mess kit—muffled
Water purification tablets, filtration bottles, and straws
Salt tablets
Fishing kit and filet knife
Fire starter kit
One gallon water: probably as four one-quart bottles
Seven days' rations if short distance, three days if it's a long haul with
    cached supplies
Two sets spare eyeglasses (if needed)
Sunglasses
Several quart and gallon Ziploc bags
Copy of the map and location notes for supplies caches
Waterproofing for boots
Surgical masks (two minimum) and nitrile gloves (ten to twenty
    pairs)
Two or three days' freeze-dried food
Two or three days of emergency rations like power bars

Worn on the person

Sidearm _and ammo_. LOTS of ammo. At least two spare magazines
    for each weapon per person plus a hundred rounds loose
Canteen for quick water access
Bowie knife
Hatchet or machete
Flashlight—small, pocket size
Pocket multitool
Clicker
Compass
Pen and pocket pad
Throwing knives
Radio (walkie-talkie)

Common items to spread out

Cooking grate
Cooking pot or pan
Utensils
Aluminum foil
Sewing kit
Suture kit
First aid kit
Small bow saw with blade guard
Axe with blade guard
Washing brush
Scrubbing pad for pot washing
Possibly enough tents for the troupe
Possibly two sets night vision goggles

Additional items for leader

Binoculars
Rifle with scope
Map
Lensatic compass
Writing utensils and pocket pad

COPIES of wills, deeds, titles, proof of purchase for weapons. The originals of all these are safe at your BoL. These copies are in a waterproof pouch.

There is nothing to say that each individual can't carry their own binoculars or telescope or whatever. But everything you add to your pack increases its weight and therefore its toll on the body. Your call.

For the pack itself, may I recommend a military-style pack that supports either MOLLE (Molly) or ALICE attachment points, plus the necessary bags and things to make those attachment points really useful.

7

Hunker Down In Place

Well, your next decisions will determine what course you will take to survive this mess. There are really only two options: hunker down in place or bug out. Pretty self-descriptive, hunh? Let's take a quick look at deciding whether to hunker down in place or not, and what your needs will likely be.

So what kind of scenario are you going to prepare for? How long do you expect it to last before normality returns? If we're talking natural disaster stuff, like hurricanes or tornadoes, things could be back to normal within a week or two. Or not. Remember how bad the Katrina/Rita debacle was in New Orleans?

Thirteen years later, I would argue that New Orleans is *still* not "back to normal," but it was pretty functional in about two *years*. People could return to their homes, mostly, within one year, depending on the location and amount of damage. But those who were displaced were at the mercy of FEMA to provide "temporary" housing, which amounted to a bunch of RVs. A large number of people just up and moved to other areas, sometimes other states.

Usually, you can return home after a hurricane or other natural disaster as soon as the utilities are restored. That is, if your home is still there. And will your goods still be there? Will your house be livable? Will you have power? Water? Heat? Black mold?

So, just as an exercise, let us assume:

(1) There is a hurricane inbound.
(2) Your house or apartment is far enough inland and strong enough to probably not be blown apart by the wind.
(3) Your house or apartment is high enough that it will not be damaged by the water.
(4) The total damage from the storm is expected to be less than catastrophic, area wide.

In other words, life will return as soon as utility service does. Your best bet here is to hunker down in place. Stay home, protect your family. Unless you live on the fourth floor of a beachfront condominium. You know. Use your common sense. Unless you have none. In which case, you're doomed. Preparing to **Hunker Down In Place** is pretty straightforward and can be accomplished pretty quickly if you are dedicated and determined.

Many of the steps are the same you would take if preparing to bug out. Many of the items needed to HDIP will be the same as those found in your bug-out bag, and this might be the ideal time to rotate some of those out of the bag, depending on how old they are.

Let's take a look at what you will need to stay alive for a few weeks. First, we have to assume that you will NOT be leaving the house or apartment. Perhaps necessitated by the bad weather or maybe the presence of crime or a criminal element, but whatever the reason, you need to remain behind locked doors for a while.

The first issue of course is food. How much will you need, and what kind? Will you have electricity during this emergency? Will it STAY on? Probably not. Although we can hope for the best, it is best to plan for the worst. Since food is our first necessity, and electricity may be an issue, you should consider that the first food you will eat comes from the freezer or fridge. Cooking it may be another issue. But that's another issue.

The point is, without electricity, all those frozen pizzas are going to waste! So, eat the cold stuff before it becomes the old stuff. There are some great camp stoves and camp ovens out there that run on propane or Coleman fuel. You might want one of each, a stove and a cooktop. At least a two-burner cooktop.

And once you get the fridge emptied out, be sure to toss out anything that was left. Pour liquids down the sink and rinse once. You do not want it stinking up the place. Then tape the fridge doors shut with a wedge or something in the crack to hold the door open one-half inch to let air circulate in it. Food box AND freezer get this treatment. Thank me later. Don't do that exactly and you WILL be sorry.

THAT said, you really need to know HOW much food you will need and what kinds. Do you have children? What are their ages? What are their usual consumptions? Is there an infant to consider? A senior? How about special dietary requirements for things like diabetes, IBS, or other disorders?

All these factors must come together to make your emergency food plan. It is not my intent in this book to cover every detail of how to do everything. Lots of this stuff I talk briefly about just to make you aware of its existence and your need to think about it, plan for it, and DO something about it.

Make a consumption plan that includes all members of your family eating three meals and maybe two snacks per day. This would be your family's full meal deal. We're not talking chicken primavera here, folks. We're looking at freeze-dried beef stroganoff and protein bars. And water. Don't forget the water.

Keep in mind that there are ways to make water more palatable. Flavorings, additives, things like lemonade mix or Kool-Aid or Mio, and instant tea or coffee. I also keep powdered creamer around for my coffee and individual packets of sugar. Once again, don't forget special dietary needs. Like infant formula. One note here…if you have figured your needs to last for four weeks, you need to reevaluate your needs at the 50 percent point, or two weeks, into the disaster scenario.

If things are not improving, you should consider going on half rations from that point forward. I figure for four weeks and keep FIVE weeks supplies at the ready. Keep the protein bars and survival foods from your bug-out bags for last, maybe. Now that you have figured for three meals and two snacks, see how little you can live on.

It might take longer than you think for things to return to normal. I also have a four-month supply of survival pack food for each person in the house. With the regular food, we have maybe five or six months' eating available. I am NOT staying in my house for five months! I hope. But I AM prepared to.

Keep in mind that not all of your food needs to be junk like K-Rations or MREs either. There are plenty of normal everyday foods that we buy and use all the time that keep just fine for a year or two. Also, there is the fact that your emergency pantry does not have to be separate from your normal pantry. It only means that you must always pay more attention to keeping your pantry properly stocked and rotated.

Foods like canned soups, cereals like oatmeal, mac and cheese, and other packaged quickies are good to have on hand and easy to prepare. **CAUTION: When figuring these foods into your pantry, _be_ _sure_ to include the extra water necessary for their preparation.**

Canned meats like tuna, chicken, and SPAM®! can stretch your protein a long way. Dried and canned fruits can help with vitamin intake. Make your meal plan, determine your stocking needs, then make your pantry.

I took one end of our normal pantry and designated it as the emergency food locker. I labeled each shelf with what goes where and how much should be there. That makes it easier to see at a glance when we need to buy more SPAM®! I also have a master grocery list that shows everything we buy like: chicken, whole; chicken, boneless breast; chicken, canned breast; oatmeal, Quaker Quick, etc. I'll show you mine in a minute.

Each item has its normal QOH (quantity on hand) in parenthesis and an underscored space to write the quantity needed. This hangs on a clipboard on the outside of the pantry door. That makes it easy to check off the things we run out of. (I make a mark every time I remove an item. Subtract checks from QOH to see how much to buy.) Organizing the list by grocery department simplifies shopping.

Don't forget to include things like aluminum foil, kitchen garbage bags, dairy, produce, etc.

Okay, let's start with what you need to have on hand in your emergency food pantry. First off, there's water. Lots of it. At the first sign of an emergency like we are discussing, you should fill your bathtubs with water. CLEAN the tub thoroughly and RINSE it thoroughly. Seal the drain. It does not matter if your drain has one of those pop-up seals or if it uses a rubber stopper or whatever. Stop it up and DUCT TAPE over that stopper very carefully. This will reduce seepage and prolong your supply. This bathtub water is to be used ONLY for necessary toilet flushes and sponge baths, and ONLY after the normal water supply is cut off. ALWAYS Keep the door to the bathroom closed to keep pets from getting to this supply.

Put a sheet of plastic over the surface of the water to prevent pet hair, dust, and evaporation. And remember, I said NECESSARY toilet flushes. You can eliminate most of those by not flushing every time you pee. You can pee in a jar, save it till you have a gallon, and then pour it down the sink and use a pint of water to chase it. Girls can use a female bed urinal and do the same. Conservation of all essentials is…well…essential. This IS an emergency.

And be on your guard. Some people, especially children and particularly teenaged girls, will want to exert their independence or display their disdain for the situation by breaking the rules. Watch for it. Catch it before it happens if you want to survive. If necessary, I would restrain and gag a recalcitrant child if it looks like an attack is imminent. For EVERY one's sake. And take up all of the cell phones and lock them away. ZERO communication with the world outside is safest, even if the cell towers are working. You don't want your daughter telling her friends that you are doing HDIP. The gangs could hit the girlfriend's house and torture the info out of her. If the internet is still on, you should disconnect your router so they cannot use any social network. Turn it on only if needed.

Water for drinking and cooking must be stored in bottles or jugs. Gallons and gallons. Under normal conditions, the average adult needs about a gallon of water per day. And that figure climbs as your activity level, ambient temperature, or stress level increases.

Teenagers count as adults here. Six to twelve years old use one-half to three-fourths gallon each. These figures are DRINKING WATER *ONLY*. That is how much *your body* needs just to survive.

Cooking needs are separate. And don't forget about powdered milk and canned milk. Not much to write home to mom about, but it can do the trick. Make up three-fourths gallon of powdered milk, then add condensed milk to get the milk fat and flavor back.

Let us not forget water and food for our pets, folks. And a means to control and dispose of their waste. For ice, we use a small countertop ice maker. Small enough that a 1,000-watt inverter and a car battery can handle it.

And here's another surprise for you. Apparently, most people think that water will last indefinitely on the shelf. NOT true! *Everything* has a shelf life. Almost ALL bottled water is nothing more than filtered water stuck in a bottle, and it will still go bad over time. You could still drink it, but you won't like it, and it might make you sick. I prefer to rotate my water out about every six months.

So, for my two adults here, figuring one gallon per day for drinking purposes and a two-week emergency duration, I should have twenty-eight gallons of fresh drinking water on hand. Add 10 percent for safety margin and you have thirty-one gallons that I keep for drinking. I figure half that amount for cooking use, and you can see that I keep forty-five gallons on hand. To keep rotation happening, I add five more gallons for a safety margin. Want to be safe? DOUBLE IT. What can it hurt?

To rotate this much water, we use refillable metal water bottles for personal drinking use, and we fill those from the emergency supply daily and that is our portable drinking water as we run around the yard, the house, town, etc. So, every day, we drink two to four gallons of our emergency supply. This gets replenished at least weekly on the grocery run. I will not let it get down much more than that. Actually, we try to pick up another gallon or three every time someone goes to town.

Yes, all this is a gigantic pain in the butt. Sometimes it is a horrible inconvenience, and quite often, it screws up our schedule to take the time to get more water, but we feel it is worth the effort. We're all going to drink water, all the time. This method keeps us from stopping off to buy yet another 8-oz plastic bottle of water that will be discarded, thereby reducing global plastic usage and waste.

Like I said, water needs to be rotated at least every six months. I prefer that my water is a tad fresher than that, so we will do a partial water rotation, which takes about two weeks, then skip a month or so, and start the process again. And don't forget to label each jug of water with its IN date, just in case you get out of sync or something.

Food should be rotated also. We keep a four-month stock of survival pack meals on hand here at the house at all times. For one thing, that ensures that if our HDIP scenario lasts longer than expected OR if it turns into a bug-out situation, we are ready. Of course, we still eat the available foodstuffs first, but if it is needed, it is there.

Most survival meals have a shelf life of about five years. So about once a week, we will each eat one pack out of the stack. It keeps it rotated and ensures that we are used to dealing with it and eating it. It pays off. Remember, when planning for an emergency, PLAN for the WORST. Hope for the best. You should also label every can and box you buy with its IN date.

Okeydoke, Smokey. That pretty much covers food and water, so what's next? Medicines? I know that there are millions of people who take maintenance medicines every day, just like I do. Blood pressure, cholesterol control, blood sugar control, vitamins, the list is endless. But, actually, most of us can do without a DAILY dose of these things.

So that gives me a chance to build a little back stock, extend my resources, without endangering my life. I do not recommend this for anyone else, of course, but if YOU decide to use this method to build your medicine backstock, you should be SURE to keep track of your vital signs and get a checkup more often, just so you know how much this regimen is affecting your cholesterol and such.

Your doctor will not agree with this and may even fight you over it, even to the point of threatening to drop you as a patient. So I have not mentioned this part of my emergency plan to ANY one in the medical field. It will go into your medical record and you will never escape it. Here's an example of how bad *that* can be...

I carry a weapon 24-7. Well, several, actually. I am always ready to protect myself and those around me. Our local hospital did not have signage prohibiting weapons, so I even wore my sidearm when going into the hospital.

One day, the pain clinic doctor that we saw there got a bug up his…nose about the fact that I was carrying. He started screaming (literally) about how it was illegal (untrue) and if HE couldn't carry HIS weapon in there, he would certainly not allow ME to. At the end of the argument, he stomped off to the hospital administrator to have her call the cops on me. She did. And the police told them it was not illegal unless there was the proper signage.

The hospital did put up the signs the next day, so I no longer carry a weapon into that hospital. But the real problem showed up over six months later. I had to take my wife to the ER of a different hospital in a city that was over an hour away. I checked her in, and we had a seat. Two minutes later, the police pulled up and took me outside for questioning, even though my wife was in great distress and was crying for them to let me stay with her.

The questioning started with verifying my name and address, etc. Then came the shocker…"Are you the guy that is always armed going into a hospital? Why is that? Do you have an agenda against the medical profession?" (Keep in mind, I am a captain on the fire department and a trained and licensed Emergency Medical Responder also!) And they searched me. They found nothing since I had left the weapon in the trunk of the car, because I knew that this hospital was signed "No Weapons," and I was eventually released to return to my wife.

So what is the point of that little story? *Any* interaction with *any*one in *any* position of authority can and *will* haunt you for the rest of your days. And in these days of information technology, you cannot win. Information spreads like measles. So don't tell your doctor or your friend the nurse or the guy next door that drives an ambulance ANYthing about your plans. Actually, it is for the best if you never discuss your prepping plans with anyone, anyway, unless you intend to include them *in* your plans.

The old adage is, "How many people can keep a secret?" The answer is…ONE! YOU! This might get to be an issue if you have children. They love to talk. They love to brag. You can just imagine the conversation, "Yeah, my dad has got all this weird-o survival crap stacked all around the house. He's reinforcing the doors and stuff, and it's really just, you know, creeping me out, like." We'll talk about this some more later on.

Back to medicines, okay? So, from personal experience, I have found that even though I am supposed to take my meds twice a day, I can skip any of them one day at a time. So twice a week, I do not take my meds. I am not an insulin-dependent diabetic, so that's not an issue, but I am a diabetic. I just take pills to keep my sugar down. You must bear in mind that I am talking about what >> *I* << have done.

Whether or not you *can* or <u>should</u> do the same is your personal decision. I am definitely NOT advocating that anyone actually DO this. This is simply the process that has worked for me.

I manage to build up two months of emergency supply medicines every seven months using this method. But you *might* decide to let your doctor help you build an emergency supply. It all comes down to this, Buck-o, if you need meds, you need meds. And you need to find a way to get them for the times when they will not be available through normal channels. If at all. So…work it out. Okay, the disclaimer is done. LOL. Just remember my little story up there.

While we're on the issue of meds, let's chat a bit about shelf life. Everyone—and I DO mean e-v-e-r-y one—will tell you that medicine does not hold its potency past one year, two tops, for certain things. I beg to differ.

My sister was married to a pharmacist for about twenty years. Then he died. But before he died, we used to talk a lot. One day we were on this very subject and he said, "I will tell you the truth, Tom. Almost every drug will last ten years. Drugs lose typically 5 percent of their power every year. So, at the end of year 1, a pill is still 95 percent effective. Year 2, 90 percent, year 3, 86 percent, and so on. Sure, as time goes by you will have to take more to get the same effect, but it can work. And the better you treat them, the longer they will last. Nitro-Pak *everything*, in other words. Shiva is not the

Great Destroyer of life. Oxygen is. I would bet that the shelf life of any medicine could be greatly extended by Nitro-Pak.

Next, we have the issue of POWER! I have an entire section in here about electricity, another one on energy, and I have to assume you will read and follow them. So this is just going to hit the high points. One of the more important issues is lighting. That part is easy.

With the innovation of LED lighting technology, power requirements for lights has dropped dramatically.

Light that used to take 100 watts of power can now be had for 15 watts! There are also plenty of camp lights and handheld work lights using LEDs that you can get pretty cheap. If you use battery operated camp lamps, I recommend that you use rechargeable batteries instead of replaceables. You might have to use a 110-volt charger for those batteries, but that is still no problem.

The idea here is that you can keep <u>replaceable</u> batteries on the shelf for a year or two, but rechargeables will last much longer. I think you should discharge them completely for storage. Then, at the first sign of an emergency, charge them up before you lose electricity.

Recharging them later is handled in the section on electricity. Plan B is to keep replaceables AND rechargeables. Discharge the rechargeables and store them long term. Use replaceables day to day. This preserves the rechargeables for when you really need them. Because once they are used, they, too, have a "life cycle" time. How many times they can be recharged before they are no longer viable.

We have one of those small 1,000-watt gasoline generators that is so light you can carry it. Once a day, in an emergency, we will fire it up and watch a DVD on the TV to keep our sanity and also to check to see if there is any news. With a satellite TV service, it's easy. (Use headphones with splitters so you don't run the speakers. Noise can give you away.) If it's a local disaster, we can keep up with the world outside. And while it is running, we recharge everything, even the car batteries we use to light and heat with. Be sure to vent the exhaust to outside.

If the power grid is down, how do I get that small amount of power that I need? Inverters. Car batteries. Solar cells. I keep four dry charge car batteries and the acid to activate them in the closet. One battery is fully charged, sitting in a closet, hooked up to a "trickle charger" to keep it "topped off." If needed, I will spread the batteries around and use smaller inverters to supply separate loads.

What else do you need power for, anyway? Hunh? Well, actually, there are a few other items that could be handy. If you are hunkering down, you probably do not have heat because you do not have electricity. Even a gas furnace needs electricity to run the fan and controls. I've had some people say stuff like, "Oh yeah, but we have these gas logs and stuff…" Yeah, but the problem there is you probably will not have gas, either, unless your house runs on propane gas. Even then, most gas log sets have a system that needs electricity. Not just to run a fan or light the gas, but other things as well.

Older-style systems had a safety valve that was powered by a thermocouple that was heated by the pilot light or the main flame. A thermocouple generates a small but usable amount of DC power. One word of **Caution! If your stove or gas logs uses an electronic ignition system, you CANNOT attempt to light it manually! You ~~can~~ WILL blow yourself to the moon.**

Most folks are familiar with the term thermocouple. Older gas furnaces and gas water heaters and stoves and grills and log sets, anything with a flame, had a thermocouple and pilot light. The pilot light is a very small flame that burns all the time. The thermocouple sticks into the pilot flame and generates about 250 millivolts (mv) of electricity. That's 0.250 volts.

This tiny amount is enough to HOLD open the pilot safety valve, also called a Junkers (Yunker) valve. It will HOLD it but will not PULL it open. That's why you had to hold down the red button while lighting the pilot light. Then you keep holding the button for thirty seconds. This gives the thermocouple enough time to heat up and start generating the power to hold the safety valve open.

Then there's the thermoPILE. Basically, it's about three thermocouple units in one package. It works the same way. Heat it and it makes electricity to use in a safety circuit. Thermopiles generate about 750 mv, which is three times the thermocouple output. Now back to the gas log that uses a thermopile.

Modern gas appliances are required to employ an oxygen deple-tion sensor that shuts off the flame in the event that the oxygen con-tent in the room drops too low to sustain life. That takes more power than a simple thermocouple can provide. So, if you have THIS sys-tem, you might have heat. MIGHT. IF you use propane.

If your home is fueled with NATURAL gas, it might not be available during your emergency period. Why? Because it takes elec-tricity to pump that natural gas throughout the distribution system. SOME where within about fifty miles of you is a pumping station. Depending on the severity of the disaster and whether or not there is any immediate damage to the infrastructure, the gas utility may or may not cut service to any portion or portions of their service area. This is done to prevent gas leaks that could suffocate you or explode or cause fires. So don't bet on gas logs for heat.

Our go-to heat system here is nothing more fancy than electric blankets powered by inverters that supply 110 volts from a car bat-tery. One battery can supply our two electric blankets all night for about a week without recharging. During the daytime we dress in layers if needed. And the cooking we do helps keep the single room we are living in warm a plenty. Should it get too cold for these to work, there is always the ubiquitous propane camp heater.

A word of caution is in order here. I use propane a lot. I like propane a lot. But I have worked with it all my life as a mechanical engineer and contractor. I was always repairing gas appliances. I am _used_ to getting blown sky-high. Just kidding. But it has happened to everybody once or twice. Usually when you get complacent and do something stupid. Like leave a fitting loose. So the word of the day here is TEST ALL JOINTS FOR LEAKS! And I do not mean with a match either. THAT can get _real_ stupid REAL quick.

Propane is heavier than air. It will sink to a low spot and accu-mulate. If the joint has been leaking for a minute or so and you come in with a match to check it, _ka-BOOM!_ Do yourself a favor, do the right thing.

I highly recommend you get a good leak check liquid at a sup-ply store or online rather than just the old soap and water trick. Most (not all) leak detector liquids are formulated to not be corrosive. Soap and water, not so much. And you don't want corrosion later down the road. Make sure yours says "Noncorrosive."

Some of these little heaters are set up to use 1# cylinders. That won't last very long. I suggest you get an adapter and hose to hook it to a 30# tank like the ones you see at convenience stores and on RVs. At least a ten-foot hose, no less. I use a twenty-footer. I want the tank a little bit away just for peace of mind. Be sure to check all joints for leaks every time you move or change ANYthing. Have a spare tank or two, also. To be safe

Security should be high on your list, also. The first thing I would do is black out the windows at night so evil cannot see inside. Even a small amount of light will stick out in a wall of dark windows. Tape black plastic over the windows.

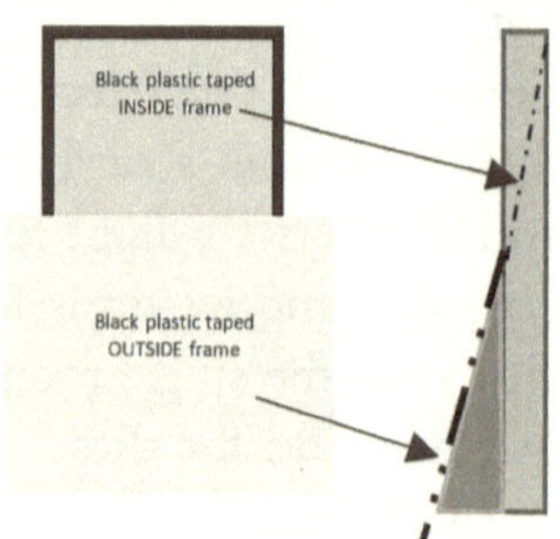

One piece inside the frame at the top, and one piece covers the frame over the bottom. The bottom piece should be taped to the top piece to prevent LIGHT from the room leaking past the joint space. That can give you away. With this arrangement, you can use a fan to blow air out of the room.

If it is hot outside, you will need to make a way for the air to get in without light getting out. Stagger the plastic sheeting to allow air flow without someone seeing in. If you are on a ground floor, you might consider using plywood instead of plastic. Screwed or nailed into place.

Again, stagger it. Put one piece IN the framing for the window, and the other piece WIDER than the frame. I use a box fan powered by a car battery and inverter to pull air in.

Windows are a prime entry point for crooks and killers on the first and second floor. If you black out the windows, do it only at night. By day it will give away the fact that there are people there. At night, it hides your lights.

Plywood over the windows is not so much a problem on lower floors, as that looks reasonable enough. Someone trying to protect their space. And crooks always look for the easy target, the window without plywood.

No matter what floor you are on, the doors are always vulnerable. Nail or screw a stop strip on the floor to keep the door from opening. Also use a brace from the floor to the knob at about a forty-five-degree angle and nail a stop strip on the floor to keep IT in place also. If you are in an apartment or condo, consider the fact that the walls in the common hallways where your door opens to are nothing but sheetrock just like the walls inside your home. You can punch right through them with your fist. And the bad guys know this too.

I would consider keeping at least a few pieces of plywood on hand that are cut-to-fit on the sides of the door. Predrilled with holes that line up with the studs inside the walls so there is no guesswork and no chance of missing the stud when things are in a crunch. Just stand it in place and run the screws through the holes. Two- to three-inch-long screws minimum. If they kick through that, you have at least bought yourself some time to get ready. I would use at least two thicknesses of ¾" plywood everywhere.

The plywood door barriers should be about 4' to 4½' tall, minimum. If the wolf is at the door, they might decide to try and shoot through the door to kill whoever is on your side of that wall. So, do NOT stand in front of the door.

Stand off to the side, beyond your wood barrier, and with your side arm or AR15, start firing through the wall *beside* the door at an angle that will have the bullets crossing the area in front of the door at a distance of about two to three feet from the door. Swing the butt of the gun in an arc to make the bullets head for differing places. Up and down, also. Do not be afraid to fire first and most. Your life may depend on it. Then you can duck behind that four feet of plywood. Of course, that plywood will only slow the bullet down fractionally. Ideally what you want to duck behind is one-fourth to one-half inch of plate steel, but even a barricade of two-by-eight pine is better than a single ¾" plywood. And be ready to repair the hole after the attack. This keeps anyone from looking in afterward.

You will not know who to trust in this situation, pal, so even if there's a voice at the door yelling, "This is the police!" you have the right to demand to see identification. A bad guy might kill a cop and take his uniform and badge, but I'd bet a dollar against a doughnut hole that they will NOT think to get his REAL ID from his wallet or pocket. And, yes, they *are* required to carry that also. If you do not have a camera system on your door (and you *should!*), they can hold it up to the peep hole. If in doubt, try your cell phone. See if you can get through to 911.

If cell towers are down but Internet is working, turn on "Wi-Fi Calling" on your phone. You have the right to verify, and any real cop will tell you that. Ask them to radio central and get verification. And a real cop will not look like five miles of bad road even in an emergency. They will do their level best to look like the professionals they are supposed to be. Do NOT fall for that "My BADGE is my ID!" crap. Like I said, a crook could kill him, steal the badge, and play "Let's Be Cops." Explain that to the voice at the door. He just might understand. If he's legit, he WILL.

You can make it for eight weeks or more if you're smart. Using HDIP, your two biggest worries will always be water and waste. Having enough water on hand is definitely a hard trick. Getting rid of trash and sewage is also tough. And if your house is in a neigh-borhood where the sewage must be pumped *uphill*, you <u>will</u> have an issue with flushing your toilets. That issue needs to factor into your decision to HDIP before TSHTF. Try five-gallon buckets with tight lids, I suppose. There is a kit that attaches a toilet seat to a five-gallon bucket to make it more comfortable. Before we leave this chapter, below is a section of my Master Grocery Inventory Control.

There are, of course, many different categories. This listing is only to represent the general type of layout that I used originally. To conform with the ideas put forth herein and to therefore yield more productive results, I suggest the following general format:

QOH is how many you intend to keep on hand at all times.
USE is removals. I mark this with a hash for each unit taken.
RQD is how many you need to purchase next shopping trip.

So when it comes time to hit the HEB or Aldi's, just take these sheets and shop from them. I keep the QOH preprinted on the form

<u>General Heading</u> (like Meat, Produce, Dairy)

ITEM	*QOH*	*USE*	*RQD*
Milk, gal, 2%	____	____	____

<u>HOUSEHOLD</u>

Alum Foil	____	Pine sol	____
Bounce	____	Scrub pads	____
Clorox II	____	SOS	____
Clorox	____	Storage bag, gal	____
Comet	____	Storage bag, Qt	____
Dish liq	____	Storage bag, Sand	____
Dish Pellet	____	Straws	____
Garbage bag, Lg	____	Toilet paper	____
Garbage bag, Sm	____	Toothpicks	____
Laundry det	____	Wax paper	____
Paper napkins	____	Windex	____
Paper plates	____	Other________	____
Paper towels	____		

<u>BREADS</u>

Biscuits, frozen	____	Cookie	____
Biscuits, refrigerated	____	Cookie	____
Bread, French	____	Crackers, Ritz	____
Bread, garlic	____	Crackers, Saltine	____
Bread, sandwich	____	Rolls, Brown-n-Serve	____
Buns, hamburger	____	Rolls, sweet	____
Buns, hot dog	____	Rolls, yeast	____
Cereal	____	Vanilla wafers	____
Cereal	____	Other________	____

MEATS

Chicken

Boneless breasts	_____
Breast fillets	_____
Breasts	_____
Fingers	_____
Legs	_____
Thighs	_____
Whole bird	_____
Wings	_____
Other_________	_____

Beef

Ground	_____
Roast	_____
Steak	_____
Stew	_____
Tips	_____
Other_________	_____

Pork

Bacon	_____
Chops	_____
Ham, whole	_____
Loin	_____
Other_________	_____

Sandwich/Other

Beef, sliced	_____
Bologna	_____
Bulk sausage	_____
Fish, perch	_____
Fish, salmon	_____
Ham, sliced	_____
Honey ham, sliced	_____
Hot dog chili	_____
Kielbasa	_____
Link sausage	_____
Salmon	_____
Spam	_____
Tuna	_____
Turkey sliced	_____
Variety Pak	_____
Other_________	_____

<u>PRODUCE</u>

Apples	_____	Okra	_____
Asparagus, Fresh	_____	Onion, green	_____
Bananas	_____	Onion, white	_____
Cabbage	_____	Onion, yellow	_____
Carrots, baby	_____	Orange, fresh	_____
Carrots, whole	_____	Potato, baking	_____
Celery	_____	Potato, Idaho	_____
Cob corn	_____	Potato, sweet	_____
Garlic, clove	_____	Salad, pkgd	_____
Garlic, minced	_____	Squash	_____
Green beans	_____	Tomato, whole	_____
Lettuce	_____	Other_________	_____

<u>DAIRY</u>

Butter	_____	Cream, whipping	_____
Buttermilk	_____	Eggs	_____
Cheese, American	_____	Half/half	_____
Cheese, cheddar	_____	Ice cream	_____
Cheese, cream	_____	Margarine	_____
Cheese, parmesan	_____	Milk	_____
Cream, sour	_____	Other_________	_____

<u>BAKING/Cooking</u>

Baking powder	_____	Flour, all-purp	_____
Baking soda	_____	Flour, self-rise	_____
Bread crumbs	_____	Oil	_____
Cooking spray	_____	Sugar, conf	_____
Corn meal	_____	Sugar, dark brown	_____
Corn starch	_____	Sugar, gran	_____
Crisco	_____	Sugar, light brown	_____

8

Mi Familia: Who Goes With Me To The BoL

Here's another inconvenient fact: You will probably not survive for long if you are alone. As the old saying goes, "There's safety in numbers." You need help, Steve. I guess you see my point, right? You need to put together a community of maybe four to eight families to make this thing work right, right?

We ARE talking about the end of the world, after all. So we need lots of people to help with the workload, but more importantly, we need to think in terms of <u>generational continuity</u>. That's a fancy way of saying "We gotta make babies!" These families make up your pack, or tribe, and if you don't make babies, it will all die out.

Think about it. If it's just your family there, what happens after you and Mom go on to the other side? Bobby and Suzie get busy making babies?? Oh HELL no. That will NOT work. So you need other people *who are <u>not</u> related to you or each other*. Because you need genetic diversity in the generations to come.

If you have eight families gathered, it won't affect things much if one of the others is related to you. But if everyone else has a related family involved, the genetics gets pretty dicey, pretty quickly. Tell your brother that he can do the same thing fifteen miles down the road from you, and he can take Sam's sister's family in with *his* clan. It would really be a great idea. Share the load. Share the tractor. You need maximum genetic diversity and more permutations is the key.

You need to be very, very picky about whom you choose to let in on your plan, Stan. Anyone you want to let in must be someone that you know inside and out. Including their spouse and kids. You are building the pack here. And like any good pack, all the animals must hunt together, defend together, survive together. And all must bow to the Ultimate Leader. The Alpha Dog.

Now, I don't care if this alpha is male or female, I don't care if it's you or your friend Frank or his wife or their twelve-year-old daughter Angie. SOMEbody has to be the ultimate leader. The ONE person who has the final say. And when that say is said, NOBODY GETS TO QUESTION IT. This is a high-stakes game of Simon Says. When Simon Says "JUMP!" everybody jumps. Losers die.

This concept is more important in a combat situation than anywhere else. If you and the tribe are in bug-out mode, traveling down the road or through the woods and you get jumped by thugs, the leader must issue orders and the tribe must obey, instantly and without question. That is the primary purpose of military training, that respect for the chain of command that tells you that no matter what the leader says, you do it, and you do it _now!_ No questions, no dissenting opinions, no "what if we do THIS instead?"

Do your invitees have good control over their kids? Do you think they can convince their children to keep quiet and not talk about this to their friends? Does his wife have a lover? (Does _yours?_) Yes? Will she tell HIM? What happens if he shows up at the last minute, willing to kill her husband (or YOU) and take his place? Hey! Crazier things have happened, right?

Maybe your wife can dig into your friend's wife's head? Would Frank rather take his girlfriend than his wife? Then Frank is out, in my book. Mary is out if she has a lover that she is not willing to drop NOW. And THAT eliminates FRANK! You need to KNOW the people involved or you cannot trust them. And the lovers will not be there training with you. Unless you are all _really_ good friends! But, again, it's _your_ call, Paul.

The whole idea is this, bub: You, and whoever you hook up with for this plan are going to be _real_ close buddies, for a _long_ time. Like...well...for_EV_er. So don't screw this up, okay? Choose wisely, choose well, choose NOW. You gotta get busy, Dizzy. This ain't no easy thang either. But it has to be done.

You all have to get along for many, many years. And the children have to _be_ children while growing up together and then they have to _have_ children. And so on and so forth. It could well be three or four generations before the country comes together enough for your troupe to be viable outside of the compound. Do NOT ask me what to do if there are eight boys and six girls among the kids. I'm not that good at math.

One more word. With this arrangement of close quarters and connubial bliss, you had better keep good genetic records. You don't want anyone closer than second cousins to have children together. A good, well-kept diary and logs of all operations of the compound can tell your story to future generations and perhaps give them something to learn from. If Bobby gets Suzie preggers, there is a lot of good to be said for him also putting a baby in Rachel. More genetic diversity. Nobody gets to keep secrets about who sleeps where. We gotta know for the records.

It might not be too hard to find one entire family that _your_ family can get along with at about a 90 percent run. Great. Now do that two or eight more times. And every time you bring another family in, you multiply the odds of it working as planned about ten times in the wrong direction!

But you have to keep working at it, boss. You have to pull together several families to make this battle plan work. Families that can work together, play together, school together, and…_ahem_…sleep (?) together.

Which brings up point 2. For maximum genetic diversity, it would be best if all of the adults of child-bearing age can agree to "cross pollinate" also. Even if there is a decade or two between them. It would be best if no one has been sterilized. Ask that question upfront before you get too deep in discussion. You do want maximum effort in this generational continuity thing, but it is not necessarily a deal breaker. Ask the guys too. Seriously. Frankly, Frank, in this situation, I would not be opposed to Sam's teenaged son putting a baby in Fred's wife! Talk it out. We're all adults here.

Try taking some camping trips together to see how everyone gets along. And personally, I think it would be advantageous, at least for the first generation, if teenagers participate also. Nothing says they can't get *married*, but let John have a baby with Suzie, even though she is married to Tommy. Then the next child Suzie has is by Bobby. Maximum genetic diversity is VITAL. Tommy is busy making babies with Janie and Luann.

Skills. You need skills. Differing skills. Keep this in mind when thinking about who to invite to Shangra-LaLa Land. Maybe the guy who fixes your car or does your small engine work. Or the fellow that put the addition on your house. If you developed a good rapport with him, you might have a candidate. Or the neighbor that builds trailer mounted barbecue systems as a hobby.

And don't think that four families is the maximum number either. Four is actually my minimum count. Many hands make light work and all that jazz. And gives more opportunities to put together the right combination of skillsets. And I think that all those who make the cut will appreciate the time and effort that you put into making the right decisions on this count.

And SOMEbody better know how to deliver a baby! And sew up a laceration. Put a dislocated shoulder back in place. These skills are available online, pal. Just do it. Get all the medical knowledge you can. It would be even better if you can corral a medical professional to join you. Download as many teaching videos as possible, of all sorts.

You might consider placing an ad in a newspaper or professional magazine looking for a doctor or nurse or dentist or even a veterinarian who would want to join your efforts. Have the responses sent to a blind mailbox to hide your identity for a while. Correspond by mail—SNAIL mail to your blind mailbox, not email—for a while, then arrange a face-to-face meeting at a coffee shop or similar venue. Maybe a few of those, to feel the person out.

I say NO EMAIL because that can be traced to a physical address. Have a few accomplices follow the prospect to make sure they do not go to a police station or meet with police afterward. You would be surprised how tricky the cops are, and people like us are prime fishing grounds for these guys. They think we're all wacko. Until they get off work and out of uniform, then half of them *become* us. But put that uniform back on and it's Jekyll and Hyde time.

While we're talking on this tack, I'll add one more possibility for you to consider. Ex-military personnel would be great. Retired *might* be too old to be genetically viable but still useful. Best to look for someone who just got out after a ten-year hitch, maybe.

Look for a grade E-6 to O-4, I think. High-level enlisted to low-level officer. High-level officers have a tendency to be too take-charge, bulldog types. But even that might not be a bad thing. At least they would have leadership experience. But they can be abrasive to nonmilitary types. Versatility and compatibility are your bywords, Wadsworth. Get busy.

9

Choosing A Bug-Out Location

If you think the way I think, it is actually *past* time to find a bug-out location (BoL). But, unless tomorrow is the Big Day, when everything goes south, you still have at least a *little* time. But I'd highly recommend you get the hell on the ball, Bub. Now, we need to remember that there are some PARTNERS in this thing. Right?

That set of three or eight other families you brought into this mess? THEY need to be involved in the selection process, too. Maybe even split the load. All of you sit down together for the initial preselection process. Pick an area you all agree is in the safety zone. A few of you go to the county that you picked to set up in, for an initial fly-by. All of you together go over data. Then split the inspection process up. Get it together. Together.

This step takes a good deal of examination about you and your current situation first, and *then* you can think about how best to prepare for the end. But here, we are thinking about where you will go. So let's begin with where you are, shall we? Do you live in a big town, like thirty-five thousand people? Or maybe a metro area of over one million souls? Or perhaps a small town of 1,600 that's thirty miles away from a movie theater? Those differences could be important to your decision-making process.

How close are you to a major city like Atlanta or Chicago? Or a military installation? And, trust me on this one, there is a BIG difference between being close by Dobbins Air Force Base and living within a stone's throw of Fort Detrick. One of these is a priority one target for war or terrorists. The other is an air force base. These things matter, really.

The proximity of your nearest target area determines how far away your BoL should be. If a conventional explosive is deployed at Fort Detrick, or at the CDC in Atlanta, there will be some *AWESOME* bad bugs let loose, and they will start killing people right away and spreading out at an unbelievable rate.

Most are airborne, though some are direct-contact-type infections. Your best bet is to be the hell and gone away from any concentration of people. So, if you live one-half mile off a one-lane road in Middle of Nowhere, Arkansas, your chances of exposure are negligible.

If you live in Philly, you might want to bug out if that happens. Something like that could wipe out the eastern seaboard to about a hundred miles inland really quickly. If you're in Atlanta and somebody pops a nuke over downtown, I personally would not want to be within two hundred miles of the place.

With those things in mind, you can start to determine where you might want to bug out TO. Let's start with the safe radius concept. Of course, the first thing to do is to determine the location of each and every base or research facility within about two to four hundred miles of your current home location. Then, based on the danger presented by each facility, figure how far away from it you need to be to remain safe. I figure about two hundred miles from a major metro area and one hundred miles from minor metro areas or minor military installations. MINIMUM.

Once you have a good idea of where, in general, you should locate your BoL, get a map out and start looking. You really do need to be within access to some area that has a few amenities and supply points, like grocery stores, hardware stores, building supply places.

These are necessary while you build and stock your BoL, unless you intend to buy your materials where you are and haul them up to the BoL yourself, which IS a viable option. So, once you have a general idea, do some online searches to see what's nearby. Also use a good map program that offers satellite views to scope out the area in question for a radius of about one hundred miles. Just do a thorough, methodical scan at a moderate magnification and then blows up to allow you to make out individual buildings.

Google the towns surrounding your location. Look for things like hardware stores, home improvement depots, grocery stores, wholesale clubs, equipment rentals. Anything and everything.

Get an idea of what is VACANT AND UNUSED land. Be sure to copy down the GPS coordinates of any likely areas. Oh yeah, while you're looking, see if your prospective areas have ponds or creeks. A water source would be _very_ nice to have. In fact, it's a necessity. Make sure it is not a "Wet Weather" source, also. It should be viable year-round.

Next, with two or six places in mind, take a long weekend to the county seat there. Try the Office of Tax Assessors first. Starting with a map of the general overview of the county, find those areas in question and then have them pull the plats for you, along with legal descriptions and current owner's name(s). Also, look into the tax status. If the taxes are in arrears, you might be able to purchase the property for a song. (IF you can sing.) Especially if it is far removed from civilization or if it contains no commercially farmable land.

Very hilly country is fine for your purposes, in fact, maybe preferred. Hills hide a lot of sins. You _can_ farm just about anywhere if you try. Look up terrace farming. Be sure to make several copies of each plat. You'll want to mark on several of them later. You might want to have a believable cover story ready in case someone gets too nosey. Maybe something like looking for an ancestral homestead that is 150 years old

Pulling multiple locations at the tax assessor's office also helps cover your trail a bit should anyone wish to see what you were up to. People _are_ nosey, you know.

Depending on your personal predilections, how far from home you are, how many properties you want to check out or whatever, you will probably want to camp out on the property, either before or after you look it over. At least after the first one, so you can get a good start the next day on the next property. Be sure to pack food, a tent, cooking supplies, weapons, radios, etc. Try to find out if you need _permission_ to camp there.

I would set up an Early Warning System around the campsite. I use four of those wireless driveway alarms, placed about fifteen to thirty yards from camp on obvious trails close to the four cardinal compass points, if possible. Be sure to label the matched pairs of units so you keep them straight.

Put tape or paint over the indicator light on the remote unit (transmitter), paint the thing gray or camo (except the sensor lens), and tie it to a tree. At camp, I put the respective receivers inside the tent approximating the relative positions of the transmitters. That way, if one goes off, you know which way to look first. Muffle the speaker with tape and cover the light with a semitransparent tape. Let it shine just enough to be seen.

You want to know if something is coming toward you, and probably whether it's a bear or a body. There's nothing worse than being awakened at 3:00 a.m. with a gun in your face. Unless it's being awakened at 3:00 a.m. by a bear in your face. Sleep with your sidearm under your pillow, loaded, cocked, and safety ON. Take no chances.

If your friends are checking out other properties nearby, and everyone has radios as I suggest, you should be able to communicate with the other parties. If you get surprised at 3:00 a.m., you could call for help, or at least warn the others. Be sure to have your radio ON, within reach, with a fresh battery in it before you go to bed. The other battery can be charging overnight, possibly in the car.

Go visit those areas, walk them over. Or use a drone, if you have one. You will probably need a handheld GPS unit to keep you on target. And maybe even to find your way back to the car. (Be sure to write down the GPS position of the car before you leave it.) Your BoB is the pack you want to take on this trip. It should have just about everything you need including a little food. But expand on it for comfort.

Add maps, plats, and colored pencils for marking the maps up, binoculars or monocular or extensible telescope or even a rifle scope. A T-square, a straight-edge, and a drafting triangle could be very handy. A lensatic compass, machete, sidearm, and definitely a rifle. Your handheld GPS, cell phone, walkie-talkie, and possibly a police scanner. Let's hope you have researched the local frequencies and plugged them into it prior to this trip. Just in case. Or start that frequency search now, even!

If you DO hear something on the scanner about suspicious activity or person or vehicle, I suggest returning to your car post haste and get out of there before the cops arrive if you can. Go to a store for a coke or something. That way you have a verifiable story that makes sense. Just in case, you know.

Please make sure you have a license to carry that sidearm. If you will cross state lines, check the gun laws for your target state as well as those in between and also check reciprocity to see if they will honor your concealed carry permit. Be sure you do not violate any gun laws in the target state.

Federal law allows "safe travel" through all states. Check it out under that name, "Safe Travel Law." Unload the guns and lock them in a box. Lock the ammo in a separate box in a separate part of the car. Do that and you cannot be arrested for carrying a concealed weapon in your car. Be ready to quote US Code to the cops by section, chapter, and verse so they know that YOU know the law about this.

See: 18USC926a Interstate Transportation of Firearms

Assuming that nothing untoward happens, like getting arrested, you should do as thorough a check as possible of the properties you are interested in. Mark any interesting points or geographical features you encounter. Show forested areas, types of vegetation, animal life you see or see signs of, ravines, caves, rock formations, creeks, etc. Mark your map with hills and valleys and their elevations above sea level.

Try to include the GPS points for these as you mark up the map. Note temperature and weather, sun position, and condition of any streams, ponds, or other water sources. *Annnnd…*repeat. You might want to not concentrate your searches in just one area if you can avoid it. Give yourselves some choices.

When you have found at least one property worth trying for, it's time to go home and digest the data you've collected. There are, of course, some main features you are looking for, TO WIT:

Hills: Hills are good because you can build beside them or _in_ them or under them, whether for shelter or cache sites. And they can hide you from prying eyes.

Water: Of course. You need a source of fresh water that is hopefully _not_ a "wet-weather" spring and preferably not within one hundred yards of where your shelter or septic system will be. For sanitary reasons.

Forest: Thickly wooded areas where you can cache weapons under some leaves for quick retrieval. Forest also gives you great cover to ambush intruders and makes it easier to set up surveillance, booby traps, and warning systems. A good forest also provides wood for heat and building materials.

High ground: Hopefully your property includes some "high ground," an area with a commanding view of surrounding areas. Of course, with today's technology, this is not so important as in years past, but it is an old habit for me that is hard to overcome. I still look for it. Keep in mind that high ground is more defensible in a prolonged fire fight.

Choke points: These are areas where, if you can lead your adversaries there, they are easier to kill. Like sudden drop-offs or ravines with a vertical dead end. Even impenetrable brush.

Secondary entry/exit point: Another place to guard, yes, but also another escape, if needed. And another way to bring goods onto the property without drawing attention.

Neighbors: While this is probably not a deal breaker, it might still be a good idea to scope out the neighborhood before committing to a property. Cruise by houses slowly if you see someone out and about. If they look hard at you, it's a good thing. Means they care about the area and are on the lookout. Might be a good time to try to strike up a conversation. Have a story in mind that might draw them out. "Hey, I was told there was some property for sale, but I can't find any signs. Do you know of any? We're planning to retire soon." Yeah, it might be a give-away, but it might be a drawing card. Your call.

At least drive-through kinda slow, and see how the other half lives. Is the house run-down? Yard trashed out with old cars? Firewood that rotted ten years ago? Does the place need a new coat of DYNAMITE to make it pretty? You can bet these guys are ready for anything and very suspicious of new people.

They will be either warm and gregarious or hanging back, half turned away as they talk to you, as if they don't want you to get a good look at their face. If every house you see is a 3Br2Ba brick ranch with a new truck in the drive, I would almost bet that there is a family who will be prey instead of predator. But they might be overly talkative about the things going on over at the old Smith place. Check your intuition.

Think long, think hard. Think, think, think. The more thought you put into selection, the less chance you will be sorry later.

10

Site Planning—
People, Get Ready

Welp, you've got a site picked out. Now what? Hopefully, you took those marked-up plats and maps, maybe some satellite views or drone imagery and made some preliminary plans, like where to put what. Considering the fact that you will be living there forever more, whether it is like Fred Flintstone or Daniel Boone or your grandparents is entirely up to you. But _as_ you plan, you should keep in mind some of the basic concepts I have presented here in this book.

Things like hidden, including from the air if possible. After a few years, this may not be so necessary, but outta the chute, yeah. I think it might be helpful to stay under cover for a while. Another one is "Get in, Get out." Get in there and get the work done. Stay there all weekend and work if you can or need to, then clean it up, hide the evidence and leave it be until the next trip.

You need to do a "camping trip" there every once in a while, hopefully with the rest of the "pack" you have elected to throw in with. And I sincerely hope they were all very active in the selection process as well. Now is the time for everybody to get _really_ active. I recommend that in the initial planning phases, you put together an emergency site plan first. This is what to do, and how to do it if— IF—The Fall occurs too early for you to get your site work completed.

I must make several basic assumptions here, such as what types of facilities and infrastructure you will need to support four to eight families, long term, comfortably. Well, as comfortable as possible under less than ideal conditions. You will probably want to amend this list to suit your individual needs and desires. And ALL the execution of these suggestions will require a TON of research on your part. I'll probably cover what and how in another section.

One of the basic assumptions I make is that at least a few of your party have a basic knowledge of construction and mechanics. Hopefully, all or most of you. AND, you simply MUST plan and agree on what goes where. That way, if you and your son go up this week to work on the water system, then next week, Walt and his boys go up to work on the solar panels, everyone knows what goes where. And there is no fight later because you buried a water pipe right across where he needs to put a conduit. Get some yard marking flags of differing colors to lay everything out.

Before I continue, let's talk access. Say you have a deal with a few tire stores where you can pick up used tires for free whenever you want. Every week or two, you drop by with a large trailer or truck and load 'em up.

Then, sometime around 3:00 a.m., you roll up on your compound and make the turn into the drive with your car lights OFF and then out of sight. Consider installing switches in your vehicles to individually disable headlights, parking lights, taillights, and turn signals from the dash. With the right switch setup, you can turn everything except your headlights off. You'll be able to see where you're driving but can't be seen from behind.

That way you have the fewest eyes on you moving supplies in. If there are no neighbors nearby, maybe you don't need to be so surreptitious about getting supplies loaded in. Or perhaps your property has that second entrance, eh? The point is, my friends, you do NOT want the whole world to know what you are doing if you can help it.

You see, there are only two ways this project gets done. Out in the open, on the up and up, with the required permits and inspections, OR, you try to keep it on the Q-T, the down-low, hidden from view. It CAN be done, but it will probably not be easy. It will require some severe thought about how to keep everybody around you from knowing about it and keep the local enforcement agencies from getting wind of your plans.

Housing

Of course, this is the first item you need, but you need to *plan* the housing so that you can build primitive and go modern as available. Meaning you need a roof, like NOW. But later on, you will want electricity and hot and cold running water and flush toilets, right? So PLAN to put those additions in. At a later date, if necessary. Plan for them now so they will be easy to install later.

Buy the toilets now, bury them for safekeeping, and use them later. Buy the septic tanks, but let them sit there until you can install them. Same with the leach field components. You need a roof first. The Fall might happen tomorrow. I built a large lean-to first, then added three more walls and beefed it up. Took me one weekend. Then I started on the main house. There are several types of rustic housing that you can do with native (meaning *in situ [meaning "in place" {meaning "where you find it"}]*) materials.

LOG HOMES: Just like our ancestors built by hand, and usually all by themselves. Log houses are sturdy and stable, with excellent insulation factors that make them easy to heat and cool. The big drawbacks are (1) it takes a good while to build one, even a small one, mostly due to the time required to prep the logs; (2) they are difficult to build by oneself; (3) they are usually larger, more distinctive and therefore easier to see from the road or air; and (4) damned hard to build without the right tools and knowledge.

COB HOUSE: Made from a mixture of soil, clay, water, and straw, this is one of the easiest and quickest houses to build. They are also sturdy and energy efficient, but they may not last as long as a log cabin. The big advantage is that they are easily adapted to blend in with the surroundings. Interiors and exteriors can be covered with plaster to make the whole thing more pleasing to the eye and touch.

CONTAINER HOUSE: Converting old shipping containers into housing units is very popular lately. The major advantage is you can be living in one within a few days or a week. Being steel, they are not energy friendly. But you can cover them quite easily with dirt, even the top. This will increase the energy efficiency and also help to hide them completely, roof and all.

With a little thought, you can even hide the entrance door, so it is not visible from anywhere. If you are going to cover one with dirt, I suggest you first cover it with some asphalt-based waterproofing material, like spray-on tar or roofing paper at the least. Burying them completely is something I recommend, but beware. The corners are very strong. The walls and top, not so much. They *will* collapse if overloaded.

EARTHSHIP: Made from recycled materials such as aluminum cans, plastic bottles, or old tires, these houses have several advantages. They take relatively unusable materials and repurpose them in an ecologically friendly way.

My personal favorite is the rammed earth house made from used tires. Did you know that tire stores will actually PAY you to remove their old tires? Line up a row of tires, _pack_ earth into the tire, and hammer it in tight, all around the inside, level with the top of the tire. Line up another row on top of that, staggered, and repeat. This method is very labor intensive and takes a lot of dirt. But there are several things to recommend it.

The house is almost indestructible, <u>highly</u> energy efficient, easily covered and hidden. And a fifty-caliber bullet will not penetrate it. The plans that I have for one include making a floor system of rammed earth tires with floor joisting and a real, insulated plywood floor with underfloor warm water heat. I'm a creature of comfort, I admit.

If things fall too fast and it catches you with your BoL down, there are no rules to say you can't do a lean-to first, then a cob house, then an earthship or log home. But as you build, plan ahead.

I said I want under floor heat, right? So, while I build whatever, I'm going to lay PEX pipe for that purpose. I will also Install CPVC pipe or PEX pipe for hot and cold running water, PVC pipe for drains, and PVC conduit for electricity later on.

Electricity planning should include boxes for receptacles, switches, and ceiling boxes for lights and fans, if so desired, and possibly separate conduits for communications or entertainment lines. Cap every open end of every pipe or conduit to keep out trash and spiders. Even electrical pipe that stops in a box. Even the black water and gray water pipes should be capped until you need them. Get a roof. First.

When planning the electrical, be sure to figure the loads that will be placed on EVERY circuit so you don't overload your inverters. In a normal home, everything in the living room, for instance, would be on one circuit from the panel box. Here, you might need three or four circuits to avoid overloading.

HEAT

A quick look at heat. Of course, you arrived with camp heaters and probably have a supply of propane set back in your stash here at the BoL. But it won't last forever. Even if you buried a five-thousand-gallon propane tank and filled it up. It WILL run out. That leaves two options, in my humble opinion: SOLAR and WOOD. (Okay, there ARE other options, just really, really hard ones.)

Solar heat is neither difficult nor expensive. Heat water. Pipe water to house. Blow fan over hot water in pipe. Wood is not only cheap, it's renewable, and it works no matter the weather. Or how about passive solar using skylights? Not as popular nor as effective, but doable and usable.

With wood heat, you can also produce hot water for domestic use or that nice underfloor heat system I talked about. I could also highly recommend a little thing called a "rocket stove" or "rocket heater." Easy to build, maintain, and run, they do a great job with little fuel. Or if you have a giant wood burning stove outside the house, great! Just plan ahead for clearances between the stove and wall, chimney, etc.

Anything you use to heat or cook can also make hot water at the same time, using the pickup coil and manifold system I talk about in the chapter on water. Now, THAT said, you should think about a combination approach to heat and domestic hot water. Something that fuses solar and wood.

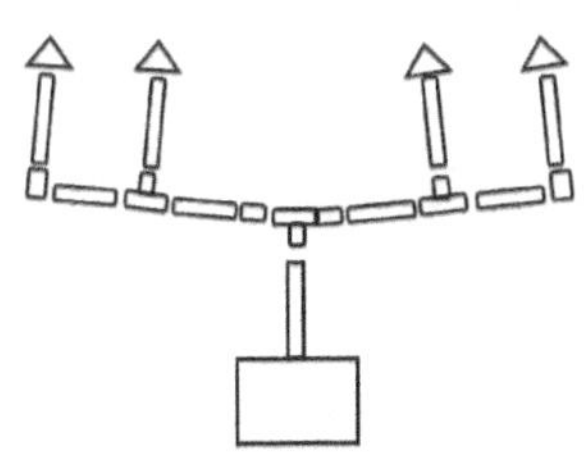

While we're here, think about this: visible signs of habitation. Like smoke. A column of smoke rising from the woods in the middle of nowhere is a sure sign that people live there. It is possible to diffuse the smoke output from a wood heater so that it is not so visible. At the top of the chimney, place a bullhead tee with the two outlets going left and right. Go about four to eight feet on each side, put another tee with one outlet facing up. Four more feet put an elbow turned up.

Take all of them up three feet or more and then put your stack caps on. You now have four outlets spread over sixteen-plus feet. Be sure to angle the horizontal runs up as much as possible to keep the smoke flowing. You will need to BRACE everything to support it and also against wind. The stacks might accumulate soot and creosote quickly since the smoke is slowed down, and therefore, it will quickly cool and the solids will precipitate out faster. Meaning they will need cleaning out more often.

I built my first hot water heat system about thirty years ago. It was a brick wood burner outside of a double wide trailer. As I was building, I put a copper pick up manifold in between the two layers of brick. A small pump that used about 30 watts of power, and I was in business. I used a lot of mechanical thermostats and electric water valves made for high-temp water.

Today you can get an electronic controller called ARDUINO that is a small computer with multiple inputs and outputs and just tons of available sensors and actuators. It is designed to interface with the real world. Build a circuit, write a short, easy program, and you have an automated control system. I'm using one now, but I have multiple backups of the controller and the sensors.

Remember, any hardware you need, like pumps, pipes, valves, Arduinos, sensors, motors, or actuators will not be available later. Get multiple backups, please. You cannot run to Ace and pick these things up. So, stock up before you lock up. At the end of this chapter, you will find a schematic diagram of my heat production, storage, and distribution system.

WATER

After housing, you probably want to consider water supply. If your accessible water source is higher than the houses, cool. Gravity is good. Gravity is your friend. And it will feed your water to you. If the source is below you, you need to figure a way to pump it uphill. I highly recommend a ram pump. Easy and cheap, it will push water to you 24-7. You need a tank. Or several. And speaking of tanks, I hope that you have by now done the necessary calculations about water needs for your growing families.

SEPTIC

Everyone is going to grow really tired of squatting over logs really soon. If you have already installed a septic system, GREAT! If not, then your best and fastest solution is an old-fashioned outhouse. Dig a deep pit. A DEEP pit. At least six feet, preferably ten to twelve feet. About four-by-eight feet. Build a shack over it with a seat and a couple of holes like a toilet. All you need now is paper. Or not. I grew up using one of these. It was a "two-holer." I am not kidding, folks, you have not lived until you have taken a dump sitting next to your grandma.

But IF you have enough time and have got the septic system installed already, then all you have to do is pipe in your houses as you build them. Before you put in a tank (or two), be sure to research sizing for both the tank(s) and the leach field(s). And don't forget that septic tanks usually need to be pumped every three to five years to remove the sludge. What are you going to do about THAT? And _do not_ EVER go INTO a septic tank to clean it out. You will **die**. It _might_ be possible to ventilate the tank thoroughly and then enter, but that thing is slap full of methane gas, among others. I personally know—from my hometown—THREE brothers who all died by violating that rule. Their dad owned a septic tank pumping company and they did the work. One day the hose got snagged. Number 1 fell into the tank trying to get the hose loose, and collapsed. Number 2 jumped in to save number 1 and collapsed. Number 3 followed, and Bob's your uncle. Three brothers. All dead. One rule. Broken.

It should be easy to see that you are going to need several septic tanks to handle the load. And more as your community grows. Tanks do not have to be pre-made. You can build them yourself. They _can_ be made of wood, but it will not last long. Coating the wood with roofing tar will extend the life. Poured-in-place concrete or cinder block is best. Do your research on caring for a septic system. Think about how you pump them.

With a little research, I am sure you can find alternative methods of construction. Don't forget that all drainpipes must slope one-fourth inch per foot of run. No more, no less. There is a reason it is so exact. Do not forget the tank baffles.

It will possibly be illegal in most jurisdictions, but you can reduce the load placed on the septic tanks by draining the gray water separately. Then again, what could be illegal after The Fall? Black water is from the toilets. Gray water comes from sink and shower drains.

You can filter solids out of gray water and use it to water plants or flush toilets. You CAN plumb the systems so that the turn of a couple of valves will put gray water to the septic system or to a catchment. If there is no authority, who is there to say no?

BUT…if, by some twist of fate, you wind up having to have everything inspected, it would be best to build to suit the building codes and inspections. Later, you can build or amend as you wish. But, legal or not, code or not, everyone will need a place to "go." And let us remember that poor sanitation was the primary cause of the Black Death, bubonic plague. Keep it clean.

One of the best investments you will make is to get a diesel tractor with a backhoe and front loader. And possibly a bush hog and plow for it. It could be very helpful in constructing all the infrastructure. No matter what you do, you will need tools. This is just a big tool. And with a diesel engine, you can keep it running for years with biodiesel fuel.

Site planning must also include things like where to put the orchards and fields and pastures and chickens and pigs and barns and wind turbines and solar collectors and on and on and on. Lay out the paths for electricity, sewer piping, septic systems and pipes, and freshwater piping as soon as possible. Don't forget that you will probably want power and water anywhere you will have animals. I recommend grouping the animal areas closely together, if possible, to simplify things.

You might want to consider fencing for the animals at some point, so plan, man. Split rail is hard, barbed wire is expensive, electric fence needs…well…electricity. Choose your weapon. And plan for it.

Let's mention here that you should plan to stock up on everything. Like pipe and valves. Couplings and adapters. Wire and fittings. Everything you need for building you will need for expanding and repair later.

11

But I LIVE At My BoL

But, BOB, you say, I'm already _AT_ my bug-out location! We've lived here for twenty years! How can it _possibly_ get any better? Well, okay. So you live in Middle of Nowhere, Arkansas. Way off any main highways, twenty-seven miles from the nearest McDonalds, and you have a twenty-acre spread where ducks and pigs and chickens call. It's an animal carpet wall to wall, and your fishing pond is ten feet tall and blue.

Let's start at the top of the list, okay? One of my primary concerns about the BoL is visibility. If you've been living there for twenty years, everybody in six counties knows you're there, number one. Which, in and of itself, is not a deal breaker. I think we can assume that under these conditions your neighbors probably like you and are all thinking like you and will support you and help you defend your place. And you will help them defend theirs. So…cool.

And let us not forget that we are also trying to stay off the government radar. Like I say somewhere else, when TSHTF, there will be _some_ cops out there who will go rogue because the government has failed. They don't actually _have_ a job anymore, and _certainly_ they likely no longer have any authority. But they have the uniform, they have the gun, the badge and <u>lots</u> of them will simply steal the cruiser they were using, and it will become "Let's Be Cops" time. Verify their identities before you submit to anything.

Most of us have been trained from the time we could walk to respect the uniform, the job, the badge. Well, okay, there _are_ some folks out there who have a built-in disdain for police and authority. If there weren't, then we would not have great TV shows like *Cops*, would we? And truth be told, some folk that live in the way back have a tendency to not be on such good terms with law enforcement.

So, you can bet the farm (literally) that you ARE on the radar. They WILL be coming to see you. Whether or not there is actually a police or sheriff's department any longer that is authorized (by a now defunct government?) to act, you can be certain that they have files on every prepper, every person who has bought multiple guns or lots of ammo. ANY thing that they themselves could use to ensure the survival of their own families. It *is* going to be dog eat dog out there, folks. Which dog are you?

All right, then, back to the show. "What do I do NOW?" you asked. Well, for starters, I would build a bug-out location anyway, if you have not already. A fallback point for when the raiders arrive. At the furthest point away from the main compound as possible. Maybe even not ON *your* property. Seriously. That's what I would do. Bunkers, caches, ambushes, booby traps, the whole nine yards. I would have it built and ready.

Continue to live in the "Big House" exactly as if nothing were changed for a while. But soon, you should move to your BoL and let the Big House run down. Great hideaway. But be sure to keep your police scanners with you and active at all times, along with your private channel radios so that should something come over the scanner that makes you nervous, the alert can be passed by radio to all others of your compound or nearby compounds, and everyone can make for the real BoL.

Of course, the details of the BoL are outlined elsewhere in this book, but the real issue with any BoL is to keep it hidden from the predators. So, the sooner you get it finished, the more time you've got to let nature take its course and hide it for you.

The last thing you want is a trail leading from the house to the BoL. You will almost certainly have trucks going to the back taking in supplies or a few containers and such. This will certainly wear a set of tracks through the fields and woods, and those must be covered.

If you are using shipping containers for caches, it would be a good idea to put at least one such container at the main compound. This could eliminate some suspicions about the delivery of containers.

Once the construction and stocking of the BoL is complete, you need to cover those truck tracks as thoroughly as possible, and let natural growth take over. If the passage to the BoL must include a bridge to ford a creek, you might want to dismantle or disable it as soon as you're certain it is no longer needed.

If there are additional forays to the Big House needed to retrieve goods or whatever, you should remember to never take that same track twice in more than, say, two months. Give your paths time to thoroughly recover from your passage before abusing the grass again.

When the time comes that someone announces via radio that there is an alert, meaning that either something was heard on the scanner or your security system caught movement on the property, or a neighbor called to warn you, everyone should head immediately for the BoL by separate paths to introduce a bit of confusion if possible. Separate, winding, nondirect paths, crossing each other in perpendicular directions, if possible and practical at the time.

Each person should carry and distribute some scent-confusion agent on their way to the BoL in such an event. Something like deer urine or black pepper or something else. Anything to cover tracks or confuse the dogs that the cops may have with them. That is a very real likelihood actually. Especially if they know you and have any understanding of your habits. And in particular if you or any member of your family have had previous run-ins or allegiances with law enforcement. Keep that scent covering substance stocked around in various places so that anyone can grab a batch from wherever they are, on the way out.

And speaking of dogs. Do you have any? How well trained are they? Will they attack intruders? I mean *really* attack, not just bark. At least attack on command. If you tell them to stay at the Big House, *will they?* Dogs following you to the BoL can be a double-edged sword. They could lead the pursuers straight to you, but they could be useful in a confrontation. Or, if they stay at the Big House, it could indicate to the "cops" that you have left but will return within a day or so. If one vehicle is missing, it adds to the story. Maybe you should have a nearby place (within walking distance) to park or hide that vehicle. Our purpose here, after all, is to confuse and deter the "enemy."

Depending on your level of expectation about why they are there and what they want, you should consider having the family positioned for a flanking maneuver. It is quite possible you may be in for a firefight. IF, as I suspect, authority has broken down and your "guests" are rogue cops, they will not be large in number. Probably four to six men, possibly as many as ten, but I would not expect more than that. And in this case, they probably cannot radio for backup. Frankly, I would *expect* no more than two guys in cop drag.

Possibly send an emissary to greet them or use a drone to drop an invitation to a parlay for ONE of them. Be sure the invitation conveys a desire for peace but a willingness to defend against illegal search and seizure operations.

Check their ID, get them to verify with their dispatcher for you to hear. A dispatcher's radio voice will not sound like normal conversation. The officer will NOT be called by name, but rather by "unit number." Deviation from this protocol would indicate to me that there is some deception in play.

Another possibility is that you can hide and wait it out. Maybe have a scout hiding in the woods off-site, carrying a radio, a 30-cal rifle and a sidearm. That way, if they are intercepted, they can easily claim to have been hunting.

Coming up from behind the intruders, your spy could keep you posted about their movements.

The whole thing is, it does not matter if you live in the best of all possible worlds, I would have a secondary location set up and stocked up. Just. In. Case.

And we haven't touched generational continuity yet, right? Or the need for more people to help do the work and shoot the bad guys. So you need to look long and hard at your individual situation. Are you close to any neighbors or is the nearest one three miles away?

Personally, I think it would be better for all concerned if you work this out with your neighbors that you would want to invite in.

My thinking on the matter is this: If they help set it up, they got a stake in it. When the end comes, they load up and join you. THEIR empty house could help throw raiders off the scent. Makes them think everybody around here has already been hit or has moved on. Suggest that to them. And after the raids have really stopped, they still have their house to move back to if they wish.

So I'm thinking that if you want to make a go of this on your homestead, you need neighbors who are willing and ready to work that property, build a cob house, and get busy.

And frankly, if I was that neighbor, I would be thinking, "Why does he think he's going to stay in that nice big house when the rest of us are living in these dirt domes? Does that make sense to you? Everyone is in the same boat, so to speak, so we ought to be pulling on the same length oars.

They are giving up something to come throw in with you. What are *you* giving up in exchange for their help in protecting your land? The land that will now be for all of you.

Another possibility to explore is if all of your neighbors like the ideas I present here and are willing to all throw in together. You help them, they help you, and everybody makes babies together. Maybe even each from their own respective existing homes. Not as safe, but doable.

12

Data Banking

There is one thing that almost every prepper I talk to agrees on, and that is when "it" happens, one of the things we will miss the most is the Internet. We are SO used to having instant access to whatever information we desire that *not* having that access will be not only be heartbreaking but emotionally and physically destabilizing as well. (Keep in mind this information superhighway has only been around like fifteen years. What did we do before that?)

For me, the real issue will be that I will no longer be able to look up videos or tutorials on the things I need to know. Like how to build a ram pump or how to make wood gas or how to capture, process, and use the methane that is produced in my septic tank. Or make biodiesel. Or tip a cow? All *very* vital subjects for a true prepper. So how do you go about getting and KEEPING this information that will be so necessary to your survival?

Think about what kind of situation you will be in at that time. You will be trapped in the nineteenth century, or very early twentieth century at best. Sure, you will be able to make your own electricity, grow your own food, and heat your homes fairly easily, but you will *still* need access to information that you do not naturally possess. Unless you were raised on a farm *and continued with that lifestyle*, it is highly unlike that you understand crops and animal husbandry at all.

How about methods of preserving the food you grow for use during the winter? I actually *was* raised on a working farm for the first eleven years of my life. If it was on our table, we grew it, with the exception of flour, coffee, and sugar. And I am certain that my grandfather could have probably managed those items also. But we bought those with the money we made selling the eggs our chickens laid and the butter we churned from the cows we had. You will NOT be able to buy flour, sugar, and coffee after TSHTF.

Paw-Paw had horses and mules that he used to plow the fields until he finally bought a 1950 McCormick tractor about 1958. I recall working in the field every day after school. Actually, our "field" was just a very large garden of about eight acres. But we all had to work it to keep it viable.

Hoeing the weeds, picking pests off the leaves *by hand*, shoveling the manure that we would spread over the fields after the harvest. "Slopping" the hogs, which was just taking everything that we did not eat and throwing it into the hog pen. They ate our "slop." Corn husks, potato peelings, pea pods, leftover food, coffee grounds, egg-shells. Everything that came out of the garden but did not go into our mouths went to the hogs.

After the first frost hit, we killed the hogs. At least one of them. Sometimes two. I was six years old when my dad made me kill my first hog with a 22 rifle. Then we had to drag it out of the pen, hang it, clean it (remove the internal organs), scald the skin with boiling water, scrape the hair off, then cut it up and process the meat. We ate, used, or sold every single part of the animal.

We had a special building called the "Smokehouse" where we would hang hams and shoulders and backs and ribs. Paw-Paw knew just exactly how to build the perfect fire to produce the most smoke and how to get that smoke into the building to cure the meat. Some of the meat went into a salt box for curing. The salt seeped into the meat and killed all bacteria. THAT is where "Country Ham" comes from. It wasn't done to make it taste good, it was done to keep it from spoiling during the long winter.

Oh, why the long ramble about farming and curing meat when we're supposed to be talking about <u>data</u>? Well, it's pretty easy, actually. If you do not *know* how to do those things I described, you need to have ready access to material that can <u>tell</u> you how to do it. And you will NOT have the internet to look it up. (I'm certain that

I would not remember the details of most of the stuff we did on the farm.) What to do, oh, what to do? Here's what to do…

You've got to start pulling that info off the Internet _right now_, is what you do. There is an absolute plethora of information just ripe for picking. All you have to do is plug the right questions into your search engine. And then be a little discerning about which of the 144,546,876 responses to your query you are going to believe. Right?

Now, there _is_ a very good, ready-made source for a bunch of this stuff you need to know. It's called the Foxfire book series. It started in the sixties at a small college in the North Georgia mountains as a class project to collect folklore from the old timers who lived in the outlying area. It soon developed a life of its own and kept growing.

It now contains about twelve volumes of absolutely fabulous information about how things were done in the old days. It is WELL worth the price. I do not know if it is available in an electronic version, but you can find out. If so, great. If not, well, how else will future generations know what a book looks and feels like? But you should keep in mind that Foxfire does not contain everything you need to know.

I suggest you read through it, maybe spread the twelve volumes throughout your pack. Then, when you all gather to discuss what you need to research for archiving, when someone mentions how to pickle okra, if one of the pack has read about that in Foxfire, they say so and you can skip that area of research if you want to. I still recommend that you get all the information that you can in electronic format as soon as possible. Putting it on CD or DVD will keep it viable much longer, AND make it available to the whole tribe.

And speaking of books, you and your pack buddies should start collecting books right away. Everything. Books on religion, _every_ religion, so the children of the future can learn about them. Classics like Plato, Socrates, Shakespeare, Melville, Thompson. _Mad_ Magazine. Everything. Paperback is fine, just get the books.

Get homeschooling books for every grade K-12 so you can teach the next generation. Multiple sets. Teach the kids to think. Losing that ability (and we are damned close to that _now!_) would be the biggest loss of all, don't you think?

Again, spread the burden out among the pack. Be specific. "John, you gather schoolbooks about math, grades K-12. Sally, you do the same for English, Frank, you need to get the science end." If you can cover college also, that would be great. Used books are cheap.

Information will be the new currency. Get all you can, any way you can. Keep it and protect it. And until you learn how to make _paper_ (which is one of the things you will want to research), you will need literally TONS of it in your cache. And pencils, pens, crayons. Markers not so much. Markers have a very volatile carrier agent that will dry out in a year or two, rendering them useless. Maybe you can do some research and figure out a way to keep them fresh for a decade or two. If you do, let me know. Maybe Nitro Pak can keep them viable. I have not tried it for that.

Paper and paper products like books can be best stored long term if wrapped in multiple layers of that shrink-wrap shipping film, or even Saran Wrap. Take a ream of paper, wrap it tight with something like Saran Wrap and cover it in several layers of aluminum foil to deter rodents. Throw a few mothballs around to kill bugs. After The Fall, do NOT use paper for just ANY thing, like keeping the kids occupied. It is too precious. School, planning, that sort of thing is where you need paper. Maybe get several thousand pocket memo books.

The best place to store your stockpile of paper is one of those shipping containers we talked about. Just make sure there is NO way for a mouse to get inside it. Do you know that most mice can squeeze through a crack of only one-fourth inch? NEVER place paper products directly on the floor. Get some pallets in there to stack stuff on. Cover the tops of the pallets with cardboard at the very least. Then tarp the load.

But we are talking about data banking, aren't we? While having a huge collection of the printed word is fabulous, you can soon run out of room if you try to keep _everything_ in hard copy. That, and paper is very vulnerable to destruction by all sorts of calamities like water, rodents, and fire. My method for your most valuable data will not fail you if you handle it correctly and work the program. I say, "Store it all on DISC!" If you can't find Foxfire in electronic versions,

I would suggest you buy one set to have, and one set to cut up and scan into the computer for archiving.

Data on a hard drive can last five or ten years, but data on a CD or DVD is estimated to have a lifespan of over one hundred years. Do not—EVER—trust valuable data to a "thumb drive," SD card, or any other type of flash drive for long term. Not for more than a few hours or a day. They are WAY too unstable to suit me. I have lost literally *hundreds* of hours of work due to those cantankerous contraptions. And, yeah, I know to close everything out and "Safely Remove" the hardware, software-wise. Which just clears the buffers out. STILL, they have just gone BLANK on me.

So what data do you need? Anything you can think of. I started with a list of food crops we would need, like corn, tomatoes, several varieties of potatoes, beans of all flavors and varieties, beets, yams, you get the idea. And I started gathering all the information I could about each one. Like wheat. Did you know that you canNOT grow spaghetti? Or marshmallows? It is amazing the things you find out when you start looking. You need to know HOW to make spaghetti and linguini. Or how to clone marshmallows.

You want *everything*. When, where, and how to plant, protect and husband your crop. What types of soil does it like? *How to change your soil to match that!* Pests and diseases that affect the crop and how to handle them. *Without* commercial pesticides and fertilizers. Growth rate? Time to harvest? WHEN to harvest? *HOW* to harvest. Temperature range. How much sunlight is needed? Rainfall? As you read some of this stuff, you will come up with a hundred more questions about each one that you need to research.

Get all types and brands of almanacs, too. They are full of invaluable information about crops of all types. They are usually regional in scope, being selectively tuned to your part of the country due to weather and so on. It might be possible to go online and download past issues. The more knowledge you have, even if it is decades old, can be useful. Everything, even the stars themselves run in cycles. So a 1959 Greir's Almanac might fit some other year also. Or contain some piece of arcane knowledge that is no longer common knowledge.

Let's not forget information about animal husbandry. All types of animals. Ducks, pigs, chickens, geese, goats, sheep, beef cattle, milk cattle, horses, mules, donkeys, rabbits. How to care for them. What diseases are they susceptible to? How to treat those diseases? How do you kill, dress, prepare, preserve, and store the meat? The milk? How to make cheese and butter. What to watch for in dressing wild game? Eating a rabbit that has Tularemia can kill you! Any videos you can find should be downloaded and saved, too. They can be lifesaving.

Does anybody among your bunch know how to make peanut butter? How do you harness a horse for plowing? How do you MAKE a harness? How do you tan leather? You WILL need these skills. ANYbody can do these things; it only takes determination and knowledge. Making paper is not even that difficult.

You will want tomes and videos on plumbing systems, electrical systems, heating, air-conditioning, and refrigeration texts. Building methods. How-tos on repairing small engines, tractors, cars, and trucks. How to change a big truck tire (it's *much* different from changing off a car tire). How to store gasoline effectively for a long term, and the same for diesel. How to make biodiesel. Come ON, folks, THINK! Think about everything you could possibly run in to or *need* five years down the road. Or twenty.

If you have a tractor or other heavy equipment on the compound, you should have a factory shop manual for it. And a goodly cache of spare parts. The dealer for that brand can help you decide what you'll likely need. Not real sure I would tell him it's for a bug-out barn, just a distant location. Like a gold mine in Alaska or something. Get some instruction on the best method to store those spare parts long term. Does it need to be covered in Cosmoline? Will Vaseline work? Do these hoses need to be coated in RuGlyde®? Or just wrapped in oilpaper? Speaking of storage, if you have a large truck you are keeping for raiding runs or whatever, if it is going to be used just once every year or two, I recommend

Drain the radiator.
Remove all hoses and allow them to dry thoroughly.

Remove V belts.
Take out the battery.
Jack it up and remove the tires. Place them in the bed and cover with
     a tarp.
Wrap belts and hoses in oil rags.
Store everything under the tarp with the tires except the battery. Put
     the battery on a trickle charge and check it every few months.
Cover all openings—heater core, engine block, radiator, air intake,
     everything. Keep the insects and rodents out.
You might consider coating everything rubber with a preservative.
     All this keeps those items in good condition. Leaving them on
     the vehicle unused will cause the hoses and belts and tires to rot
     and the battery to sulfate. This also prevents the engine block
     from freezing and bursting.

Now, there are still other things most folks do not consider,
like…

Medicine. Not just how to treat sprains and strains, but how
to do minor surgery, like digging a bullet or arrow out of someone.
How to stitch them up. What can you use as an anti-biotic if you
have no penicillin to stave off infection? (Hint: Bees make it.) GET
VIDEOS on how to do these things. They are available! Herbal remedies and homeopathic treatments. What tools and supplies will you
need? Medical textbooks? Surgical tools? Suture kits. Lots of it is
available on Amazon. I know. I have bought it there.

Think about alternative medicines. Marketed for pets and often
sold as aquatic antibiotics, common antibiotics such as amoxicillin,
penicillin, and ciprofloxacin are sold under product names such as
FishMox®, FishPen®, and FishFlox®. Maybe talk to your vet for recommendations, or the local co-op can possibly help. Here's a few
more ideas to get you thinking in a different direction:

Garlic (and more specifically the allicin produced by cutting or crush-
     ing garlic) has been known for centuries to be a potent antifun-
     gal, antiviral, antipathogenic, and antibacterial substance. And
     with the recent scientific studies done into allicin, including the

first patented, stabilized, and fully bioavailable allicin extract (trademarked under the name *Allisure®*), it is now gaining wider acceptance in the medical community and has even been used to treat MRSA (methicillin-resistant *Streptococcus aureus*).

Cinnamon is a potent antibacterial, antifungal, and antiinflammatory spice that can also act as a natural food preservative when used in cooking. In addition to a raft of other health benefits (including a significant reduction in the pain associated with arthritis), cinnamon has been shown to have great promise in regulating and stabilizing blood sugar. **Arjuna** is an herb that has shown promise in the treatment and managements of diabetes, particularly type II diabetes.

Hawthorn has been a used in traditional medicine around the world for hundreds of years as a strengthening tonic for the cardiovascular system, as well as for its potent effects on high blood pressure and hypertension. Extracted into an alcohol-based tincture or steeped as a tea from the fresh or dried leaves and or berries.

Curcumin is one of the active components found in turmeric and is a potent antiinflammatory capable of reducing the symptoms of arthritis.

Wanna get *real* kinky? DMSO (dimethyl sulfoxide) is a universal solvent so powerful that if you dissolve a sugar cube in it and touch it to your fingertip, you will TASTE sugar within a few seconds! My wife once contracted MRSA in a hospital. We were lucky at the time to have a physician who had also worked for the CIA. He told us to make a mixture of DMSO and WHITE IODINE (decolored iodine) and paint the MRSA spots three times daily. Problem solved within three days. Iodine is powerful stuff. Stock up on it. Especially the decolored version. At the first sign of a cold, paint a square area on the underside of both wrists, the size of your wrist, with iodine three times daily. Works great.

So make your list and check it twice. Then, divvy the research duties up amongst the entire pack. Your pack should probably round table this whole idea about *what* info to dig for, also. Twelve heads being better than one and all that. And that way, everyone is involved in choosing who does what. Mary may be a closet pig farmer, who knows? So she already has a wealth of information and knows what to look for. Let HER research the pigs. And tell her she doesn't have to keep them in the closet.

Who knows how to make flour from wheat? How to spin cotton into yarn for weaving? How to build a spinning wheel? Or a gristmill to grind corn for meal and wheat for flour? Is John a weekend carpenter or an electronics type of guy? Suit the job to the person, I always say.

So what to do with the knowledge once you have it on your computer screen? Well, for the most part, you can *copy* and *paste* it into a Word document. Then print that document as a PDF file. That's what I have done. MS Word may quit working without Internet, but if you have Adobe Acrobat Reader, you can ALWAYS read a PDF. Even on a cell phone that cannot be used for communication!

For instance, if your search takes you to Wikipedia, I hit <u>Ctrl + A</u> (Hold down the Ctrl key and hit "A") to select everything on the page, top to bottom. Once you have it all selected (highlighted), hit <u>Ctrl + C</u> to *COPY* it all. Then swap over to the WORD document using <u>Alt + Tab</u> (hold down the ALT Key and tap the TAB button to switch between documents or applications.) and then hit <u>Ctrl + V</u> to paste the page into your Word document. Then use SAVE AS to save the document into the appropriate location.

And if you spend more than about five minutes working in any one document (meaning one subject, like "Pear Trees," be sure to SAVE the document frequently using <u>CTRL + S</u> so you don't accidently erase a bunch of your work. There's not much in this world that hurts that bad and is that frustrating, is there?

I usually edit each page, sometime later when I'm sitting around watching TV, but I'll edit out any useless stuff like ads or links that won't work later, mastheads, and stuff like that. Remember: SAVE AS gives a document a new name and tells it where it lives. SAVE just updates your work. These commands are also found under the FILE menu item. I only mention this stuff because someone may not know it yet.

Myself, I don't use the default folders available with Windows. I prefer to make my own. The reason is simple. There ARE limits to how long a file path can be, even in 64-bit Windows 10. They don't tell you that, but it's there. Also, shorter filenames result in quicker file access. Every time the PC has to change something, it has to spend several hundred clock cycles just finding the file NAME so it can go to a table and find where, exactly, it is on the drive. Shorter filenames, shorter access times.

So I open a File Explorer window and find the folder for the **C:** drive. In Win10, it is called WINDOWS(C:). Then I make a new folder under that, like "Prepping." Open that folder and make sub folders for each subject, like "Energy" or "Food" or "Weapons." You see it, right? So the folders are already made and ready for your use. And if not, you can always make a New Folder on the fly in the Save As dialog box if you need one. Just look for the NEW FOLDER button or menu item somewhere. Point being, save your work in a folder related to that issue. As close as possible to the *root drive.*

I could also recommend that you BUY a copy of Microsoft Office to install on your computer. These "subscriptions" to Office might or might not be available once there is no Internet. So your copy of WORD might suddenly shut off after thirty days of no Internet. Who knows? I know I wouldn't trust ANY body's word on this issue. But if you OWN your copy, it should be good as long as you have the original disc. If you buy it online and download it, you need to find out how to make a loadable install disc. It might take a bit of looking to find that but do it. And while I'm here, be sure to get Install discs for every piece of software you need, including your operating system. Just in case.

And just for the skeptics among you, yes, I *have* gone through these issues myself. I just don't recall exactly how to make a loadable install disc for Office. And you could use the practice.

Or try *OpenOffice.org* for a suite that is compatible with MS Office. But I am NOT sure they sell an install disc. Ask them. Maybe even have spare computers that are not used, just held in reserve?

One other thing you can do to protect yourself against data black-out is this…Once you get a bunch of data accumulated on a subject, PRINT it to a PDF file with a program that makes PDFs from a print command. They look like a printer to the computer and are really easy to use. I use DOPDF, but there are lots of others to choose from. This way, you should always be able to read the file on any computer or tablet. Or cell phone.

When TSHTF, cell phones won't be worth a Tinker's Damn for anything related to communication, but you will still be able to use them for lots of other stuff. Music, movies, books, games, stuff like that. Your beloved cell phone will become nothing more than a portable document reader and music player. Things that do not require it to talk to a cell tower. Unless, of course you or someone in your pack is a cell tower technician. Now THAT could be a handy person to have on board! They could set up a mini tower for the compound! One that might even be able to reach the outside world when comms come back up.

Don't forget about videos. All the video services have loads of information available. And most have ways to download the videos so you can save it to your computer. Most will also have means to keep you from using a BOT to capture their stuff, so you have to do it all manually.

Get a couple of external hard drives. At least a couple. One terabyte minimum size, and make sure it is a DISC-based HD (HDD), NOT a solid-state drive (SSD). You'll want one in use all the time while you do your research. Once a day, drag the contents of your PREPPER folder from the C Drive to the external drive to make a copy of the files. (Be SURE it says "COPY TO" instead of "Move To." If it does not, holding Control (or maybe Shift) while you drag and drop will change it to Copy.) At least once per week you want to copy THAT external drive over to the SECOND external hard drive. And when you drag _that_ Prepper folder over to the drive, be sure to change the name to include the date. "Prepper 10-28-18."

That second external drive is your Secondary Data Bank, folks. Your safety deposit box of information. Wrap the drive in six or ten layers of aluminum foil, wrap that in six or twelve layers of paper towel (for moisture abatement) stick it in a Ziploc, wrap that in more aluminum foil, and put it in a _metal_ ammo box. This box should be kept somewhere safe, away from the house. This is protection in case of a fire, flood, gang looting, or EMP attack. Just keep backing up to this Drive #2 on a regular basis. And you could also Nitro-Pak it as described in a later chapter.

Your primary data source is, of course, your C Drive. Secondary is External Drive #1, and External Drive #2 is the Failsafe Backup. Adding some packets of silica gel to the ammo box could be a good idea, too, to help keep moisture down. Do NOT use one of those El Cheepo PLASTIC ammo boxes! The main idea here is to protect the data from corruption or erasure due to an EMP and also from rodents.

Plastic cannot do this. Here's another tip: Every time I bury my backup in an ammo box, I place the hard drive in the box, then I coat the rubber lid gasket with a petroleum jelly like Vaseline®, shut the lid, clamp it, then I coat the main hinge thoroughly with Vaseline®. This protects that steel hinge pin *that you cannot see* from rusting.

Once a month, it is time to make the archival copies. If your computer does not have a DVD *BURNER*, you will need to get an external version. But you DO want to make copies of your data on DVD. A DVD can hold about four to ten CDs worth of data. Make several DVDs and store them in the ammo box as well. *This is a vital step.* My personal data file archive takes *fourteen* DVDs! Sixty-six gigs.

Yes, you already have double-redundant safety on your data, and that's great. But hard drives can also take a dump on you at any time. Putting your data on an optical disc (and taking CARE of that disc) will keep your data safe for about a hundred years. Several copies of your optical discs would be even better.

And don't forget to have a few spare DRIVES, suitably protected. Be sure to keep your dates straight and use only the LATEST dated data to make your DVDs.

Please be sure to keep the optical discs in covers or at least sleeves to prevent scratching. A scratched disc is lost data. And that is irreplaceable. Also keep in mind that if you change a file on your current working copy, it is now different from all of your backups. So anytime a file is changed in any manner, it should be saved under a new, dated name.

The method I use is to combine the file description with the date and time and my initials. That way, anyone coming behind me can tell who did what to whom and when, and how many times and in whose backyard. Like "Silver Queen Corn 10-14-19 tjm." When naming files and folders, you canNOT use a "slash" in a filename. It must be a "-" or "_."

Burn a new DVD every week or so. Several copies would be best. Hand them out to the rest of the pack. Bury some. These still need to be in METAL ammo cans, for rodent protection. Unless you would rather put the rodents in the metal can. Then you can bury the DVDs in plastic. Be sure to instruct all researchers on how to name data files to avoid confusion. And label all discs with MagicMarker.

You should also have a scanner or three. Just in case you run across some printed material you want to archive. And you can use your cell phone to photograph important stuff, too.

I can still feel how overjoyed I was the first time I realized that I could use my cell phone to take pictures of a machine that I was taking apart for service. I would now know where every cable, tube, and odd length of bolt went. And that can save your bacon when you are on your own, friend. You most valuable asset is your mind. Your ability to think and figure out what you need to survive long term on the BoL. EV-Ry-thing. From asparagus to zippers. Aspirin to Zithromycin. List it out, research it, get it, store it.

13

Communication Skills

Whether you are in the planning, building, or bug-out phase, COMMUNICATION is a must, whether on site during research, planning, and building, car-to-car during bug-out, or hiking through the woods at night bugging out, and even around your home and town before TEOTWAWKI.

When thinking about private communications, most people would think of something like CB Radio (Citizens Band) or FRS (Family Radio Service) radios that you can buy at truck stops, Wal-Mart, Amazon, just tons of places. While they have their uses (I have systems of both of those types, handheld, mobile, and base), I find the most effective, most versatile, most secure, and most powerful is the VHF/UHF amateur (ham) radios.

Yes, everything you have heard about Ham radio is true. Current United States law says you must have a license from the Federal Communications Commission (FCC) to own and operate radios in these frequencies, but it is not well policed and you are not likely to be noticed unless you irritate some local hams by stepping on their frequencies. Then they will report you.

After The Fall, who knows? Who cares? So, I say, get on it. (Wink, wink. Nudge, nudge.) But of course, you know that I am kidding because I now recite this legally required disclaimer telling you to fully comply with the law and get your Amateur Radio Operators license from the FCC so they are sure you actually know how to operate the damned thing.

That said, the probability is that if you do not play on it, if you use it only for those necessary communications, it is very unlikely you will even be noticed. And now I can safely assume that you are in possession of a First-Class FCC license and are fully qualified to own and operate a ham radio.

The biggest deal about ham radio in my eyes is POWER. The maximum power for a CB base station is 5 watts. Ham radios operate at higher powers than that even in the handheld units. Ham base stations right out of the box are 25–50 watts or greater. And watts are watt it's all about! (Pun intended.) More watts mean farther distances can be reached with greater clarity. And that is vital. "Real" ham operators are typically electronics-oriented guys who do long-distance radio communication as a hobby.

They can even send television signals over their radios! It's called SlowScan TV, and it is not actually moving pictures as we know them. The point is you can do a lot more with ham than just make a sandwich. Some of these guys even use their radio to pipe the Internet into places where it does not belong. If you want to really get into ham, by all means, please do. It IS fun, and you learn a lot. And you actually CAN talk all the way around the world using special techniques and equipment.

Lots of smaller police and sheriff departments still use analog radios that are in these ham frequency bands. If you find those, you have a built-in head start, because if they decide to "check in" on you at your house or compound, you have the ability to know about it before they get there.

Law enforcement in larger metro departments are moving toward a system called "trunking" radio. These are much more difficult to monitor with scanners or other radios. Instead of always talking on one frequency, each department is issued a "batch" of channels for use. Whenever any unit calls another unit, the computers in the towers select one frequency out of the batch and assigns it for this transmission. The receiving unit shifts its frequency to match. So you never know where to find that radio. There are scanners that can follow trunking radios, but they are not cheap.

Ham radios used to be prohibitively expensive, but now they are within everyone's reach. Handhelds can be had for as little as $25 each and a base/mobile radio for about $130, plus antenna. I suggest that you put a mobile in each vehicle of your entire entourage that will be involved in the bug-out—all the families. And one handheld per person. Even preteens can be taught to use them, and if you restrict the frequencies installed on the units, you should have no issues with going out of bounds and getting the local gendarme involved.

One note here, if five people in a car each have a handheld radio and you pick up the car mounted radio mic to check in, all those radios are going to squeal with feedback unless you do some diligence and properly assign frequencies. Also, IN the car, they should not have their radios ON. But everyone must remember that if they exit the car, turn it on. A radio that is off is about as useful as a gun with no bullets. It makes a good hammer.

I say one radio per person because if Little Johnny is in the woods relieving himself and a bear comes up on him or the cops come up on you out at the car, the situation can be communicated to the others. By the way, there are certain situations where a reply is not only unneeded, it is ill-advised. Put a little thought into that and draw up some guidelines that will work for *your* party. I use a single "click" on the transmit button for "Yes," two clicks for "No." Three for DANGER—STAY PUT.

There are many brands available, but the biggest seller is the one made by the Chinese company Baofeng (pronounced pow-fuhng). I have even seen large lots of these available on Amazon where you buy ten handhelds for about $15 each. The smaller handheld unit they have is the UV-5R model. It holds about 140 channels and is what is known as a "Dual Watch" radio. This means it can monitor (listen to) two separate frequencies at the same time. This is a very handy feature.

Notice the two different frequencies in the picture here. These are the two frequencies this radio is "listening" to. Also notice the little caret to the left of "430.000." That caret indicates that this is the "active" channel. If you press the transmit button, this is the channel you will be talking on. Press the 'A/B'

button to change this to the bottom channel and talk on that one instead.

Also, in this model, as with most of their units, the display can show channel NAMES instead of frequencies, and these names are programmed in by you. These are very versatile units!

There are base/mobile units that will monitor three or four frequencies at once. Most of them also have a SCAN mode where they will scan through whatever frequencies you select just like a police scanner. The difference between monitor and scan is that in dual watch (or QUAD watch) you select two (or three or four, depending on the radio) frequencies to monitor. These frequencies will appear in the LCD display window and are available instantly to talk on. If you have a party working down at the stream on a pump and another out in the woods cutting trees, you can hear both.

If the woods team calls, you hear it, and if you press the transmit button within a few seconds, your radio automatically selects that frequency to transmit on. (This depends on your specific model of radio.)

SCAN means that the radio will operate like a police scanner. It will look at every frequency that you select (when programming the radio) and check it for activity. If there is any activity, it will break squelch and let you hear what is happening. As before, with dual watch, if you press transmit within a certain time, you can talk back on that same frequency. See the manual for details.

The big difference between this type of scan and a regular scanner (like the Uniden Bearcat) is that a regular scanner can check several <u>hundred</u> channels *per second*. Using the Baofeng in scan mode only checks THREE frequencies per second. I *do* use mine in scan mode quite often, though. I will set the top display to the channel I most want to monitor, then set the bottom display to anything and press SCAN. That way, the bottom is scanning, and the top is set solid on the one I *must* hear. One word of caution, though, I never program more than six channels for scan in my radios due to the three-per-second scan rate limitation.

If you have fifteen frequencies scanning like this, you would be checking each channel only once every five seconds. That might be the difference between life and death. Also, with the Baofeng, you must program into the radios what channels to scan while they are hooked to a computer and you are doing other programming duties.

Another good thing about the Baofeng is that they are easy to program, and the radios usually come with the programming cable and a software disc. I use a free program called CHIRP for programming my radios. CHIRP was written by a ham radio group and it is available at *www.danplanet.chirp.com*. Anytime a new radio (one that is not on their list) comes out or is purchased by a member, it is sent to one of their coders as a courtesy for research.

They then determine how that radio talks to the computer, and they include that coding into the latest "build" of CHIRP. Every time I want to program a radio I go to CHIRP and download the latest build to make certain that any bugs for MY radio that have been found and corrected are included on my computer.

There are full instructions available for CHIRP, but the process is really easy. Open Chirp, plug the radio into the PC, select your radio from the list, turn it on, and turn the volume on the radio all the way up. Hit DOWNLOAD and let the computer read the radio.

Make any changes or additions to the frequencies list that you wish and hit UPLOAD to send it to the radio. By the way, the adapter cables you use to go from PC to radio actually have a computer chip in them that handles all the translation from radio to PC, and vice versa. Some of the cheaper ones use a knock-off or "clone" chip that sometimes does not function as planned. I suggest you splurge for the high-priced spread on this one.

I'm going to give you a tip about programming these buggers. Each radio must be "read in" to the computer to establish its identity. THEN you make changes to the programming and read that back to the radio. IF you are programming ten frequencies or fifty, doing that for forty radios can get old. Here's how to do it quickly:

Do one radio. Read it in, make programming changes, upload it to the radio. Then select all of the data on the frequency page by selecting the upper left data box, hold down SHIFT, and select the lower right data box, then hit CTRL + C to Copy it. "Save As' the radio info, with a name like "Tom's UV5 10-28-18." Close this radio off. Disconnect it.

Connect the next radio and download it to the computer. Click the top left spot in the programming field. Hit CTRL + V to paste the information you copied from the last radio. Upload it to the radio. Save it "AS" and close it. That's it.

You just keep pasting the information into each radio that you hook up. No need to type it forty times. Note that any changes you make to the SECOND tab (I think it says "Settings") will have to be manually entered for each radio, but that will be very few items. You need to write them down as you *will* have to put those changes in manually for each radio.

This Copy and Paste operation will allow you to quickly alter the frequency list and Quiet Tone setups for each radio without having to manually input each and every one of them. The big caution here is, just like any other document you have ever worked on, if you copy this info, you can paste it as many times as you want, *but you cannot copy anything ELSE until you are finished with THIS data.*

Since each radio that you "Read-In" to CHIRP opens a new tab, you *can* simply switch to the tab of the first radio, select all of its data, and copy it and then switch back to the tab of the radio you are working on and paste it in. That works too. Also, I like to save each radios data to a new file with a name that lets me identify it easily and usually contains the date the file was made, so I can always pull up the latest if anything happens.

Say Bob dropped his radio in the lake, and it is not working. If I take a spare radio out of stock, I can just plug it up and drop the data from his last update into this new radio. This method also allows me to keep private channels straight. If I assign three Private frequencies to John's family, I don't want those frequencies to be the same ones that I use for MY family.

Everybody needs to practice *using* the radios. It seems that some-how, *every*body wants to start talking before they press the transmit button. Until they get practiced up on it. The process should be: PRESS the button, count to ONE, then talk, *count to one*, then release the button. A helpful habit is for everyone to say "Over" at the end of each transmission to indicate that the other person may now talk. (It was originally "Over to you.")

I suggest you assign unit numbers to everyone to avoid using names on the radio. Don't give away any information you don't need to, right? Everyone in "Family ONE" should have unit numbers beginning with "1," Family Two begins with 2 and so on. Dad would probably be "101" or "201" and Mom could be "102" or "202" and so on. The houses would be "100," "200," etc. That prevents mistakes in case there are multiple persons with the same name, like "Chip" or whatever.

Initiate a radio conversation this way: The person starting the conversation states THEIR unit number, followed by the unit number of whomever they are calling. Such as "Three-zero-three to two-one-two, over." Two-one-two would respond by saying "Two-one-two, go ahead, over," or maybe "Go for two-one-two." And then back and forth. At *the end of the entire conversation*, each person says their unit number followed by "Clear." This indicates they are finished with the channel. But getting used to pressing that button a second before you speak seems to elude a lot of people. Work on it. Otherwise you're gonna hear a lot of "Can you repeat that?"

I recommend you install a BASE unit in at least one of the houses on the property. In ALL of the houses would be best. That way, instant communication from house to house is possible, and each household can keep track of its individual members. But at least one house should have a base unit.

I say this because all the handhelds must be recharged every night. ALL night. And while I'm on that tack, it is a good idea to order spare parts for your radios. Belt clips, extra batteries, and antennas. These things WILL break or wear out, and there will be no way to replace them. Extra radios would also be a plus to anticipate growth of the tribe plus those radios that go bad. At least three or four changes of clips and antenna for each and every radio. With several spare batteries so you can have a battery charging all day, then charge the radio at night.

With a base station antenna fairly high up in a tree, you will be able to communicate farther from the base unit to the handhelds.

The higher the antenna, the longer the reach, especially if the terrain is hilly. In the case of hilly terrain, the handhelds may not reach each other over the hill. Radio communication is always "line of sight." Each antenna in any conversation must be able to "see" the others involved.

It depends upon many factors, and you will find that you might be able to bounce a signal over a small hill or whatever. But as a rule of thumb, if you cannot stretch a string from one radio to the other, they will probably not talk. So, obviously, the higher the antennas are, the greater the possible range.

Oh yeah, consider having a mobile radio unit installed on tractors and four wheelers, also. Or horses and mules. It CAN be done. Use a motorcycle battery to power it. Strap the battery and antenna to the harness, saddle, whatever. Motorcycle batteries are gel-cell type and will not spill acid out.

When I was nine years old, my dad got CB radios for his business. Big, bulky, vacuum tube models. There were no transistors in 1961. One of my friend's dad did the same thing. But HIS kid had him put a radio on his pony cart! We would spend all day on Saturday riding that pony cart all over town talking on the CB.

With a little effort, you can learn all you need to about telephone systems and even build your own. Something that will talk from house to house or house to barn or whatever. Not as versatile as the radio, it can nonetheless be useful, and cops or neighbors cannot overhear your conversations with a scanner.

Having a "telecom test set" and a little knowledge means that I can stop at any little green box sticking out of the ground and clip onto a telephone hard line and make a call to anywhere the phones go. For as long as the telephone company is still operating, that is. All knowledge is a good thing, my friend. Learn all you can.

I mentioned the police scanner earlier somewhere. There are plenty to choose from, from lots of places. Personally, I like Uniden Bearcat line. Versatile and easy to use, they can be indispensable.

Read the manual thoroughly and start looking for all the frequencies in use in your home locale. And also, the area around your BoL.

Keep a thorough log of date, time, frequency, traffic (what is said, what is talked about, and any other information you can garner from the conversation). Monitoring for several days or weeks on any frequency is best so that you get a good idea of what that channel is all about.

After a while you should know all there is to know about the radios used by your local police, fire, EMS, and whatever. You will also, if you are patient, find a lot of the frequencies used by the local ham radio buffs. That can be handy info too! You see, the _real_ purpose of this exercise is to determine what frequencies are NOT in use in your area. Those are the ones that YOU can use.

Let's talk a minute about one aspect of radio communication that is vital to understand. Squelch. If your radio should output to the speaker everything that the antenna receives on whatever frequency you have tuned to, it would be a constant hissing sound called "white noise." Very irritating.

The squelch circuit monitors the received signal and turns the speaker OFF until it reads a signal level that exceeds that white noise. It is an adjustable setting, so you can determine how high a signal level needs to be in order for the radio to "break squelch," or turn the speaker on, and it depends on many factors.

Your radio might be receiving a signal from a distant transmitting unit, a signal that is just barely loud enough to override the squelch system and annoy you with a signal that you can barely hear and definitely cannot understand. Turning the squelch level UP a notch would keep that weak signal from coming through, leaving you uninterrupted until a stronger signal is received.

Ham radios also have a means of making your communications more "private," at least to a degree. It is commonly referred to as "quiet tones." For our example, we'll use a frequency of _one hundred fifty-four point four hundred megahertz_, written as 154.400 MHz. ONE hertz means the radio wave cycles up and down one time per second, so our example frequency cycles 154,400,000 times per second.

If you are set to 154.400 MHz as a main frequency, you can select from several different *types* of quiet tone technology, and in each of those, maybe up to twenty different "channels" within the main frequency. The net result is that you kind of have channels within channels. Which means that if you are set to 154.400 MHz and have a quiet tone of sixty-five set, no other radio could hear your conversations unless THEY were set up exactly the same way. The odds of that happening are, well, they're big. Read everything you can find on this.

The point of all of this is…suppose you are scanning for police frequencies. Once you have identified those frequencies, then you can possibly set your scanner to *search* for the quiet tones that are in use on those channels. Not all scanners can do this. Be sure you select a scanner that can scan for quiet tones. It will say so. When searching for a scanner to buy, if it does not mention this in the description, get the model number, plug it into an Internet search engine, and download the user's manual. There, you can determine for definite if that scanner can do it. If it will not, move on till you find one that will. Why? Those quiet tones will enable you to put the police frequencies into your ham radios and monitor them more closely without everyone having to have a scanner.

I know of one compound where the situation did not permit the residents being secluded from the neighbors. Every house along this particular road was RIGHT up against the road, usually within fifteen to twenty feet of the edge of this one-lane road. Almost all of them thought just like I do about how things were going and were eager to band together for mutual protection and production in case TEOTWAWKI happened. So each family bought a handheld radio. In programming the radios for them, I set up one common channel that they all used to call one another. The other channel in these dual watch radios was for that particular family or person.

With this setup, Dan could call for Mary on the common channel. Mary would respond on that channel and then both of them would switch to either the Mary or the Dan channel for the conversation. Since all radios kept one of the two Dual Watch channels constantly set for the common channel, no one need ever miss any call for conversation, or an "All Call Alert," indicating there is a danger approaching that could affect us all. It is one of the things you set up in programming to have the radio "power up" with one particular channel in the top position of the display or otherwise. That ensures this frequency is always ready when you turn the radio on.

A perfect example of that need occurred once when the first person on the road (where the road turned off a main highway) noticed dump trucks traveling WAY too fast down this winding one-lane road that has many small children living along it. She issued an "all call alert" on the common channel. Frank heard it and called Dave to meet him in front of his house, which he did, armed as he always is, as was Dave. When the next dump truck came barreling down the road, they stepped into the road and stood there. Let's just say they took care of the problem. Because they could communicate and help each other quickly.

One more tidbit about quiet tones...They do NOT give you _exclusive_ use of a frequency. They only allow you to use that frequency without someone overhearing you _easily_. In reality, if you are using 154.400 with a quiet tone of 65, and someone else wants to use 154.400 with a QT of 72, the two of you will be "stepping on" each other all the time.

If you are transmitting on a frequency, that frequency is in use. Period. Anyone else trying to use that _frequency_ can only override your transmission if their radio is stronger. Or closer. Point being, don't share frequencies thinking the quiet tones will give you exclusivity, it will not. So you actually need quite a few frequencies to contain all the personal channels that you might want to use. And _conversely_, if you notice your radio lighting up like it's receiving something, SOMEbody is ON THAT CHANNEL! Might want to look into that. But keep in mind 154.400 and 154.405 are different channels. There is LOTS of room!

Also, in your radio research and purchasing, don't forget to include antennas. How many base antennas will you need? What type? I recommend that you get one _really_ good base radio, like a Yaesu or similar. The type real hams use for long-distance (DX) communications. You will also want a linear amplifier for ham bands, like a 500-watt or 1,000-watt. And a directional antenna with rotator and a mast or tower to hold it up.

A directional antenna—called a "beam" antenna usually has three to five additional elements to it. These are reflectors that increase and direct the transmitting power and also amplify the received signal. This is how you get real long-distance communications. Like hundreds or thousands of miles. Don't forget the cabling to go from the radio to the antenna. Also extra connectors in case you need to adjust the length of the cabling and a standing wave meter (SWR Bridge) for adjusting things. Look it up.

With this setup, you can contact other groups like yours. You should be very selective about divulging where you are. Over the radio, you cannot tell anything about the person on the other end. It might be a trap.

And get a book on ham lingo so you can fit in and understand when you tune to a frequency and hear someone saying "CQ, CQ. CQDX." What on earth could that mean? It means that someone is on that frequency looking for a new contact. They "seek you." *DX* means "long distance." (*X* replaces the "istance.") You've got a lot of stuff to learn, Vern. Get busy.

And while we're talking about communications, let us not forget the fine art of <u>*silent*</u> communication. Like using hand signals to convey a message. Clickers can also be handy. Only you and your bunch will have them. That is almost a guarantee. They can be heard in the woods for a surprisingly long distance, and a simple code system can get a lot of message across that anyone following you will not understand.

For instance, you are bugging out on foot and have just fallen asleep. Your watch hears footsteps in the distance and clicks three—a warning. You jump up and touch everyone to wake them. One click, pause, two clicks, and they all disperse in a prearranged pattern to encircle the invaders. Not a word has been spoken, but everyone knows what is happening and where they are supposed to be. Your pursuer may have heard the clicks, but you can bet he's got no clue what's meant by them. Intricate moves like this require lots of practice.

Now, let's discuss radio security measures. You have your frequencies set up and programmed into the radios, and if you followed my cut and paste instructions, all radios are programmed identically. So, if all of you are on "All Call" or whatever, if everyone goes up one channel, they should all still be on the same channel, able to communicate.

Now here's a scenario: A gang of raiders has made their way into your neck of the woods. One of them has a scanner running, looking for communications that would indicate there are people nearby. They hear something and call for a stop. They camp. And over the next few days, they monitor and plan, and search for you and your compound. Once they are ready to pounce, they have already identified at least your basic comm channels, and they can listen in to your directions and plans.

So let's set up a scrambling system that would be difficult, if not impossible, for them to follow. It is called "frequency hopping," and it works like this: One of your members, perhaps out hunting a few miles away, runs across the gang of raiders working their way toward the compound through the woods. He has just enough time to report the contact to his base by radio before he is either taken or has to go radio silent. To go radio silent, I first announce my intent to base like this, "401 to base, going dark. Repeat, 401 to base, going dark." Base now knows that something's wrong and they cannot call me. I turn my radio off.

Now the compound knows trouble is on the way in. One command from the leader should put everyone on the same page of action. At my compound, I would issue a command by radio—"Condition RED! JUMP! JUMP! Condition Red! Jump! Jump! Acknowledge!" I now expect to hear each person respond using their unit number and responding IN ORDER (to avoid confusion). Like this: ("100" >pause< "101" >pause<) until all are accounted for. If 403 does not respond for fifteen seconds, 404 should go ahead.

Every member of the team knows that in this situation, after they have acknowledged the jump command, they are to GO to a channel called "JUMP 1." That is the starting point.

The next transmission that occurs is a triggering event. At the end of that radio exchange, if it lasts ten seconds or ten minutes, the conversants sign off as usual: "Then, that's where I will be, 412. Over. 302 clear." "Roger that, 302. 412 clear. **JUMP, JUMP.**"

That last word, *JUMP*, tells EVERYONE to go up one channel in the JUMP sequence. Your radios will hold about 140 channels, so you have plenty of room for like FIFTY or more "go" channels, should you need that many, so you should not run out. If I said "DOWN 3," what should my pack do?

When programming your radios, you need a list of JUMP channels. Like the first JUMP channel would be 173.65 MHz with a QT of 35. The next could be set to 446.750 MHz and QT 75. THREE can be 165.135 MHz, QT 82. See what's happening? I'm jumping all over the place, frequency wise, I'm even switching bands from VHF to UHF. And the only thing my people have to do is hit the channel UP button one time for each jump after the first one. And by giving the jump channel destination (GO SIX!), everyone knows where they should end up, since the radios display the channel NAME in the LCD display, not the actual frequency. And if they miss one? It is easy to move up and down the GO channels looking for the active one. I would switch to GO 5 and announce my presence, like "602" is all I would say.

If someone hears me, they repeat my number, so I know that I was heard, and this is the currently active GO channel. Your opposition would need computers hooked up to scanners plugged up to a psychic's…whatever to keep up with this and find your frequencies. Using JUMP, all transmission MUST be essential. NO CHATTER! Keeping in touch can save your hickory-smoked bacon. Plan it well.

One more thing to mention about radios. You should really consider getting some of those earpiece/mic things that clip to your lapel. With that, you can communicate almost noise-free. At least your radios are not blaring out through the speakers for the whole world to hear.

This can be very useful, perhaps even necessary, in an evade and pursuit situation. There are also "laryngophones" available. Throat mics like fighter pilots use. I prefer the standard over-the-ear type that has a mic on a stick next to your lips. You can speak more quietly like this. And in the scenario that I described above, I would not have to turn my radio off or "Go dark," since communication would not be coming over my speaker to be overheard. IF YOU ARE ABOUT TO BE CAPTURED, turn your radio to an unused channel so they cannot overhear anything.

14

Packing For The Long Haul With Nitrogen

The enemy is _not_ "Time." It is oxygen. The giver of life and also *The Great Destroyer*. Without oxygen, there is almost nothing on this rock that can live. Yeah, sure, there are some anaerobic bacteria, such as those that live in sewer systems, compost heaps, and similar places. But for the most part, everything living needs the big "O." And without oxygen, most chemical reactions cannot take place. Like rust, for example. Rust is OXidation.

If you think about it long enough, you will see that rust is nothing but "slow fire." The steel is actually burning. The carbon in it is combining with oxygen, just like carbon atoms from wood gas combine with oxygen in a fire. The difference is only in the speed of the reaction.

I am going to hit a sidetrack for a moment to tell you all that I don't give a FIG what you *believe* or what you were told or taught. _OXYGEN IS NOT FLAMMABLE!_ Despite the abundance of signs in every hospital in America that says "CAUTION! FLAMMABLE!" everywhere oxygen is in use. Oxygen is the ONLY "constant" in the fire triangle, which says "Fuel + OXYGEN + Heat = FIRE." The fuel can be anything from wood to plastic to gasoline.

The heat can be anything from an electrical spark to concentrated sunlight to suddenly being struck (because the energy of the moving hammer turns into heat upon impact). But ALL fire requires oxygen.

The fuel is what BURNS. Gasoline, acetylene, propane, kerosene, cloth, lumber. All those things are fuel. They are hydrocarbons. You need the carbon molecules from the fuel COMBINING with oxygen to create carbon monoxide and carbon dioxide, and the hydrogen combines with leftover oxygen to make water. H2O. You can subject oxygen to all the heat you have and the oxygen will not burn. Don't let anyone tell you otherwise. Not only am I a fireman (captain, actually), I am also an engineer.

Oxygen SUPPORTS combustion. _IT_ does NOT burn! THAT said, here's how they fool you. Oxygen is lighter than air, it rises. Turn a glass upside down and blow some O2 into it. Then strike a wooden match. Hold the match under the glass and move it _into_ the glass and _WOOOF!_ Explosion. Idiots will tell you that that proves the OXYGEN blew up; therefore, it is flammable. Not true. Oxygen _accelerates_ combustion so that the burning gases coming off the match suddenly have the chemical reaction of fire <u>accelerated</u> by the presence of the oxygen. THAT was the WOOF.

Here's the secret to all this falderal. Oxygen is just about THE most active element in our pantheon of chemistry. It will combine with almost anything. And change the thing it combines with into something totally different. And it supports all forms of living things that _feed_ on other things. Like bacteria that eat meat and cause it to rot.

But, Roy, boy, you say, "How can we keep the bad ole oxygen from doing these nasty things?" The answer is really simple, actually. Replace it with something else. There are some gases among the elements that are **inert**. Nonreactive. We call these the NOBLE gases, because they seem to be "above" the need to react with the more "common" elements.

Helium, argon, and NITROGEN are among these. But of them all, nitrogen is the most abundant by far. Our atmosphere is comprised of about 20 percent oxygen and 78 percent NITROGEN. All the other gases combined only make 2 percent of our air.

It is the fact that nitrogen (which literally means "to choke" in Greek) is inert is what makes it so useful in protecting our foods and equipment. If you put a piece of metal into an airtight enclosure, remove the air inside and replace it with nitrogen, it will not rust!

EVER. There is no oxygen inside to combine with the steel, so iron oxide cannot form.

If you have a bucket of, say, wheat flour and you remove the air and replace it with nitrogen, the insect eggs that are _always_ present in this product cannot hatch and grow into larvae to eat your wheat. Sorry, it doesn't work with fresh meats and vegetables. But for the most part, nitrogen-filled packaging will protect dry foodstuffs and metals.

One of the simplest ways to keep the oxygen away from food and other goods is to remove it and replace it with nitrogen. It is really easy. The hardest part may be accumulating the gear necessary to do this. I'm lucky there, I have been a mechanical contractor for over forty years, so I already have the necessary gear.

The list of gear is pretty short, but some of it is also pretty pricey. Like the vacuum pump. I use the same vacuum pump that I use to evacuate air and moisture from a refrigeration system before charging it with Freon. Basically, it just sucks the air out of any closed vessel you can connect it to. I paid over $300 for the one I use, and that was nearly thirty years ago. When you "pull a vacuum" on a container, any moisture in it will evaporate and be sucked out.

I just found that you can get a vacuum pump from one of those discount tool places for about $90, and a hand vacuum pump for probably $30. Next you will need a nitrogen source. Unfortunately, that only comes one way. Pressurized tanks that you get from a welding supply store. They _might_ rent you the tank, but they will probably want to sell it. About $150 for a 25-cubic-foot tank.

Then you need the pressure regulator. Another $100–150. This device screws into the tank outlet and reduces the tank pressure to a safe level. The nitrogen in that tank has been compressed to 2,200 psi.

That much pressure can kill if released unregulated. I have seen that happen twice in my life. Watched people die by having a part of some equipment shot through their body by unregulated nitrogen because some idiot wanted to save thirty seconds. So YOU put a regulator on that tank to give you the 2 psi you need to nitro-pack stuff.

And do NOT try to use unregulated nitrogen! You can NOT "crack" the valve open to get "just a little." When that valve opens, you have 2,200 pounds of pressure blowing your skirt up.

Next you need some hoses and a valve manifold to connect the nitrogen tank, the vacuum pump, and your product hose. The product hose is the hose you use to connect to whatever you want to nitro-pack. It should usually terminate in a football needle for your application. And you must hook to the tank, vacuum pump, and product at the same time.

Given all that, it is only natural that I lean toward using a refrigeration charging and testing manifold for all of this. That same tool outlet store has those for sixty bucks. Which is really a bargain. You get two valves on a manifold, two pressure gauges, and three hoses.

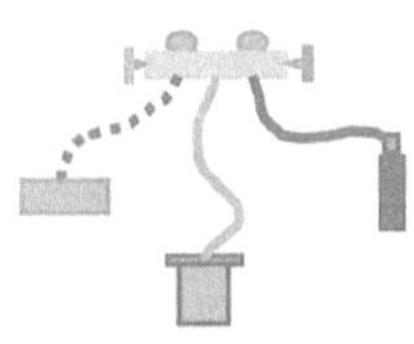

In this diagram, you see how to hook it all together. The manifold pictured above is at the top, the vacuum pump is on the left, the nitrogen tank is on the right, and the bucket of wheat is at the bottom. The hose colors are pretty much universal as blue–yellow–red, from left to right.

You will need to buy some adapter fittings from a hardware or plumbing supply to complete the set up. The hoses on the refrigeration manifold terminate in female ¼" flare fittings. The nitrogen regulator outlet is either ¼" or 3/8" FPT (female pipe thread). The vacuum pump will have a ¼" MALE flare fitting, which the blue manifold hose will screw directly to with no adapter.

To get from the nitrogen regulator to the manifold hose, you need an MPT × ¼" male flare half union with the MPT part either ¼" or 3/8", depending on the regulator outlet size. It's called a HALF union because the two ends are different. A FULL union (or just "union") would be the same size AND THREAD on both ends.

Then you have to adapt the football needle up to the ¼" female flare of the manifold hose. Be sure to use Teflon thread sealant tape on all PIPE thread fittings but NOT on the flare fittings. Okay, now hook the red hose to the nitrogen tank regulator, hook the blue hose to the vacuum pump, and the yellow hose becomes your product hose with the football needle on the end.

First, a short course on pressure. Pressure is expressed in various ways, depending on how much pressure is being measured. We are all used to seeing PSI, which means "pounds per square inch," which is, actually, an incomplete description. The air above us exerts pressure on everything you see. At sea level, this pressure is 14.7 psi. So all the gauges that *we* use to measure pressure are calibrated to exclude this 14.7 psi. If your tire pressure gauge reads "30 psi," it is really saying "30psi**G**," for "gauge."

Laboratory gauges read in psi**A**, for "absolute," which means they do NOT exclude atmospheric pressure. In our setup, we are using GAUGE pressure, so the ZERO line on your manifold gauge is really at atmospheric pressure. BELOW that zero line, we use "inches of water column" or "W.C," to express the <u>*negative*</u> pressure of a vacuum, because it is in much smaller increments. It takes about 29.9" W.C to equal 1 psi.

Set up the rig as shown and insert your charging needle (yellow hose) into your product can or bag. With both handwheel valves on the manifold closed, start the vacuum pump. Crack open the nitrogen tank valve and adjust the pressure regulator output (left gauge) to about 2 psig. You also need to crack the red hose fitting at the manifold a little bit loose so some nitrogen can escape while you adjust the regulator. Then close the red hose fitting when you're set to go.

Open the RED valve to blow nitrogen through the red line and the manifold body. This bleeds any air in the line from the tank out. CLOSE the red valve. Open the blue valve fully and watch the gauge. It might take several minutes, but it should bring the needle DOWN to about 25–29" W.C.

Let's say you want to pack away some oatmeal so that it will keep for years instead of months. Fill a zip lock bag with oatmeal. Or a five-gallon bucket if you have that much. Zip the bag almost closed and put the football needle in the opening just before the zipper hits the end. If you wrap the needle in Teflon tape or a pinch of dental wax, it will seal better.

Open the blue valve to connect the vacuum pump to the needle in the bag. Pinch the bag tightly around the football needle. The bag will rapidly collapse as the air is pumped out. Hold the bag tight over the needle stem, being careful to not block the needle openings while <u>you turn the blue valve off</u> and open the red valve. The bag will expand as it is filled with pressurized nitrogen.

Turn the red valve off. Quickly remove the needle from the bag and immediately zip the bag shut completely *as you squeeze the bag flat.* This squeezing action reduces the volume of the bag, and the expulsion of some of the excess nitrogen as you zip it shut ensures that no dirty old air gets back into the bag. Your bag is now filled with nitrogen instead of air! As long as that zipper seal remains intact, the nitrogen will be there protecting your oatmeal. Or your ammunition. Whatever.

You should get a LOT of uses out of that nitrogen tank. When the pressure on the tank gets down to 25 psi as shown by the right-hand gauge on the regulator, you need to take the tank back to the welder's supply and trade it for a full one. And always remove the regulator when not in use.

Yeah, I know. You give them a tank that you just paid $150 for and they give you a used one. Them's the breaks, Jake. Thousands of welders have argued that point for a hundred years. You will lose. Give up. Now. While they are still willing to sell you nitrogen. And don't forget—don't tell them what you want the nitrogen for. Tell them you put it in your car tires. They'll buy that. "Yes, sir, I DO have a regulator and all necessary hoses and fittings."

In all truth and fairness, simply vacuuming the air (which contains oxygen) out of any storage system will extend the shelf life of most foods and greatly improve the long-term viability of durable goods like bullets. As for food storage, there are many various means and methods of vacuum sealing foodstuffs that are available on the market. Just pick one. Reusable zipper bag with a valve in each bag and a hand pump or a machine that uses special bags and sucks the air out then heat seals the bag.

But there is one, very *large* difference between vacuum sealing and nitrogen filling a storage container. Vacuuming out the air will

ALWAYS leave *some* air inside. Your zip lock bagging system described here is certainly NOT a perfectly sealed system and you would do well to achieve 20–25" W.C vacuum with the setup I describe here. But keep reading...

What this means to *you* is that there is always some air, some oxygen left inside your vacuum sealed bag, even if you managed to achieve a 20" W.C vacuum. And some bacteria, some moisture. Bacteria is the scourge of food storage. Moisture, the bane of metals and gunpowder. The advantage of the system I give you is that it replaces the life-giving oxygen in the bag with death-dealing nitrogen. Not many bacteria can live in an atmosphere of nitrogen. So, given the choice, I choose the nitrogen method.

I have known many people who purchased five-gallon buckets of raw flour, meal, rice, beans, etc. That was their food stash. And it worked well, but you must make sure you have food grade cans. One five-gallon bucket of rice can last you a year, probably. And actually, I think they should be easy to Nitro-Pak.

 First, you need some valves like you find in a sports ball. And a needle used to pump up a ball. You might also want the two most commonly used needle valve tools, the  inserter and the remover. You will have to adapt the needle to your hose from the refrigeration manifold as above.

Drill a hole in the lid of the bucket, put the valve in (I suggest you put a *small* dollop of silicone sealant around the _valve_ prior to insertion), and replace the lid on the bucket. The lids have really good seals in them, but I would recommend that you coat those seals with a good grade of petroleum jelly. This will help make a better seal and also help prevent the rubber drying out. Now you can insert the needle, vacuum the can out, and fill it with nitrogen. Easy peasy, possum's greasy.

You can also do this process to an ammo can. They also have great seals (better than the buckets) and are designed to last a long time. At least the military versions are. So, drill the top, deburr it, silicone the valve in, and grease the lid seal, and you should be good to pack your ammo or anything else in nitrogen. You can use plastic ammo cans (if they have a lid gasket) to bury your ammo in. But I would suggest covering the metal hinge and latch with petroleum jelly very thoroughly then wrap the whole thing in several layers of clear wrap. That is after it is nitro packed and right before you bury it.

Thank you and good night.

15

Map The Path To Freedom

You have your BoL picked out and purchased. Next step is to make sure everybody knows how to get there. Whether it is in a vehicle or on foot. Because you never know what will happen. You might have your vehicle prepared and even have a spare PCM for it. But what if someone steals your car? Maybe even halfway to the BoL. How do you get there now?

For sure, it will take a LOT longer to walk there. Even if it is only twenty miles, it will likely take a full day or more. Trekking through woods is slow going, especially wearing a full pack and dragging a couple of kids along. Now what if it is a couple of *hundred* miles? You're going to cover ten, maybe twenty miles a day. Four hundred eighty miles will take you a minimum of twenty-four days to hike that distance with your family. Or your entire pack.

So let's get ready for this. Take a map, preferably a topographical map, one that shows the height of the land using concentric rings. The smallest rings will show the tops of hills and mountains. Spreading out from those will be rings showing decreasing altitudes. Topos are really good for helping you pick likely places to find creeks or rivers or lakes and ponds.

If your map does not show roads, you should consider getting one that does, then take them both to either a FedEx store, UPS store, Kinkos, or Office Depot. They can scan the maps in and merge them, producing one map that shows the topography AND the roads. You can do this yourself if you're good. I suggest you at least let them scan the maps for you. One other path is to take your topo and hand draw the roads in using a satellite image from a maps app to see them.

With your map spread out, begin working out the path to your BoL from your home. I have never found a map that did not have an indication of which way was north, the "Legend Compass." So start picking your direction of travel and marking it lightly in pencil on the map. Be sure to mark the heading every so often also, particularly when there is a change in direction. This you get from the map. Open your lensatic compass fully and place it flat down on the map. You might need a T-square to draw some lines down from the top that are square to map north.

You will need to make sure your compass is pointing to true north ON THE MAP before you take down a heading. Consider also that north on the map may NOT be straight up and down to the page. If this is the case, use a long straight edge to draw a north–south line through the legend compass (the one printed on the map), then use a drafting triangle and straight edge to extend lines that are parallel to the N-S reference line across the map to where you are marking.

Once the preliminary route is marked, you and your other pack leaders should plan a trip to walk the trail and drive the roads to get familiar with the route. Stuff your packs with food and tents and clothes and radios, and start walking. Probably from the house of your pack member that is closest to the BoL.

Check the accuracy of your selected trail as you go, making any necessary corrections as you run into obstacles or whatnot. Like houses or whiskey stills. (You might want to avoid those.) Unless a much more direct route takes you otherwise, try to stay within one to two hundred yards of a major road and as close to a creek as possible. And fer the love of Mike, carry some bear repellant, please? And your weapons.

Stay sharp and alert. Everyone should practice NOT talking or using cell phones at ALL. Keep your eyes open and your heads on a swivel. Look out for game trails, nesting or resting areas for big and small game, roads, and human sign. Look up and check for congregations of squirrel nests. And DON'T forget to constantly scan the ridge lines above you for signs of predators, both two- and four-legged. Also be on the alert for any DANGER signals that the wildlife put out there. If a hundred birds suddenly take flight past the top of the ridge to your left, it is probably worth checking out. Or watching. Carefully.

Mark all these on your map at exact GPS coordinates. These are the places that hunters will frequent and particularly after The Fall when food is scarce. It would not be a bad thing if you and your buddies actually killed a few squirrels or rabbits to eat along the trail. Good practice. But don't forget to check the carcasses for disease like tularemia before you cook them.

You are also looking for places to cache food and water later. If your BoL is a many days' journey, you will need them. You will depend on them to stay alive. So no more and no less than the space of one's day's journey apart, you should have a set of caches large enough to support everyone.

If there are eight families in your pack, you might want to have eight caches at each location, designated by family, so you know where *your* stash is and that is the one that *you* will use. This is in case you all get separated from the others. The bad guys will not expect you to have multiple caches at each point, so if someone stumbles upon one of the places where you have a cache, they are not likely to even look for the others.

If you reach cache point 7 and find that the food stash for your family has been raided or destroyed, well, that is the reason everyone is carrying emergency rations and water filtration straws and bottles. And even if you miss a meal or two, all you need is water to survive for seven days.

You are going to mark potential cache points along the way. Now do you get why I want you to stay close to roads if possible? When you come back to bury supplies, you don't want to have to carry 100# of stuff for three miles into the woods. You need to know how many cache points you will need for your entire pack to make the journey. Also, be sure to mark the spot on the ROAD where you leave it to carry goods into the woods. Ideally, this should be out of view of a house or other gathering point for people. You do NOT want folks to see you going into the woods with a lot of stuff and then coming out empty-handed.

I should probably caution you to make the best time possible, but we must consider that you will be traveling with people and not everyone can keep the same pace. If the practice run takes multiple trips to complete, so be it. It would be better to try and take four long weekends to get this right than to rush it and try to stuff everything into one eight-day journey. You cannot get it right if you rush.

The cache points you are looking for should be places where there is some major feature that will be easy to see, like a rock out-cropping or a large fallen tree with an unusual shape. I'm not saying to put your cache AT the rock or the tree, just that you use such a thing as a marker that there is a cache nearby.

One method is to have several directions and distances that are consistently used. Like one set for each family to find *their* cache. So you find your tree, mark it on the map, and note the starting point. Like, you put a line on the map for the tree, with an *X* at the end where the root ball is. Standard procedure for *you* is if the marker is on the south end of something, *your* cache is located forty feet due west (180°), if a marker is on the north end, go due east to find the cache. Frank's cache is fifty feet at a bearing of 250°.

You should not put any type of marker over the cache, like paint or tape or even an old jug. But you could consider burying a metal can with your cache. That way you can use a metal detector to exactly locate the stash. Even a cheap detector would do this for you. Cheap and light, easy to carry.

Your entire troupe must also practice good woodsmanship on these forays. Try _very_ hard to not disturb *any*thing. *TRY* to not even leave footprints. Do NOT blaze your trail. NO markings of any kind. Leave no trash, no sign of your presence or passing. If you camp overnight, you can have a fire on this trial run, but if it were the real thing, you should probably not have a fire. You _can_, but it could get risky.

But even on this trial run, if you have a fire, leave no trace of it when you depart the area. Put it out thoroughly, scatter the remains far and wide, disperse the rocks used as a fire ring, and cover the burn completely and thoroughly. When you are finished, step back and see if you would notice it if you walked by it. And for the love of Mike, do NOT camp anywhere near your cache point. You'll just likely mark the spot for two-legged predators. Fire or no fire on the real bug-out walk has gotta be your call. You have my opinion.

The same goes for the rest of your campsite. No sign of your passing shall remain. Not one cigarette butt, not one candy wrapper, scrap of toilet paper, or soda can. Why? Because some backwoods Bob, walking around, looking for game trails and squirrel nests for his next hunting trip will stumble over your campsite and think, "Who the hell has been in MY woods?" Then he will start following your trail. He might track you all the way to your BoL or your next campsite.

He *might* linger a half day behind you, just so you won't know he's following you. If he has to call Frank to meet him at Burls Road with some grub to take with him, he will do that. These people can be relentless, especially if they think "their" area has been "violated" by some outsider or if they think there is some gain in it for them. Keep this in mind. People, especially woodsy types, can be very territorial. And it could cost you your lives if you do not believe it and live by it.

You also want to keep track of how long the trip takes to each point. Use a pedometer to count your steps. Measure your stride and calculate your distance. Mark it on the map. Knowing how to use a sextant to determine your position by the stars could also come in handy. Who knows whether the GPS satellites will be working after The Fall? I believe they will, but I like to have multiple means of accomplishing anything.

Also, consider that your cell phone GPS does NOT use satellites, they reckon off of cell towers, and *those* will likely NOT be working after The Fall. Think about that.

Your path through the woods would ideally run pretty close to the roads you would take if driving to the BoL. Or maybe vice versa.

Your chosen road should run close to your woodsy path. Why? If, during the actual bug-out, you run into an ambush or insurmountable obstacle such as a blown-out bridge, you can leave the vehicle, traipse a hundred yards into the woods and pick up your trek. Redundancy rules, dude!

In this mapping process, you should also locate and designate locations to dump your vehicles when you bug out. These should be about five to ten miles from your property and not clumped together. You've got eight vehicles and the van in your troupe? Send two of them five miles toward each of the four compass points. They should even park their cars a mile or two apart. Park one, then the two drivers ride in the second car to the second drop point where the van will pick them up.

After all drivers are accumulated, go back to the property in the van and get out. Two or three go with the van driver to drop the van several miles away, then they will all hike back to the compound. BE SURE to remove all tags and any identifying material from the cars, such as warranty info, inspection stickers, or repair receipts.

Your trip through the woods here will accomplish two things. The most important one is to familiarize yourself and your tribe members with the path, the terrain, the cache points, everything about this part of the bug-out process. When you stop for the night, why not all of you explore, without lights, for a mile or so around your site? Learn the pitfalls, as it were, of traveling at night through this particular wood. The more you know, the better off you are.

16

Tracking And Evading

Okay. So you're bugging out on foot. Your family, all six of you, are en route. The Petersons and the Smiths are with you, for a total of seventeen people in the woods. If the Jones family is lagging behind by an appreciable amount, they may need to be left to their own devices if the situation is dire. In this case, the tribe members with you should go ahead. If there is no immediate danger, by all means wait for them and put the whole troop together. But we're talking about tracking and evading here, so let's get to it. For this exercise, we will assume you are all walking to the BoL.

When you are in the process of walking the path and marking your cache points, you should practice tracking. Hopefully you won't *need* to evade anyone at that point, but you *can* practice it with your buddies. Let three of you drop back and play "hound" while the rest are the "foxes." The hounds will do their level best to remain silent and stealthy and still catch up to you. Agree on an amount of time that they will stay still before beginning the pursuit.

In a real-world situation, the first question is how do you <u>*know*</u> you are being followed? Were they close enough for you to hear before you found out about them? Then you probably lose. If this is a real bug-out, you need someone walking drag. This is one or two persons or maybe two teams of two persons who are five to twenty minutes behind you, flanked off to the sides about ten to twenty yards. If they encounter hostiles, they are within radio range and can notify you. Your choice now is to either engage or evade. For me, that decision would depend upon the demeanor and intent of the hostiles, if that can be determined.

First off, to successfully evade pursuit, you need some intel. You need to know where they are, how many there are, the "heat" of the pursuit and the capabilities of the pursuers. The way to do that is for four of you to peel off, two to the left and two to the right. The main body, the "tribe," will be unit 1. The pair on the left are unit 2, and the pair on the right are unit 3.

They should continue in your general direction of travel but at a 45° angle off from it until they are maybe ten to twenty yards off the trail. This keeps them moving in the right direction but falling back slightly. STEALTH is the byword here, guys. Walking softly in the woods can be difficult, especially if it is dry. Keep your eyes downward 60 percent of the time, looking for sticks that you want to avoid stepping on or holes you want to avoid stepping IN. Or trip wires. Them good ole boys might be thinking ahead and booby trap "their" woods.

Step softly by landing on the outside edge of your boot and "rolling" your foot to the ground. It takes practice. Duck under branches if you can or gently lift them over your head if not. Try to pick the path of least resistance to your travel. I like to avoid briars. Remember, stealthy walking through the woods will greatly reduce your speed.

When they have each reached a point about ten to twenty yards from the trail, stop. Acknowledge to the tribal leader that they are in position by clicking their transmit button with their unit number. Unit 2 clicks twice, and unit 3 clicks three times. Tribe leader clicks transmit once to acknowledge.

The intel team should avoid using their headlights if it is night, even in green mode. IF they have a HANDheld green light, they can keep it low to the ground, never shine it upward and use it sparingly. The intel team point (lead) should be careful to warn the sweep (rear) of obstacles, holes, branches, etc. If he encounters a branch that must be lifted, he should signal sweep with one click on his frog, lift it over his head, and then HOLD it until sweep takes it from his hand.

The intel teams carry on internal communication using the frog clickers while in transit. When stopped, soft speech will work. But when walking in this stressful situation, breath and speech become labored, therefore more audible. If sweep must signal point, two clicks. You'll work it out.

Once positioned, the intel teams (ITs) wait there until the pursuers come into view or earshot. If they cannot be seen, the units converge toward the trail, again at a 45° angle, until the pursuing group is in sight and identifiable. It MIGHT be the Jones family trying to catch up, yes? If not, their mission is to gather the missing information that you need. How many? Are they armed? How? Are they camouflaged? Are they stealthy, normal, or boisterous? That could mean they are probably drunk, by the way. Are they talking about YOU? Any chatter about "did you see movement to the right?" means they might have seen <u>you</u>! If you get a drift of *THAT*, do NOT drop to the ground quickly. That is sure to draw attention. <u>*SLOWLY*</u> lower your body.

The teams should acknowledge contact with the enemy ASAP. If using earpiece mics, they can transmit, just be sure to turn your back to the enemy and cup your hand over your mouth and the mic to muffle your voice. The leader does the same in replying. Once you have the intel, you can decide what to do about the problem. Personally, if you are in bug-out, I say kill 'em. It's harsh, yes, but it's them or you, right? The downside to this approach is that they may have friends who will come looking for them in a few days.

If you have to kill anyone, make sure they can't find the bodies. If they find them, they will pick up the pace and the pursuit will be relentless. So you could have to kill thirty of their cousins or get the hell out of dodge. If it's RUN, stop at your next cache just long enough to get your goods and get moving again, IF you can. Always be sure to cover where you dug. The enemy will be moving fast and won't look closely but don't give them something to catch their eye. You might even consider missing one and moving on to the next, for speed. If the troupe MUST stop, I would want everyone to take individual paths off to one side and congregate maybe a quarter mile off the trail. But when you set watch for the night, maybe set one to guard the camp and another to watch the trail.

Here's a possible scenario: Two intel teams drop off, left and right and wait for the pursuers to catch up. If it looks like a fight is likely, they should alert the main group that is about five to twenty minutes ahead, and then fall in _behind_ the pursuers by about two to five minutes, staying on high alert for the hostiles stopping for any reason. If one of them is ex-military, they will know the advantages of stopping every so often to check for followers like you. The main group has stopped and dispersed. When the hostiles approach, the main group engages, and YOU come up from the rear. You are also there in case the hostiles turn tail and run. Don't let them escape.

If you choose to NOT engage for a fight, your only option is to scatter. Everyone starts walking at an angle, off into the woods, being as careful as possible to not leave a trail. Lift your feet high to avoid dragging leaves or sticks that will disturb the area and leave a clue. Stay quiet. And this could be an issue if you have small children.

Kids over ten or twelve might be able to hold it together. If you have any _ether_ with you (add that to the list) or fast-acting decongestant, it might save your life to sedate the small ones and carry them. Your call. Engine starting fluid is mostly ether, but I am unsure if it works on people.

It is THIS issue alone that makes my decision be one to kill the intruders. I want to live. I want my family to live. Your pursuers don't want that. If you scatter to the woods, you want the hostiles to pass by you without noticing you. You must be low to the ground and absolutely quiet. In a bug-out by foot, you should consider wearing camo and applying camo makeup to everyone's faces.

Well, we've still got one issue here, don't we? Is the rest of your tribe with you? Are or they lagging behind?

One of you should climb to the top of the ridge and try to radio them if you cannot "raise" them normally. Let's say that they entered the woods four hours behind your pursuers, so the thugs do not know of their presence, hopefully. The decision of whether or when to fire a Berry pistol to warn them is strictly up to you. But you better do it before you lose the round, if that's the way it's heading. Berry pistol is ONLY for issuing a SCRAM order, to warn others of your tribe that there are hostiles in the area.

So your intel teams have identified the threat as extremely hostile, well-armed, and in an alcohol-fueled rage. If you decide to fight it out, here's the plan, Stan:

A predesignated team takes the small children and moves ahead down the trail as fast as possible. Dump the packs out of sight. Put as much distance between themselves and the hostiles as possible. Hopefully about a mile. Then they peel off into the woods to the side. And they wait there a minimum of two hours before moving on without you. Then they should send a recon team to see 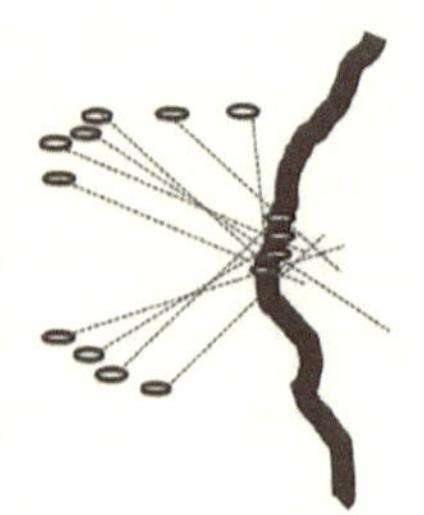 what happened. They will need to recover their packs, at least. This troupe should include at least one or two men. The rest of you lot will immediately split into two factions. Team 1 will continue forward twenty yards down trail, then go off to one side about ten yards or until there is sufficient cover. They will signal team 2 as to which direction off trail they went. Team 2 will go off trail _to the same side_.

That way, when the attack goes down, nobody is shooting into their own people. Everyone concentrates their fire toward the trail from converging angles. Team 2 goes about twenty yards into the wood or until sufficient cover is attained. Even if that is only five yards. You want to be as close as practical without being visible. Get low to the ground, prone if possible. When the hostiles enter the kill zone, the tribal leader signals and everyone commences with withering fire.

Okay. I get it. I got distracted. Kinda. But the truth is, this is _your_ likely scenario. No evading. You're going to have to duke it out. But the chapter is EVADING and tracking. So let's take another stab at it, okay? SO…evading, right? Most likely a process you will have to engage in when you are alone and under pursuit by likely unknown assailants. YOUR job, should you choose to accept it, is to get away from the bogie without being tracked.

The two major components of evasion are, oddly enough, mutually exclusive. Speed and stealth. It is hard to be quick and quiet at the same time. But that is what you must practice until you can do it in your sleep. And about the only thing I might be able to help you with is the stealth part. Stealth in the woods is simply passing quietly while disturbing your surroundings as little as possible. And doing that while wearing boots is a bleeding miracle. But it can be done. There are videos on the internet demonstrating walking silently through the woods.

The most basic thing is the most counterintuitive of the bunch, I think. We have become so lazy that we drag our feet from step to step all day long. Check yourself and see if I'm not right. In the woods, you have to *lift* your feet. Well, your whole *leg*, actually. Your goal is to get off your last step point and to the next one without moving one leaf. Or cracking one twig on the ground or breaking one single branch of the trees overhead.

I find it easier, especially if I am moving quickly, to bend over at the waist *slightly*. About forty-five to seventy degrees. Helps me keep my balance. Start slowly, walking. Raise your dominant foot until that thigh is almost parallel with the ground, extend the leg to where you want the foot to fall, making sure to avoid twigs, rocks, and holes. *LOOK* where you intend to plant your foot, then plant it as flatly as possible, transferring weight to this foot proportionately as you step down. TRY to not roll onto the *ball* of your foot as you shift your weight forward for the next step. T'ain't easy. Practice. The reason? In that split-second that you are almost motionless in mid-stride and your full weight is on your entire foot, you are placing about five to six pounds on every square inch of your footprint.

If you flex that foot onto the ball, you reduce the contact area from roughly thirty square inches to about EIGHT. That raises the footprint pressure up to around twenty-five pounds per square inch. Big difference. Much bigger depression in the ground.

The amount of impact that makes on your trail depends upon the ground conditions. If the ground and covering leaves are dry, your print will be barely visible within one minute. Sure, there will be some cracked leaves in the shape of your boot, but they will rebound soon enough unless you broke a twig. Which will make a large, loud cracking sound that will be audible for a long way in dry weather.

On *wet* ground, you leave a trail two inches deep unless you move *really* fast. It sounds wild, I know, but it is true. The depression you leave is also a factor of how long the weight is applied. So, if you move very quickly, you leave less of a hole in the ground.

I have always believed that the most important part of evasion is confusion. Confound your enemy by changing directions as often as you can. If you can safely and quickly manage it, make one DEEP impression intentionally with your OFF foot, then step on a rock or dry tuft with your dominant foot and take a leap to the opposite side and <u>backward</u>. Try to twist in mid-leap also. That puts your landing *behind* that deep footprint. That deep depression sets your direction of travel (DOT) firmly in your enemy's mind. Leaping to a place behind that and then changing your DOT will lead him in the wrong direction until he figures out he has lost the trail. It will cost him time. Time you use to get OFF your chosen line of flight.

My main desire at this point is to get as far away from this nutcase as possible in as short a time as possible. That means going in the *opposite* direction if I can. So, once I get turned onto a new DOT, I will go perpendicular to my original DOT for fifteen to thirty yards, if possible. If I can see or hear my pursuer as he passes behind me, I will crouch and hide for a minute until he passes. Then I will start moving in the direction opposite his DOT. Try to cross the original trail and into deeper woods for about thirty to fifty yards. Then you can slow down and work a little smarter. Step softly, purposefully and quietly. Keep doing that until you reach somewhere safe. Unless your intent is to kill your problem off. Which is not a bad idea, come to think about it. But to do that, you need a place where you can get off a good, steady shot.

TRACKING? Tracking is basically looking for those things I have just spent so much time and energy telling you to not do. I guess it kinda depends on what you are tracking. If you are tracking game, you must first know your quarry. Deer? Rabbit? Bear? Are you KIDDING me? WHO tracks BEAR?

As a matter of fact, I have only one piece of advice regarding bears. If you come up on a bear and it acts aggressive, I would first try backing slowly away. If the bear continues its aggression, my fallback position is to slowly pull my sidearm. If the bear is fairly still and you are a good enough shot, shoot him in the eye. A bear's skull is too thick for a 9mm to penetrate, so if you land a shot in his eye, he will drop like a stone. If he charges, keep aiming for that eye. You could get lucky. Or empty a clip into his throat. Try to sever the spine.

Anyway, know your quarry. There is a really great plastic-coated, trifold pamphlet for the woodsy mammals in your region of the country. You can probably pick one up at the local outdoor shop. It shows photos of the animals and pictures of the scat and tracks. But you will still need to read up on the habits and habitats of your prey. Like looking for scrub marks on trees where a buck has marked his territory with his antlers. Large pellet-type scat is a deer. A pile of scat with a tennis shoe in it is definitely a bear.

Tracking involves total concentration on your part. Coupled with the situational awareness to know what is going on around you at all times. Don't want that bear creeping up on you, right?

Since you are tracking, there is no real caveat against trying to not leave tracks or break small limbs, but you DO want to be as quiet as possible. If you're looking for supper, you don't want to scare it off. And animals have incredible senses of hearing and smell. Which brings up point 2.

ANY time you are in the woods for ANY reason, the last thing you want to do is go into the forest smelling like soap or cologne. Because even if it is a person tracking YOU, you don't want to be smellable.

Scanning ahead of you a few yards can often reveal the hidden. We live in a world full of mirrors and shadows. In the city, window glass and shiny surfaces can help you keep track of what is happening all around you, if you pay attention. In the woods, shadows are your friend. Look at the ground five to ten feet ahead.

Well, actually, it's like driving a car. You keep scanning from where you want to see, back to where you *are*, then to the sides, and so on. So you look at the ground directly in front of you, then up to a point ahead and back to your feet. The SHADOW in an animal's track can often show it up more clearly than being right on top of it. But you have to keep looking at the ground from straight overhead also. At the same time, you are looking left and right for the same signs.

Don't forget to stay alert for signs of human passing also. Footprints, cigarette butts or wrappers, soda or beer cans, campfire remnants or pieces of rotted tarp. All these point to the passage of the human animal at some point in time. A close inspection of any artifacts will tell you how recently. Most people, even hunters are not really careful about what they leave behind them in the woods. But YOU need to be REAL aware of it, because <u>these are not your woods.</u> This actually gives you a large advantage. When you are traipsing through "his" woods the first time, you are very likely to see all sorts of detritus indicating where Billy Joe Ray Bob and his buddies have been drinking and/or hunting. That's your advantage.

17

Defense

Wow. This one should be a doozy. Frankly, I was just thinking that I have pretty much covered everything. Didn't you think so? But let's give it a go, shall we? Actually, I think I *have* covered pretty much everything about personal defense in previous chapters. So let's think in terms of defending the compound, what d'ya say? Hunh?

MAYbe I forgot to bring this up earlier, maybe not, but when you are laying out your BoL, you should consider where you want your choke points, booby traps, and killing fields kind of things. There must be certain points and places where you can lay traps and use passive weaponry without impacting your life and operations too much.

Let's start at the entry point, eh? This will *usually* be the road, especially if your primary concern is the traveling band of rats that will roaming the countryside in a raping and pillaging rampage once the system goes down.

They will likely walk (MAYbe drive) along the roads looking for soft targets. And they will find them. A house here, a small town there. Isolated and mostly defenseless people. Yeah, there will be some firefights and both sides will experience losses. But I think that numbers will be on their side. Once they conquer an area, they will keep some of the populace as conscripts to bolster their army.

The point is, they will typically travel the beaten path. First the major roads into medium-sized towns, then smaller roads, smaller towns, and then the one-lane blacktops that crisscross the country-

155

side. They will be looking for signs of habitation. Like walking paths or dirt driveways leading up a hillside, a gate. Someplace where the vegetation looks thin or new. An abandoned car. Anything out of the ordinary. Then they will send a scout team up the hill to look for you.

Your first point of defense is always detection, isn't it? You cannot fight what you cannot see or do not know about. Hopefully, you have chosen a piece of land where you must go over a hill of maybe twenty feet in height before you can even *think* there might be something further on. And that first hill is where your first detectors should be. You want to funnel any entrants into a small area.

The first thing I would do after I get a modest housing unit to live in would be to take some small pine tree seedlings or similar from your forest and transplant them to that first hill. Offset two lines so  that they overlap with a hidden entryway between them. Notice how I made the lines not straight? That makes it look more natural.

In that small entrance, you can capture any movement easily. And for short range, I use those wireless driveway alarms that I mentioned a few chapters back. They use ultrasonic detectors that sense motion within a certain range, usually twenty to thirty feet. I know for a fact that they will transmit at least a hundred feet. I have done that.

But you are going to be much farther away, I guess. So you should look for something to extend that range. Like add an antenna to both the transmitter and receiver. It might even be possible to find something similar with a much longer range. I know one guy that used a thin clear fishing line. Anchored at the trees, it ran through a series of eye screws mounted to trees all along the way to the house. It was almost a two-hundred-yard run. At the house, it was stretched tight and a weight was hung from it. If someone tripped on the string that hung knee high, it activated a switch that rang an alarm bell inside.

Such things are, of course, prone to false alarms. But what you are looking for is a first response alarm. Something to get your attention. THEN you can check the cameras you have mounted about.

There are many multicamera security systems that are wireless. Most only transmit about one to three hundred feet, but some can go much farther.

I have found that you can set up several cameras at a more distant location (three triangles lower right trees). Address those cameras to a particular wireless router. That router (in the upper left tree) is used in bridge mode as a range extender. Mount it high in a tree with a rain proof enclosure. Attach a  larger external antenna. Power it from a motorcycle battery that is recharged from a solar cell. Both are in that same tree.

At the compound, you have a large external antenna going to another wireless router. This should enable you to keep an eye on things. The alternative is a wired CCTV system.

Okay. So now you know there is someone poking around your hidey hole. What now? Well, number one, it depends on the size of the party coming in, right? If it's like ten people, you could invite them in and see what's up while you send an intelligence team over the hill to check out the surroundings. If they are part of a large group, you can bet they will deny it. But if you hold them long enough, group two will come hunting them within a few hours, a day at most. Your IT should be back by then with a good count.

I will assume, at this point, that you have planned far enough ahead to have designated several crossfire points close to that initial landmark hill. This place will secret four fire teams of four to ten people each. All with radios, of course. You, the general, will direct the fight from a vantage point somewhere nearby. The purpose for that is to keep everyone from firing at once. And keep their lines of fire from hitting each other.

You want to initiate the combat from one direction. That will draw their attention, and they will start firing and moving that way. That is when you tell team 1 to duck and team 2 to open fire. The opposition is now confused and starting to look around to see if there are more. As soon as they start firing on 2, 1 comes back up. Then 3 fires. They will probably start to circle, congregate, and back away.

Then everyone bears down on them. And about this time, team 5 has come around to the entrance to block it off. Your fire teams are coordinating themselves so that one or two people are firing while the other two are changing magazines so that the bullets never stop flying.

One of my favorite things is what I like to call the "Ring of Fire." Handy, effective, and very dangerous. But as a last resort, it is a wonder drug. I take a ½" PVC pipe and build a line across a field. Usually about a hundred feet long. Start by taking your ten or twenty foot lengths of pipe and drill 1/16" holes about ten inches apart down the length of the pipe. Be sure to keep them lined up on one side. Dig a trench to bury the pipe JUST beneath the surface.

As you assemble the pipe, make certain to use the purple PVC cleaner and then apply the glue liberally. Line the pipe up so that one set of holes is 90° offset from the other piece. Apply glue, push the joints together and TWIST them until the holes line up. Cap the very last piece. You get one shot at this, so make sure all the joints are glued very well. Now, put a small piece of dental wax OVER each hole, NOT "IN" it. You just want to cover it enough to keep insects and rain out. Tape may also work. Just not tight.

At the beginning point of this system, adapt the glued pipe to screwed pipe and then flex pipe and connect it to a 30# propane tank hidden away. Maybe even buried. The system needs an electric solenoid valve to let the gas into the pipes so that the tank can remain open all the time, ready. Run your firing wire to your remote location, probably the house.

I suggest the whole thing be operated by a key operated electric switch. Set your gas pressure regulator to about 30 psig if you can. If NOT, and you can find a solenoid that can hold the tank pressure, just let tank pressure into the line. THAT will make an impressive fire! When the switch is activated, a voltage is sent to the ring of fire firing center.

There, the solenoid opens, letting gas flow into the system. Once the pressure builds up in the pipe, the dental wax will lift off and gas will start seeping from the ground. Propane, unlike natural gas, is heavier than air and it will stay on the ground. Until the pressure in the pipe matches the tank pressure. About one minute, I would say. Then, an ignition system, similar to the automatic match used to keep a pilot light going if it blows out, will ignite the gas along the ground. The ignitor MUST be above ground, NOT inside the pipe.

Or you can set it off with a flaming arrow. And then those large flaming jets will erupt from the earth. Burning everything around it. If it is installed halfway up the hill they are coming down, the gas will fall down then hill, engulfing them all. The downside is you might wind up with a grass fire. Clean sweep ten to twenty feet on both sides of the field to prevent the fire spreading into the woods.

On a more practical and less destructive note, there is always the ever-popular tiger trap. The old ones were designed to catch one or two men at a time. Here, we might want to plan to catch thirty or more. Maybe. My plan is to dig a trench about thirty feet long by ten feet deep by five feet wide, seen from the end. The tiger trap consists of sharpened sticks in the floor of the pit. The pit is covered with tree trunks about four inches in diameter, stretching across the width of the pit, edge to edge. They are covered with branches and that is covered with dirt and the wild grasses are allowed to overgrow it. Sowing grass on it will look unnatural.

In the pit, there are stringers made of tree trunks that support the covering. And there are pilings, resting on larger trunk sections, holding those stringers up.

A cable system runs the length of the pit, with attachment points located at every row of pilings. At the end of the pit, the trip wire enters a pipe that protects it as it travels an additional thirty feet or so to a box. In the box is a pulley that changes the direction of the cable from horizontal to vertical through another pipe.

The wire then exits the ground pipe and proceeds into a tree. Up to a pulley and then to a weight sufficient to yank the supports out from under the pilings in the pit. The weight is held up by a support cable attached to the tree and released by a quick release system. Possibly electrically operated so it can be dropped remotely. Just lure the jerks into the zone and drop the hammer. Or you could dig a dozen one-man traps that will collapse under the weight of one man. Scattered about the killing field.

There are simply loads of information online about this kind of stuff, but one of the most complete references you will find is called *The Anarchist's Cookbook*.

18

Security

Wow. After defense, security should be a cake walk, right? Especially since we have covered many of the essentials already under other headings. But let's see what we find, okay?

Security is about awareness, intelligence, and information more than anything else. HOW you get those things is the key. We just talked about security cameras in the last chapter, so you know what you can do with that.

One thing we did *not* discuss is RC Drones for surveillance. They are marvelous and very well-suited for this purpose. There are several different methods used to stream the video from the drone back to the operator. Most operators get pretty good at flying the drone in LOS (line of sight) mode, but this requires that you maintain eye contact with your craft at all times.

This is not always practical, like, at night. Which is probably when you will need it most. Once you get good at LOS flight, you should work on FPV (first-person view) flying, which lets you look at the live feed from the camera and control the craft as if you were actually in it.

Most of those systems use an RC system frequency of about 5.8 GHz and require a separate controller/screen unit, instead of controlling and/or viewing from your cell phone. If you have people on patrol around the property, a drone of this type could be a great adjunct, allowing them to check out any noise or disturbance without putting themselves in danger. The downside is that the intruders will likely hear the drone and know they are on the right track. Unless the drone is flying REAL high.

The best intel you will get in these situations will be by putting people out there to check things out. Teens and preteens from about ten years and up would probably love to do this for a few hours a day. It would make them feel important, also, and that is good for a kid's ego. For starters, you might pair a kid with an adult, possibly a senior if you have any in your tribe. For support, company, and training. The adult can remind the kid of the basics of tracking and stealth, and possibly they can get in some target practice at the same time.

The hard part is that you might need patrols out 24-7. That takes a lot of manpower and wastes time for the most part. But if you need it, you need it. There is another way to do unmanned surveillance—sound. It would not be difficult to mount a microphone near the road, at the first hilltop, around the property at various points. But it WILL take a lot of wire and some line amplifiers for audio.

First off, you will need what is known as a low-impedance microphone. Most mics that you are familiar with are high impedance (Hi-Z). Impedance is the word that describes resistance in an AC circuit. High impedance is about 10,000 ohms. Low impedance (Lo-Z) is 150–600 ohms. The advantage is distance. Lo-Z lines can run about five hundred feet without a relay line amplifier. Hi-Z is only good for about thirty feet.

Mount a mic in a tree and run a mic wire out five hundred feet. Lo-Z mic line is what is known as "shielded twisted pair" cable. The connectors are commonly called cannon plugs, though that is incorrect. Cannon designed the system originally, but the connectors are available from many sources now. The male version has the holes and the female has the pins. It is the casing that determines the sex of the connector, not the pins. The connectors are identified by their type designator A3M and A3F for male and female. You can look up the way to wire them. It's only three wires that have to be soldered. And they are NOT waterproof!

One drawback, of course, is that every five hundred feet you have to put a Lo-Z amplifier to boost the signal for another five hundred feet. These, like the Wi-Fi routers we talked about using to transmit camera signals long distances, can be powered by a small motorcycle battery pushing a 100-watt inverter and recharged by solar cells. A 100-watt inverter can be had for as little as nine bucks.

I actually like sonic surveillance a lot. Once you get the audio signal to the house, it could be coupled to a radio transmitting on a special channel that you can monitor from a scanner or a ham radio. Let's say you have ten mics scattered about. All the wires come to a central point, and then you have ten separate signals to monitor.

You can combine the signals with a device called an audio mixer. You can also get several smaller mixers, like ones that handle four signals, and stack them together. That could save a few clams. But if a suspicious signal is detected, you have to push some buttons to determine which mic it came from. And to do that, you have to be at the mixer station.

Okay. Now let's talk about THE most practical means of area surveillance. Take a regular motion sensitive security light, mount it in a tree. Leave out the bulb. Take the bulb socket mounts out of the box and cover the holes with the special plugs made for that. Inside the mounting box there are four wires. Black, white, green, and red. Black is the 110 volts power to feed it. White is the 110 volts neutral. Green is the ground wire. RED is the money ball. Red is the wire from the ultrasonic sensor. When the sensor detects something in its field of vision, it makes that red wire hot to feed 110 volts to the bulbs. Those bulbs that you removed.

There are two ways to do this thing. One is you run a cable that contains three wires from the house to each sensor. Hook the black and white to 110 volts power. The third wire hooks to a light bulb or a signal bell. At the sensor, hook black to black, white to white, and RED to that third wire. This is returning 110 volts to the house in the event the system is alarmed. At the house, Red and White go to some signaling device like a light or bell.

Method 2 requires our old friend the motorcycle battery, a solar cell, and a 100-watt inverter. You still need a wire from the tree to the house, but this time it's just two wires. Pick a tree. Mount the sensor. Above that, out of sight, and protected from the elements, mount the battery and inverter. Above those, mount the solar cell to charge the battery. The battery feeds the inverter. From the inverter, power the sensor. Black to black and white to white. Connect the red wire from the sensor to one of the two wires going to the house. The other wire from the house goes to the white wires. In the house, just hook those two wires to a light or bell.

Let us not forget that the farther you run electricity, the larger the wire needs to be, due to voltage drop losses. But there are limits. On the other foot, you are not using much current (amps) to keep the sensors running, so you could probably run a 16/3 wire (with or without ground) for a thousand feet, five hundred feet each direction.

If you do this multiple times, it will simplify things if you mount a map of the sensor placement on the wall and label the lights or bells to match. That way you can tell at a glance where the intruders are entering. Use 25-watt bulbs there.

Certain plants can make an effective barrier against human intrusion. Planting a thick row of these around your property can be an effective deterrent. Doing this might make it seem unnatural, but I think if you make a hedge that is both thick, front to back, and uneven on the front, it would appear more wild looking. If your property has only one entrance, you should plant with the thought in mind of overlapping that will hide a driveway access through the hedge. You can plant to completely cover this after you have completed the compound and no longer need vehicular access.

Of course, when you get settled in a bit and your routines developed and other security measures just about in place, you might want to consider building a stone wall around the compound. I would think maybe the suggestion to keep all the houses in a tight bunch would not be out of line. Barns and fields and all can be outside the wall, but keep your people close by inside the wall. It's just another layer of defense against the Dark Arts when that time comes. About ten feet tall, I should think. With broken glass imbedded in the cement along the top. Or nails. Nails are good, also. But I prefer glass.

Nice, stout doors at all entrance points. Four to six inches thick and solid wood. Keep those closed and barred shut whenever possible. You will have to access the fields and such daily, of course, but you can keep that front gate shut 99 percent of the time. You might consider some firing slits at appropriate heights about the sides of the doors and along the perimeter also. Of course, your feel for your situation will always be the deciding factor, and let's remember that my purpose here is to give you things to think about.

And there is always the ever-popular electric fence. Similar to the ubiquitous electric cattle fence common across America, I would build a system that first senses that it has been contacted, like those lamps that you touch to turn on, and then it will energize the wire with 110 vac. An animal that touches it will back off or jump over. A human that touches it…will die. An alternative is a standard electric fence. The charger unit at the house or barn will suddenly draw more current if something hits the fence. You can sense this electronically and fire an alarm off.

19

Go Long—The Bug-Out

I guess we're looking at a major event here, Buck-o! The excrement has impacted upon the oscillating rotational air moving device. Either the terrorists were turned loose or the banking system went kaput or maybe the island nation of Salacia dropped a nuke on Secaucus. Something bad has happened. And it don't look good for the home team. We're gonna be out of business for many years to come.

Already the grocery stores are empty, and the doors are hanging open. There is no gasoline or diesel fuel to be had anywhere at any price because the nuke knocked out a major grid point and brought the whole damned thing down. Wow. Who'd a-thunk it? But HEY! You're ready for this, right?

Okay, so your BoL is 480 miles west by southwest of your house because you live in Philly. You're prepped up and ready to jump. The BoL is stocked up and waiting for your arrival. You have a full tank of gas and another twenty gallons ready to strap to a carrier on the hitch of the SUV. It's time to rock and roll. First, take the tag off your vehicle and keep it handy.

The VERY first thing you want to do is get everyone assembled. If Suzie is out at the mall with her friends, call her home, if the cell phones are still working. Maybe you will take my advice and you have a radio system that can reach her, and she has enough sense to keep it on. If not, let's hope she has enough sense to leave there as soon as she hears anything weird. That should have been part of your pre-bug-out training.

Get her home any way possible, and right away. Send Bobby to her friend's house to check there and advise Mary's parents that Suzie is needed at home right now, WITHOUT telling them WHY. If nothing else works, YOU get in the spare car and go hunt her down while Mom and Bobby pack.

When you find her, do NOT chastise her, thank her for being easy to find, no matter how hard it was. Then book it back to base.

ARM UP! RIGHT NOW! Whoever is available. If Bobby has to run down the street looking for Suzie, he does not carry a weapon at that point. Once he and Suzie are back, THEN they can arm up. But you and Mom need your sidearms on NOW. And from this point on, you brook NO interference with your departure. If a neighbor comes over and starts begging to go along, tie him up, gag him, and do not let him loose until you're loaded up and ready to pull out. You can throw him in the front yard just before you pull out. Still bound and gagged, of course. Someone will find him. Eventually.

Cops? That's gotta be YOUR call, but unless you have jumped the gun, the world outside is in chaos and NO one is to be trusted, not even most cops. If they come to the front door, everybody hides. _You_ answer the door. They canNOT enter the house without a warrant, and they know that. If they INSIST on entering without a warrant, you can pretty much take that as proof that they are gone rogue. TRY to not allow them in under any circumstance.

There are, actually, a few circumstances where police are allowed by law to enter without a warrant. First is a "welfare check," where they are answering a call placed by a concerned relative or neighbor. Typically, there must be a specific person they are looking to check on. Insist that they furnish the name of the person they are checking on and the name of the person requesting the check. If it is not a family member, tell them the person who made the request is a "little off," then offer to assemble the family for their inspection.

If the named person is one of those present, they will probably insist on talking to that person in private. Whether or not they are allowed to remove that person against their privately stated will is a question for a local attorney, but I am inclined to say that they cannot. Your feel for the severity of your situation will dictate how you respond to this incursion. Talk to an attorney and get answers before you need them. In writing. With citations.

Another reason for a warrantless entry is what is known as the "Plain Sight Doctrine," which states that any officer who actually sees physical evidence of a possible crime has the right and duty to collect said evidence and investigate the situation. For example, while standing at the front door, an officer sees what appears to be marijuana lying on a table, or a pack of rolling papers, they then have the right to walk into the home and inspect that artifact to determine if it is, in fact, an illegal substance. I suggest you speak with a local attorney regarding warrantless entry. Oh. If guns have been outlawed and you are wearing one, that's "plain sight."

One other item that might save your bacon in this type of situation is the fact that, contrary to popular belief, many jurisdictions have one exception to the rules against assaulting an officer. I know this from personal experience and personal research to clear my name following an incident that resulted in being charged with assaulting an officer.

This exception revolves around the officer's actions that allegedly caused you to assault them. The particular wording that I found was included in the legal description of the offense of assault. It stated that "It shall be an affirmative defense against a charge of assault on a law enforcement officer if the officer is attempting to arrest a person and said arrest is not based upon an infraction of the law but rather upon a personal prejudice or act of personal malice perpetrated by said officer."

In other words, if an officer tried to take you into custody just because he is pissed off at you, you might get away with assaulting him. But you will have a hard road ahead of you. Again, check on this with a local attorney before the need arises. They will probably say "NO WAY!" right off the bat, but if you explain it as I did above and insist that they actually do the *research*, they will. Also have the lawyer check out whether or not "resisting arrest" is a "stand-alone" charge, meaning you can be arrested for resisting arrest even if no other charges are filed.

I actually beat that one too. Cop got pissed off at me just because he thought I had a "bad attitude." There was NOTHING he could charge me with, but he cuffed me and hauled me in on resisting arrest. When I went to court, the judge ripped him a new one. I turned around and sued him and his department. Got him busted from sergeant to patrolman.

If it happens to you, think really hard before taking any action. What POSSIBLE reason could they have for being there? Does it sound legitimate to you? How is their dress and demeanor? If they come across as legit, you might want to deal with it in a civil manner, courteous, and acquiescing. Maybe you can get them to go away. If not. You might have to resort to drastic action.

Be aware that cops have to check in on a regular basis. If they do not, then their communications people call *them*. If there is no response, they will send every cop in five counties to their last known location. Your house. Don't forget to verify IDs! IN FACT, if you do NOT hear them communicate with dispatch, it is pretty much a sure sign that they are not for real.

If you know that you have done nothing wrong, then there is no reason for them to be there giving you crap. It is possible that they have responded to the wrong house. It happens all the time. About the best chance for survival that you have is to get the heck out of there, fast and incognito. Incognito at this point has no name other than—stolen tags. If this raid is illegal and you can come to no other resolution, tie the cops up, gag them, and get out of dodge.

Because this is what is going to happen, assuming either they are legit or the whole force is rogue:

Within five minutes of their arrival, the 911 dispatchers will be calling these cops to check on their welfare. If these officers do not reply, you can bet that every cop in the area is roaring your way, looking for YOU. Part of your pre-planning needs to be to locate a vehicle very close by, in your neighborhood if possible, hopefully one that is the same weight class and type (like SUV) if not the same make and model and even color if you can manage it. Your tag receipt shows your Honda SUV is champagne, not maroon, and if a cop gets behind you and runs your tag, his computer will tell him the tag is supposed to be on a 2015 Maroon CRX.

So you have a target vehicle picked. Know what tools are needed to swap tags with that vehicle. Probably change YOUR tag mount hardware to match THEIRS so you only need one tool. Bobby can take care of that. One afternoon riding around on his bike, he looks for the right car. Maybe you and he confirm it together later. You can probably determine the tag hardware with binoculars from the other side of the road. The point about the hardware is to get both cars where only one tool is needed to swap tags, like a Phillips head screwdriver or maybe an 11/16 nut driver, or whatever. But VERIFY it so there is no issue at the wrong time.

At the first sign of trouble, you give him some code word or code look and he grabs the tool and your tag that you have already removed and runs down the street to swap the tags and then books it home, hopefully by a back way so the cops do not see him. Put the stolen tag on your car and haul it out of there, NOW. He does NOT have to tighten the screws all the way on the car he takes a tag FROM. Just a few turns to hold the tag in place for a while.

You canNOT leave your old tag lying around your garage. That will tell them you have a stolen tag on *your* car, and they will figure out which one in about five minutes. They just have to look for a car without a tag, right? So SWAP the tags. If THEIR car has no tag, it will be no time before the cops know someone has a stolen tag. And they know the stolen tag number. If YOUR tag is on <u>their</u> car, it all goes unnoticed.

You want to be fifty miles away by the time the police figure out what has happened. For crying out loud, do not wait around there for the rest of your pack. They are probably not in danger. YOU are. Do not leave any evidence of where you are going lying about in your house. Nothing. Not even a book of matches from the bait shop fifty miles from your BoL.

Anything that could give you away or point in some direction must always be in a jump bag that goes in the car first. Maps, drink cups, ink pens, match books, napkins, ANYthing with any logo or other clue as to your destination or direction. Keep your house spotless of these things ALL the time. Take out the maps and books and planning notebooks from the jump bag each time you need to work on something, put it BACK in the bag and the bag back in the garage. Every time. Without fail. It could save your life.

The thing here is this, sport: you are now in the fight of your life, FOR your life. And that of your family. You can let nothing stop you. If things are as bad as you think, then government has broken down and it is every man for himself. Cops can go renegade, just like everyone else. Maybe these two heard from the grapevine that you were prepping? And they decided to take *your* stuff for THEIR families? Who knows? But if order has gone out the window out there in the world, they _may_ be legit, but you cannot _count_ on them being legit.

The government will *try* to remain operative. Did you know that the federal government has underground bunkers stocked to support one million people for ten years? TRUE. They want all the sheeple to believe they have everything under control, and it will all be back to normal any day now. If you have already decided to bolt, they are just in your way. BUT…and this is a big butt, IF things do come back within a month or two, you do not want to come home to a murder charge. So just try to work it out as best you can, Dan. That's what I'd do.

Be sure you BACK your car or SUV into the garage or carport, even if it is just far enough to get the back door inside. Why? You do NOT want your neighbors to see what you're doing. They are already in a panic, and they are looking for any straw to latch hold of. Like a good friend who apparently has supplies and a plan and a place to go. BACK the car in. All the way in and shut the garage door if possible. But try to not look suspicious doing it. _Put Bobby's bicycle in the driveway_ halfway down the drive but directly in front of your car. Or use a trash can.

This prevents anyone pulling into your drive and blocking you in. Like cops. All you have to do is drive around it to get out, even if it means jumping the curb. When you *do* pull out, try to do it gently. So it doesn't hurt. Don't attract unwanted attention. Maybe even move the trash can first so you don't have to jump the curb. Or not. Your call.

Load all the BoBs so that they can be accessed quickly, without digging through a bunch of other stuff. If you want to strap the BoBs on the roof rack, fine. Just be sure to cover them with a tarp and strap it down tight so it will not come loose. Mom will probably want to throw blankets and pillows in the seats to keep the kids comfortable. That's fine. You're going to live out of those BoBs for a few days, maybe even after you arrive at the BoL.

Load food, ammo, supplies, and water that you have predetermined to carry in the event of a drive-out bug-out. Load all the water you have room for. Then put the extra guns in on top of the supplies and cover it all with some blankets or clothes. I want those guns easy to get to. Right? And everyone should be wearing at least one sidearm.

I would suggest you try to take everything you can, guys. Do not leave ANYthing essential to life, like weapons, food, water, and fuel. Not if you can possibly help it. After that, you can add clothing or bedclothes as you like. I don't think furniture is a good idea, though. But frankly, I intend to grab my movie collection of over eight hundred titles (in soft cover cases that hold one hundred each), the DVD player and a 32" LCD TV. And our four laptops.

OH! And don't forget that special waterproof, tear-proof envelope that contains your vital info. Like copies of birth certificates, identification for everyone, copies of the deeds to your house, and your BoL property, titles to all vehicles, bills of sale for every valuable thing you have with you, as well as weapons, laptops, TVs, four wheelers, dirt bikes, whatever. Keep it within easy access. Mine stays in my BoB.

Speaking of that, don't forget that in one of these chapters I describe how to back up all of your data to an external hard drive and protect it? Well, now would be the time to grab anything you have buried in the back yard, which you should have done already, really. You never know. I have heard rumors of some gangs that have EMP guns to disable cars passing through their turf so they can attack the occupants. I don't know if that's TRUE or not, but what the hey? If something happens and your car won't start, changing the PCM out just might fix it. You need to be sure and know exactly where it is on your car and the best way to access it. You can get a spare PCM from an auto junkyard pretty cheap. **_CAUTION:_** Some PCMs require special "training" to work on a car other than its original. Check with your dealer and learn how. Do it in advance.

Now that everything is loaded, and everyone is here and ready to go, it is time to put that hitch-mount carrier on the back and throw the gasoline cans on it, plus the cooler or whatever. Cover it with a tarp, tie it down well and we're off. First, take a peek out the front window to check on conditions in your immediate area. Presumably you have been monitoring the radio or television or a police scanner for news reports across the region ever since the "happening"…uh… happened. If all looks clear on the outside, let's go.

Let me give you two different versions of how things could happen as you travel, and then you decide what to do about departure times. Day or night, you are in danger from gangs, rogue cops, normal people who are just scared shirtless, and the occasional AB-normal person who is just antisocial. And maybe military. Or Muslim extremists. Sorry. It's a real possibility, not a racist comment.

If you want to travel by day, it would probably be best to leave REAL early in the morning, like 4:00 or 5:00 a.m. This puts you on the road before any unsavory persons are awake. They may be night owls, but even owls sleep sometime. Most gangs and weirdos stay up until 3:00 or 4:00 a.m. then pass out. So leaving about the time they drop off gives you a head start on the bunch in your area.

If you must travel far or through deep country, you might be better off to make that portion of the trip in daylight. If you think you can manage to maintain 50 mph average, you're gonna be able to cover about four to six hundred miles per day, or more, and I have to hope that your BoL is not much farther than that. Maybe MUCH closer. But that is really going to depend on where you live.

If it is a BIG city, like Philly, NYC, Atlanta, DC, Seattle, LA, you might _want_ your BoL four to six hundred miles away. Because _those_ cities are on the target list. Anybody who shoots at us will shoot at those cities first. Plus a few more, but you get the point. So you might just be in for a long drive, Clive. There is one more thing to think about, maybe I should have brought this up in an earlier section, but I just thought of it so…(and I'm not saying this is mandatory, just think it over…)

Your car. If you live in Pittsburgh and drive a brand-new SUV or anything that would stick out badly as you travel through the back country to your BOL, you could consider having an old panel van parked somewhere as a backup. In one of those locked and secured U-Stor-It-type places. Get an older model that does not have a PCM or ECM (computer). If it DOES have a computer, be sure to have a backup as described elsewhere and protected against an EMP. Have a mechanic go over it thoroughly and get it in top condition mechanically.

You don't want the brakes to go out or the transmission to go tits-up halfway there. New belts, new hoses all over. Maybe a new water pump and alternator, too! You want something that looks like John Dirt drives it but NOT something that looks like he deals dope out of it.

This vehicle is much less likely to get you assaulted by thugs along the way. Before you park it in the storage, be sure to put enough STA-BIL in the gas to keep it fresh for a year or two and run the engine at least thirty minutes to get it through the carburetor or fuel injectors. Put the STA-BIL in the tank first, then fill the tank with fuel. This mixes it thoroughly. Be sure to crank it and run the engine for thirty minutes each and every month. Use this van for camping trips two or three times a year to run the gas out, then refill with STA-BIL and gasoline. It IS a good, viable part of a plan to cover your tracks and provide maximum invisibility, but it might not be right for you. Food for thought.

Drive your car to where the van is hidden, then one to three people get in the van. The van, equipped of course with its own radio, always travels at the back of the pack. One person at least in it should be a very good shot. You want at least two five-gallon buckets of oil with lids on them, at the back, and maybe 10–20# of caltrops or nails, also.

If you are pursued, the shooter goes to the back, opens the door, and starts firing. IF YOU ARE PURSUED, that is. If you think they are just driving along, or maybe even following you, see if you lose them by turning off. If not, a few warning shots to the off-road side of their vehicle should suffice.

If not, if your observation says that it IS a full-on pursuit, kill the passenger first and then the driver. Make the shots count, but DO NOT STOP TO CHECK your work, radio the tribe to speed up. If there are multiple pursuers, keep it up. If shooting is not working, toss half of the caltrops out. Or open a can of oil and spill it out the back. I say SPILL it because if you try to push it or throw it you will just wind up getting it all over you and the van.

There is one more advantage to having a van in the caravan. If someone's vehicle is captured or disabled, that family can pile into the van. It would be real hard to cram six more people into four more cars that are already packed full of kids and supplies. The van is perfect. Oh yeah, do something about shielding against gunfire at the back door.

As you travel, no matter how or when, the rules are the same. Nobody uses electronics. No phone, no music, no iPods, no games, or DVDs. No books or playing cards either. Everyone from nine to ninety has to be an active sensor. Eyes open, heads on a swivel. Looking at everything in their watch quadrant. And don't forget that someone must check out the rear every minute or two, minimum.

Things can come out of the woods at any moment. The sooner you (the leader) know about it, the better your decision-making process can work and the safer you as a family are. The one exception to the no electronics rule is your ham radio. I hope you took the base unit that you had in the house. It's just unplug it and load it anyway. If you leave it behind, they now have a list of the frequencies you will be using. You should already have one in your car to communicate with the rest of the pack, but take this one anyway.

If you want to travel by night, that's okay, too. The big difference in my eyes is that night travel is best done on big highways. They could be crowded if lots of people are trying to get out, but hopefully you are ahead of the curve AND the traffic on that one. Also, on the big road, it is easier to run without headlights. Remember to flash them on every minute or so to check the road. The sooner you get out of dodge, the less time everyone else has to block the roads to capture prey. Big roads have the advantage of speed, of course. You can really book it and cover tons of ground. Big roads are also harder for locals to barricade. And if they are out looking for prey, they *will* barricade roads. Big or little.

The trick is to not get caught. Particularly at a choke point like a bridge. In the back roads, if you can manage it, drive without headlights. Or use them intermittently. I have put a switch on my taillights, including brake and turn signals so I can shut those off from the front seat, including the right headlight. I am almost invisible. But if you are in the pack traveling, the ones behind you might need something to follow as well as some indication if you slow or turn. Perhaps put masking tape over the taillights to dim them. Try it, see how it works, before you need it.

Day or night, big road or back trail, watch out for choke points and barricades. What looks at first like a few abandoned cars on a bridge can turn out to be a barricade that you cannot back out of. If you see this situation, it would be worth your while to stop a half mile back and scope it out before you approach. Get up on the car for a better view. A spare rifle scope works well for this. Be sure to check outlying areas as well as the approaches to the bridge. That's where they will hide.

If it happens at night, look for red lights or a red reflection glowing and dimming. Watch for smoke rising from behind a car. They will be sitting there, smoking, waiting for you. While you are checking the way ahead, you need at least two people outside the vehicle watching all around you for potential trouble. IMPORTANT: In any situation during the bug-out, if you must stop and exit the vehicle, DO NOT shut your doors! Leave them open for quick ingress to the vehicle and a faster get-away.

ALWAYS, always, _ALL_ ways, leave yourself a way out. If you HAVE to stop in traffic, even if it is light, stop at least a full car length back. And NEVER stop on a bridge, if you can at ALL avoid it. You want to be able to turn your car out and get moving the other direction in a hot New York minute. Do not stop for an injured dog, a crying child, or an old, limping woman reaching out to you. If you do, YOU die! I guarantee that EACH of those scenarios was planted by someone trying to trap you, take your goods, rape your dogs, and kill you all.

If you must stop along the way for a relief break, there are rules. First, ONE OR TWO PEOPLE AT A TIME. While anyone is in the woods, everyone else is on guard, guns ready, in a circle, and scanning everything everywhere. Hurry it up, folks. Time is life, here. If you have people to spare, someone should accompany the one going potty, at least partway. And NO one leaves their gun behind. Leave the car doors open for a quick ingress and retreat. And…Butt on log, gun in hand. NEVER be caught unprepared.

If you are traveling with the rest of your pack, all vehicles could start and stop together for mutual protection. Or you could adopt a hop-scotch system where three or so cars stop for whatever and everyone else keeps going. I'd say they should go no more than five miles before stopping to let the stragglers re-mount and get on the road. Spreading out like that could be good for protection. If the leader gets hit by raiders, they will not expect the cavalry to be only five minutes behind and ready for action. Radio communication is essential. But let's keep the chatter to a minimum.

"They" will likely have scanners. But every ten or twenty minutes, each vehicle should call in with just a simple unit number to let you know they are there and okay. Don't forget to implement my frequency jumping technique as outlined elsewhere, if needed. It would be way easier to travel in a nice tight pack, I know. But I would prefer to travel with one or two vehicles in the pack running together, then the next two spaced about two minutes apart. Then if any small group gets in trouble, there is help just two minutes away.

If one or more of you has to leave quickly like the scenario above where I said do not wait for the others, you should have agreed on a gathering point where one or two can wait for the rest to arrive before continuing onward. And this could be especially needful if your members are scattered over a larger geographical area. This assembly point should be someplace where one or two or four cars could wait safely out of sight of the road, monitoring the radio for the approach of the others.

Of course, I assume that everyone has been in communication for the preceding several days as conditions in the world outside deteriorated and have agreed on a departure time window for everyone to meet.

If you actually make it to the BoL by car, all well and good. Especially if one or two families were lagging behind for some reason. But what if you do not make it? If, at any point along the path you find you must abandon the vehicles, there are a few things to keep in mind. Number 1, stay out of sight if possible. No. NOT "if possible." Stay out of sight. If you have to back track three miles, get out of sight. Number 2, before you enter the woods, point your vehicles in the OPPOSITE direction from your original line of travel. This is to confuse any pursuit.

They will naturally assume that you entered the woods intending to travel in the direction your car is pointing. If you can get off the main road and into a side road before abandoning them, all the better.

Spread the cars out as much as practical. Pull them all up to the unload point and get all your gear into the woods out of sight. Then, one driver per car takes their car to a predetermined drop point and parks it, being sure to check for identifying information including vehicle tags and inspection stickers. Leave nothing behind. The van driver makes the rounds to all the drop points and collects the drivers, returning to the unload point and dropping off all but two. Those two accompany him to drop the van at its designated point a few miles away. The three of them can then hike back to the assembly point to meet up. Stay out of sight!

The rules and procedures for a walking bug-out are mostly the same for mapping the path, with the BIG exception of **no campfires**, if possible. But if you really need one, okay. Be extra vigilant. Hopefully, you all had the chance to practice this trek at least once. Move stealthy, move fast. As fast as possible, considering the fact that you probably have some pissed off people in pursuit.

One more piece of advice here, Ace. If someone is coming up on you, campground, trail, car, whatever, **GET YOUR GUN OUT!** And if this person or persons says, "Drop your weapons." **>>>FIRE<<<**.

BEFORE HE FINISHES THAT SENTENCE. *NEVER* give these idiots a chance to get over on you. If you hesitate, YOU ARE FOOD!

You're standing there with your gun in your hand, hanging by your side he says "Drop your weapons." YOU fall backward and to your off-hand side. That means if you are right-handed, fall to your LEFT. As you are falling, bring your weapon up and unload the clip into them. Have standing orders with the rest of your troupe, Suzie shoots the guy on the left, Bobbie takes the scumbag on the right, you shoot the leader. Or something like that. Point being, make sure someone is covering everyone with no overlap if possible.

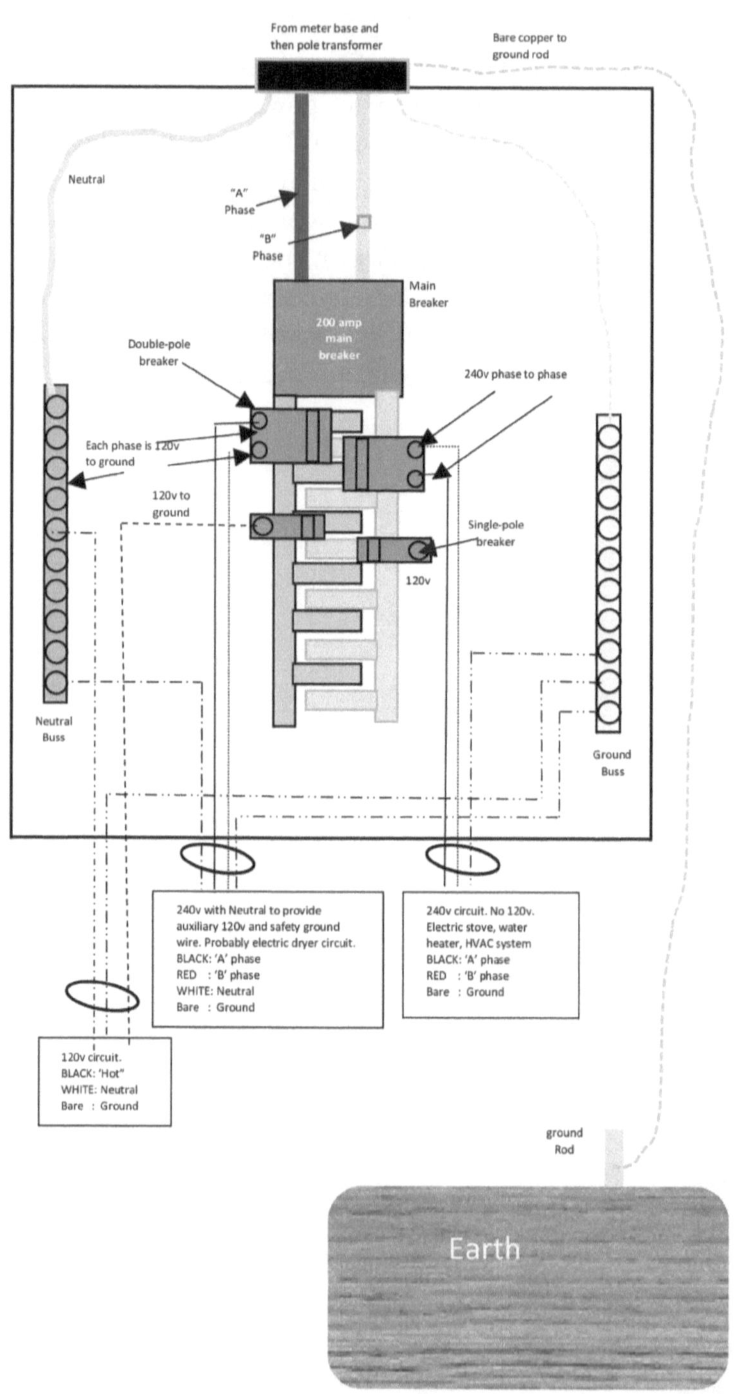

From meter base and then pole transformer
Bare copper to ground rod
Neutral
"A" Phase
"B" Phase
Main Breaker
200 amp main breaker
Double-pole breaker
240v phase to phase
Each phase is 120v to ground
120v to ground
Single-pole breaker
120v
Neutral Buss
Ground Buss
240v with Neutral to provide auxiliary 120v and safety ground wire. Probably electric dryer circuit.
BLACK: 'A' phase
RED   : 'B' phase
WHITE: Neutral
Bare : Ground
240v circuit. No 120v. Electric stove, water heater, HVAC system
BLACK: 'A' phase
RED   : 'B' phase
Bare : Ground
120v circuit.
BLACK: 'Hot'
WHITE: Neutral
Bare : Ground
ground Rod
Earth

20

Electricity

To understand electricity in its whole, let's start by examining a typical home electrical breaker panel, like the one on the left page here, as it contains all the elements of AC electricity. Travel with me from top to bottom, left to right.

At the very top are the **service entrance** wires. These are two, typically very large gauge (one-aught [1/0] to four-aught [4/0]) aluminum wires, called "phase A" and "phase B." Though usually it is not designated, the B phase is typically the one on the right, but it does not matter if they are backward. In modern systems, there is a third, smaller wire called "neutral" that is part of the service entrance from the meter base.

These service entrance wires are encased in a plastic insulating cover and wrapped in a braid of bare aluminum, which is the neutral wire, and the entirety is often covered in an insulating sheath. These service entrance phases are the HOT wires and attach to the **main breaker.** The neutral wire attaches to the **neutral buss** on the side of the panel box. WHITE wires from the house circuits connect to the neutral buss.

The outlet of the main breaker attaches to the two **hot busses**, labeled A and B to match the phases connected to them. Note that each hot buss has "fingers" that extend into the center of the space. It is to these fingers that the individual circuit breakers attach to draw their power. This arrangement is such that a **double-pole** (240-volt) breaker may be inserted at any point and still contact both phases A

181

and B. This is necessary to provide 240 volts at the breaker outlet lugs. A **single-pole** breaker will engage only one of the phases, no matter where it is inserted, thus providing 120 volts at its outlet lug.

This is a diagram of the voltage waveform of 240-volt alternating current, so called because the voltage goes first positive (above the zero-voltage line that divides each diagram horizontally) and then negative, below the zero line, and thus _alternates_ positive and negative sixty times per second. 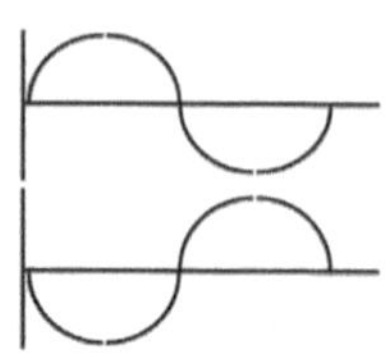

The top diagram represents phase A, and the bottom represents phase B. On either diagram, the peak of each wave, whether up (positive) or down (negative), represents a voltage of (about) 120 volts difference from the zero line. Since the two diagrams show the **A** phase going positive at the exact same time and rate that the **B** phase goes negative, we say that the two phases are 180° _out of phase._

Therefore, from the first positive peak on the A phase to the first negative peak of the B phase, there is a voltage difference of **240** volts, peak to peak. If you were to measure from the topmost output lug of a double pole breaker to the neutral bar, your voltmeter would read 120 volts, and the same is true from the bottom lug of the same breaker to neutral. But measuring from the top lug to the bottom lug you read 240 volts. An AC voltmeter cannot differentiate between phases, so phase A and phase B read the same way, and reversing the voltmeter leads makes no difference.

Two hundred forty volts is used to feed high-power devices like electric stoves, clothes dryers, water heaters, and whole house air-conditioners. One-hundred-twenty-volt circuits feed our wall receptacles where we plug a lamp, a clock, or a television. It is also used in lighting circuits. Practically everything besides the four devices mentioned as needing 240 volts will run on 120 volts.

Some 240-volt devices require both 240 and 120 volts by design. For instance, the motor in your clothes dryer that tumbles the drum uses only 120 volts, but the heating element that supplies the hot air for drying the clothes needs 240 volts. This is accomplished by adding a neutral wire to the two phases that are run to the device from the panel box. The dryer motor will connect to the neutral and phase A while the heat element contacts only the two *phase* wires.

This is an important point to remember. Any phase wire plus the neutral wire supplies 120 volts, and two *different* phase wires always supply 240 volts. But they have to be an "A" and a "B." Connecting two "A" phase wires to a device that needs 240 volts will not work.

In our reference diagram, there is a fourth wire. One that is not part of the service entrance wires, although it may come in through the same hole as they do. This is a bare copper wire. It connects to the GROUND buss on the other side of the cabinet. (Note: The positions of the neutral and ground busses may be reversed in some boxes.) In almost all four-wire systems like this one, the neutral buss is a silver color, while the ground buss is brassy looking.

This ground wire goes out to the meter base cabinet and connects to a lug attached to the meter base box itself, and then out of that box and to a ten-feet metal rod that is driven into the ground very nearby. This is the ground rod. Its purpose is to drain off any stray voltages that occur due to short circuits or equipment malfunctions.

Notice that in the breaker box, the neutral buss is **insulated** from the breaker box cabinet, while the ground buss bar is *attached* to the cabinet. The neutral buss will have only WHITE wires attached to it, and the ground buss will have only BARE (or green) wires. Note that some older systems will still have a combination neutral/ground buss and both white and bare wires connect to it.

Electricity is not to be confused with energy, which is a separate chapter as well as a separate idea. But electricity can be confusing, so I figured I should devote a chapter to explaining the hows and whys of electrical calculations. Even though we all deal with electricity to some degree every single day in our lives, very, very few ever understand it. And frankly, I have met many "master" electricians who's only skill was a memory good enough to keep up with how many #12 wires you could put inside a four-by-four junction box and stay within code. And electricity is *much* more complicated than that. (Not ALL masters are like that!)

Electricity in a wire is often compared to water in a pipe. They are very similar in two very important ways. Volume and pressure.

Pressure in a water pipe is measured in pounds per square inch (psi). The pressure of electricity in a wire is measured in VOLTS. Volts is NOT *how much* electricity is there or available, it is only the amount of *push* or pressure behind that electricity.

The amount of water *flowing* in a pipe is measured in *gallons per minute* (gpm). Electricity flowing in a wire is measured in *AMPS*. Amps is the actual <u>amount</u> of electricity or number of actual electrons that are flowing. See the analogies?

It's actually pretty important to keep these comparisons in mind so that you can keep the concepts separate. This is where most people screw it up. *Way* up.

The third term used daily in electricity is WATTS. There is no easy analogy of Watts in water, even though such a comparison does exist, but electrical watts are easily calculated and understood. Watts is the actual amount of *POWER* or work that can be done. And the relationship is very easy. Volts × amps = watts and is sometimes written or referred to as VA, which means "volt-amps." If you remember your grade school math, all of this can be rewritten as "watts/volts = amps," and "watts/amps = volts." That's lesson 1. W = V × A. V = W/A. A = W/V.

Lesson 2: There are two flavors of electricity in common usage. AC and DC or alternating current and direct current. The term *alternating current* means that the electrons in the wire are moving one direction for a while (about 1/120th of a second) then they reverse and flow the other way for the same amount of time. Sixty times per second, the current alternates, the flow changes direction. That is sixty cycles per second, or sixty *hertz*. This is the frequency of the power in our American society.

<u>How</u> this AC electricity is made is the key to the fact that it is alternating, <u>*and*</u> the frequency at which it alternates. That is not our story here. But before I move on, let me explain one other small concept, just to give you something to worry about at night.

AC alternates direction sixty times per second. Electricity moves at about 0.9c, or nine-tenths the speed of light, which is 186,000 <u>*miles*</u> *per second*. So, in that 1/60th of a second that the electricity is moving "left to right," each electron can travel about 3,100 miles.

So, if you live twenty miles from a substation, for each alternation of the electricity, each electron makes **155** round trips to that substation and back in 1/60th of a second. And it does that sixty times every second.

Wiring for 120-volt AC is almost always three wires: black, white, and green or bare. There are some older systems left out there that do not have the green or bare wire (safety ground). Black is called "hot," because it is at the highest potential from ground. White *used* to be called "ground," now it is referred to as "neutral."

The green or bare wire is the "ground" or "BOND" wire now. It is also known as the safety ground. If something shorts out in an appliance, that ground wire is supposed to carry the current straight to earth ground, tripping the breaker and saving your life. In AC power, if you touch the black wire and any grounded object, like an appliance or plumbing fixture, there is a high likelihood that you will die. One hundred twenty volts will kill you quicker than 240 volts.

The reason is that 240 is so powerful that it will usually KNOCK you loose! But 120 volts will *grab* you. It causes your muscles to contract, and you cannot let go of the wire or pipe or whatever.

Now then, on to direct current (DC) electricity. The electrons in DC electricity do not alternate. They are always moving in the same direction, from a negative pole to a positive pole. This is backward from what logic tells us *should* be happening, but there you have it.

DC was the power system proposed by Thomas Edison, while the AC system was discovered and patented by Nikola Tesla. There was a huge fight over which system would be used for power transmission in the US. AC won for one big reason—you can use a transformer to step the voltage of AC up or down, but DC cannot pass through a transformer.

AC is much easier to transmit over long distances. After a long trip through a wire, voltage decreases appreciably due to the resistance of the wire. Put the electricity through a transformer and step it back up to account for the losses. You cannot do that with DC. It actually requires a *generating plant* about every five miles, I think it is. Some ridiculously short distance like that. But AC can travel for thousands of miles.

DC is the electricity of choice in vehicles because it is easy to store in a battery for later use. DC power is simple, just black and red. Red is positive, or hot. Black is negative, or ground.

The reason for all this rambling about the differences between AC and DC is because *your* electrical system is going to be a *combination* of DC and AC systems, and you need to know these things. Everything in our lives today, televisions, computers, refrigerators, stoves, lights, battery chargers, cell phone chargers, fans, whatever, runs on AC current. The only way to make AC is with a machine called an alternator.

All those standby power units that people buy at the home improvement stores, etc., are advertised as <u>generators</u>, but they are actually *alternators*. They make ALTERNATING current. A <u>generator</u> makes DIRECT current. ONLY. And solar panels? They make DC also.

Another large difference between AC and DC is <u>storage</u>. You can store DC very easily, but AC, due to its nature of changing direction, cannot be stored. Storage is important. Let's say you have a combination generation system, one that incorporates a wind turbine, a water wheel and some solar cells. The only reliable one is the water wheel, and <u>it</u> could drop out if the water level falls. The others will produce electricity on and off, as the sun or wind is available.

The idea is to store the electricity that you make *now* for use later. One reason for this is the fact that your ability to make power is far outstripped by your ability to USE it. So you make power all day long, a little trickle here, a trickle there, and you put it in a storage device. Then you have a LOT of power to use later in a short time.

How do we do all this? That's the easy part. You make DC power and you use that to charge batteries. Standard lead-acid batteries like you have in your car. Or something better, perhaps, like Tesla's Power Wall®. To USE the power you have stored, you take the power stored in those 12-volt batteries, and you feed that power to INVERTERS.

These things take 12-volt DC and turn it into 120-volt AC that you can use in your house. That is where we run into the need for some math. You see, what we _actually_ use is POWER, not VOLTS, not DC or AC. Not even Amps. WATTS is the keyword here. Let's use rounded numbers for our examples, okay? It makes the math easier to see, and the concept of the RATIO easier to grasp.

Let's take a regular, incandescent 100-watt light bulb. If it is fed by a 100-volt source, that 100 watts divided by 100 volts means that 1 amp of electricity is flowing through the wires and the lamp. If we need to power FIVE such lights, we need 500 _watts_ or 5 AMPS at 100 volts. (Remember we are using round figures here for clarity.) Now, what does this 500-watt draw mean at the _supply_ end, where our batteries are putting out TEN volts (actually twelve, but round figures...)?

It means that we are _still_ pulling 500 <u>WATTS</u> out of the batteries, but at ten volts that means FIFTY amps, not FIVE. That becomes an issue when you're talking about wire size and length of the wire run.

The big deal is, **_watts will always be the same, whether from the batteries or from the inverter._** One-hundred-twenty-volts AC or 12-volts DC, the WATTS will remain the same. And if we're talking about 120-volts AC coming from 12-volts DC, then the RATIO is always going to be 10:1. For every amp that you need of 110 vAC, you will need to supply TEN amps of 12 vDC.

Ever notice that wires are not all the same diameter? Big current, big wire. Most of the wiring in your house is fourteen gauge (#14 AWG). This is because most of your devices use only small amounts of power. The circuit feeding your refrigerator may be #12 wire because #12 can carry more power than the fourteen gauge. Your electric stove requires about a 50-amp service, so it uses probably a #6 wire, a much bigger wire, to carry that much current. Wire size is directly related to power consumption of the device.

To supply the electric range at my compound from my 12-volt storage batteries, those batteries would have to supply _FIVE HUNDRED_ amps of 12 vDC electricity. Take a good look at the wires coming into the breaker panel in your home. Take the front cover off and look at the wires coming in from the top. They are the feeder wires that bring the power to your home from the transformer outside.

Those *very* large wires are sized to carry about **two hundred** amps of electricity, and at 240 volts that is about *FORTY-EIGHT THOUSAND* WATTS. Enough to power a blowtorch of a radio station! And that is 200 <u>amps</u> at **240** volts. This is the average service entrance size for the average American home. Two hundred amps. Not five hundred amps. To supply the entire house at 12 volts would mean…they don't make a wire that big. (Actually they do, but…)

So, if your battery storage system is one hundred feet from the house, your choices are as follows: (A) Run two wires that are about ONE INCH in diameter for one hundred feet, then feed the inverters to make 120 volts. That will cost you about $300 PER FOOT, or $30,000.

Or you could choose door #2: Put some inverters close to the generating source and battery. Make the 120-volts AC there. Then you can run some #10 wire to the house. That'll cost about $100. Let me state that another way.

Let's say you have solar cells three hundred feet from the house, because that's the closest location where there is sufficient sunlight. Those solar cells are supposed to charge batteries. So, to keep wire costs down, the batteries need to be there, at the solar cells. NOW we need to get the power up to the house, where we intend to use it. So. Let's put an inverter there at the solar array. Probably a 3,000-watt inverter. At 120-volts AC, that 3,000 watts, or 25 amps that can be sent to the house over a pair of #10 THHN wires with a #14 THHN bond wire in conduit. Actually, for a three-hundred-foot run, you might want to use #8 AWG wire. Look it up in *<u>wire ampacity</u>* tables.

Ampacity tables are specified by the National Electrical Code and tell you which size of what type wire you must use to carry how much AC current for *<u>one hundred feet</u>*. You usually find instructions close by for what to do if your wire run is *over* one hundred feet. You can safely fudge the ampacity tables by a small amount. Let's say, 110 feet instead of a hundred. Or 33 amps instead of 30.

To move your power from point A to point B, you *can* use what is called <u>direct burial</u> wire (type UMB), which is meant to be placed underground in a trench without the protection of conduit. Otherwise, you will have to put PVC conduit in the ground with wires inside that, like type THHN. THHN is just a kind of wire. Look up *wires types*. If you do use PVC conduit, <u>be sure</u> to use PVC cleaner on the joints before applying glue, put <u>*plenty*</u> of glue on the joint then *twist* the joint while the glue dries. This will make a waterproof joint. And, trust me, you want any conduit with wires inside it to be waterproof. Unless you like fireworks.

Different wire *types* sometimes have different ampacities. In the example, if we used THW wire instead of THHN, it would **have** to be #8 instead of #10, and the bond wire would be #12, not #14. That third wire, the bond or ground, is very important. This is the wire that saves your life if something shorts out. Do not EVER cut that little round prong off a three-wire plug-in. You're taking your life in your hands to do that. Really.

The big deal here is this…in figuring your needs for battery storage, solar cell capacity, and power needs at the house, you must always be conscious of the relationships between your *stored* amps and your <u>required</u> amps. The POWER (watts) will be the same everywhere. The amps relationship will always be <u>*roughly*</u> a 10:1 difference. Man, I hope that was clear enough. **whew**

I am going to recommend that you DO plan to use electricity for lighting, running fans, washing machine, maybe even a clothes dryer, water pumps and, maybe cooking in summer. Because unless you put a wood stove in a separate shed outside of the house proper, you will not be able to stand the heat to cook in the summer months.

The old-timers used to do it that way. A summer kitchen outside. In the winter, of course, a wood stove in the house is a triple blessing. Cook your food, heat the house, and heat water all at the same time. But in summer, it is tough. I remember, folks. We had an outdoor and an indoor cooking area when I was a kid. Until we got electricity in the house about 1959. Then Dad bought an electric stove for Maw-Maw. Never saw an old woman that happy before.

To supply all that need, you'll need to have many, many storage batteries. You will need many inverters, and you will need multiple feeds to the house. We will talk about all this in ENERGY.

Well, while we're here in electricity, let's talk about solar for a bit, eh? Solar panels are pretty good at converting sunlight into electricity, but they ain't cheap, friend. The prices are coming down, though. I think they are at about $2.00 per watt right now.

When I started playing with solar cells, they were way more expensive, like thirty to fifty bucks a watt. So I started accumulating those solar-powered yard lights solar calculators, anything solar that was being tossed. I could pick stuff up cheap at yard sales. People throw those things away when they quit working, even though it is usually just the rechargeable batteries are dead. Or the spring tail connectors for the batteries are corroded.

I would take them apart, being careful to not damage the cell proper. Each cell puts out about three volts, so if you wire five of them in series (black #1 to red #2, black #2 to red #3…black #4 to red #5. black #5 and red #1 are the output terminals), you get fifteen volts. That's enough to charge a 12-volt car battery. Slowly. This arrangement puts out about 0.5 amp or so. So now you take those strips of five and wire them in parallel with each other. Strip 1 red to strip 2 red, etc., etc. All reds together, all blacks together. Before you know it, you have 100 amps of power available. About 1,500 watts.

Another concept you need to know about batteries and power is the idea of AMP-HOURS. A battery that says it can supply 350 amp-hours means that it can supply 350 amps at 12 volts for one hour. Or 1 amp at 12 volts for 350 hours or any combination thereof. This is AMPS, not WATTS. And again, this difference is well worth remembering.

If you have a solar panel rated 12 volts at 100 WATTS, and you expect ten hours of sunlight today, you could be putting 1,000 _watt_-hours into your battery system. <u>NOT</u> _AMP-HOURS!_ Not enough, is it?

Let's look at just one appliance, that one appliance you are most likely to want, your refrigerator. The typical refrigerator will use about 2.4 kWh (2,400 watt-hours) per day, or 100 watts each and every hour.

Watt hours at 120 vAC is the same as watt hours at 12 vDC. It is power. The difference is how many amps it is. 2,400 Wh/24 hours/

day = 100 watts for an hour. Every hour. Which is a little inaccurate. The fridge will run about twenty minutes, then off for thirty, something like that, and it depends on how many times it is opened.

So, all in all, you should be able to run a fridge on a 1,200-watt invertor. Which means it will pull about 100 amps from the battery. If you have a 100-watt solar panel charging the batteries for your fridge, they must charge at least as much as the fridge runs. Meaning, this 100-watt array should be able to keep up unless you have a cloudy day.

A better bet would be to have 200 watts of solar array feeding about four batteries. That might be enough to keep you charged up. But that is just one appliance. You do the rest of the math. That's what this book is all about, gang. Show you what's happening, tell you how the math works, and let you take it from there. Don't forget, there ARE refrigerators that do NOT need electricity! (MORE homework!)

As for how much power any given appliance needs, I would first look for what is called the "nomenclature plate," a sticker or metal embossed plate that gives all the particulars about the device. You could also take a clamp-on amp meter and just read the amp-draw for the device. But if you do that, remember: the amp "clamp" must clamp around _only one wire_, and that wire *must* be the hot wire on 120-vAC stuff. Either phase wire of a 240 device will do.

You know, I almost forgot. In a pinch, you can use a stationary bicycle to turn a car alternator to charge batteries or a "generator" head to supply 120 volts directly. It would be best if you set up a flywheel system to keep the speed to the gen head as stable as possible, and a voltmeter reading the output so the operator knows when the target speed has been reached. This way you can get exercise while making power for your house.

All in all, I think the best system will have multiple generation means scattered about. Each generating site will have a couple of batteries and an inverter of say, 1,500- or 3,000-watt capacity. Put some research and math into deciding which one you need where. Each generating system is making 12 vDC and charging the batteries.

The inverters are feeding from those batteries and sending 120 vAC to the house where it goes through regular battery chargers to charge a bank of storage batteries right there at the house. These batteries feed several inverters that make the 120 vAC that the house needs. You'll find a diagram of this in the ENERGY chapter.

But while I'm on that subject, think about this, kids. Say you have a waterwheel driving an old truck alternator. Add another alternator to it. Maybe a third one. Keep adding alternators until the waterwheel slows down a bit. (Oh, the alternators have to be _loaded_ during this because loading the alternator makes more work for the waterwheel.

So if you figure out that your waterwheel will turn three loaded alternators, at a capacity of, say, 65 amps each, then your waterwheel will produce 195 amps to charge the batteries there. At 12 volts, that's 2,340 watts. So to get this power to the house, you need a 3,000-watt inverter. You will need a wire that will carry 25 amps to the house. With a little extra work and figuring, you have just tripled the output of your waterwheel. Live a little. Experiment a little. Get shocked a little.

Three-phase electricity. If you go off raiding for things, like propane, especially, you might run into the need for a different sort of animal, called three-phase electricity. Most large commercial electric motors are wired for 3-phase. Black, Red and Blue tags on the wires for A, B & C phases. Those motors will not operate without the right electricity. Three-phase is just a little wrinkle beyond the 240v electricity we just talked about. THAT is _called_ "Single Phase". I have always thought that 120v should be single phase, regular 240v should be TWO-phase, and THIS rascal would then make more sense. Look at this diagram:

You can see the three different curves that represent the three phases. Notice that they peak at different times. Those peaks are 120 rotational degrees apart, because electricity is generated by rotating machines. To contrast, here is a different look at single-phase 240-vAC power:

The only difference it makes to you is if you should run up on a motor driving a pump somewhere that requires three-phase power. There *is* a device that will convert single-phase to three-phase, it is 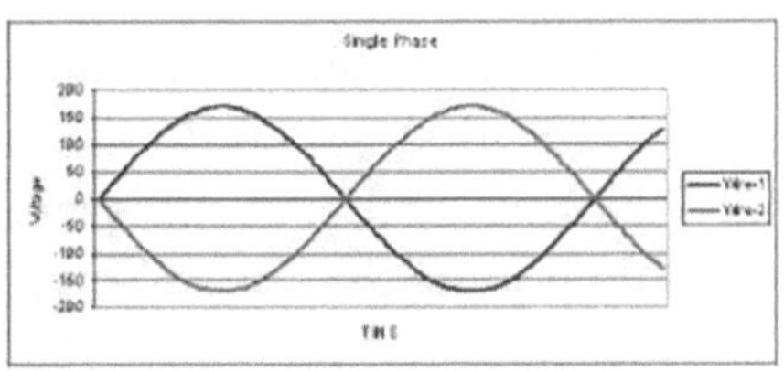 nothing more than a single-phase motor driving a three-phase generator. Works quite well, actually. But finding one can be an issue.

A *single*-phase motor is a peculiar animal. You see, *no* motor can actually begin to rotate on its own unless there is a phase difference on the power wires *other* than 180°. So, in a single-phase 110- or 240-volt motor, the B phase (or neutral wire in 120-volt motors) is connected to the leg that is common to both the start and run windings (called, oddly enough, "common").

The A phase connects to the start (main) winding and to a capacitor that connects to the run (auxiliary) winding. The purpose of the capacitor is to introduce a 45° phase shift to the A phase. This creates the rotational torque needed to turn the motor. 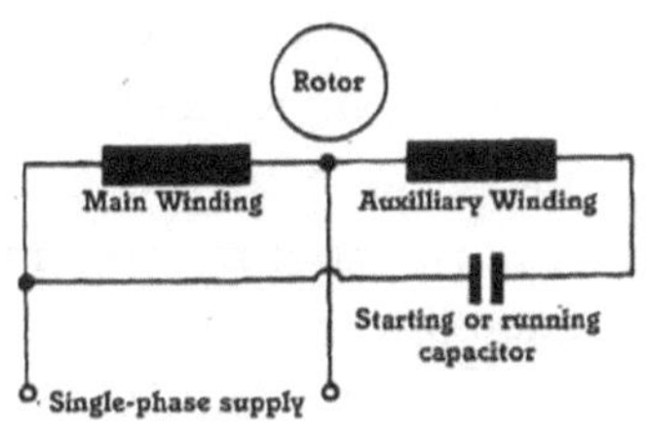

The three-phase motor does not need a capacitor to make it turn, as the phases are 120° apart. Simply connect the three lead wires to the three motor lugs and you are good to go. There *IS* one odd thing about three phase motors, however, and it *will* affect most pumps, particularly a screw or scroll 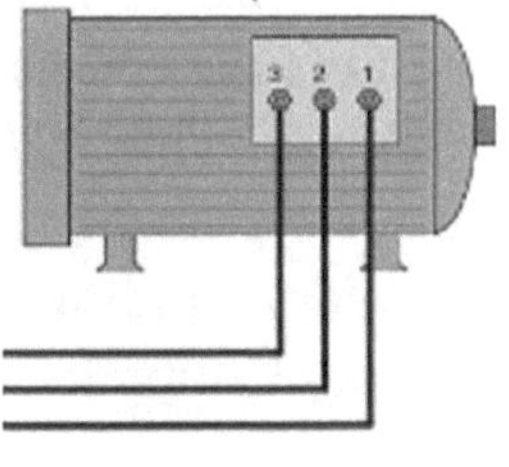 pump, and also some mechanical devices that are direction sensitive.

If any two of the three wires are reversed in position, the motor will turn backward, or, rather, in the opposite direction. Should you find this situation and it creates a difficulty, simply exchange *any two* of the three wires. So if you DO run up on a three-phase motor and figure everything else out, *bump* the power to the motor and listen for loud noises, which could indicate a phase reversal. If it happens, swap two wires.

There are several varieties and voltages of electricity, ranging from 120/240 single-phase systems to 120/208/240 three-phase systems and then 277/480 three-phase systems

Now let's think about *controlling* things a bit. Most control systems do not use the same voltage as they system they are controlling. For instance, the common voltage used to control a heating and air conditioning system in homes and small businesses is **24 vac**. We get this voltage by using a **transformer** to reduce the **line voltage** that the system is using for primary power.

A transformer is really simple, just two coils of wire wound either on top of each other or placed side by side. They usually have a **core** that the windings are placed on, made of steel plates. This core enhances the magnetic coupling between the two windings.

To explain electromagnetism quickly: any time a current flows through a wire, it creates a magnetic field around the wire. And any time a magnetic field cuts across a conductor—like a wire, or piece of metal—it generates a current inside that conductor. So one coil of the transformer makes a magnetic field. That magnetic field makes a voltage in the other coil. One factor in the strength of the fields and voltages is the number of windings in the coils. I am going to just make up some arbitrary numbers here, but they are accurate in the ideas they convey. Trust me.

Let's say you have a gas furnace whose input voltage (line volts) is 120 vac. That 120 volts is fed into the **primary** winding of the control transformer, and this winding has 1,200 turns of wire. The **secondary** winding has 240 turns. The rule is that there is a ratio that is the same for volts and amps and watts and number of turns of wire in the windings. So, using these figures, we expect to see an output from this transformer of 24-volt AC. I know I keep saying "AC." It is just an old habit. You must keep in mind that DC (direct current) canNOT be transformed in this manner. "Why" is a very complex issue, so just take it on faith, please.

It does not matter what your line voltage actually is, it can be transformed. The caveat here is that if you have a transformer marked "Pri: 120 vAC, Sec: 24 vAC," you can*not* put 240 volts on the primary, you will burn it out. Every winding in every transformer is designed to "see" a particular voltage.

This is determined by the size of the wire used and the number of turns in the coil, plus about a dozen other very esoteric factors like "interwinding capacitive reactance." In other words, everything has its own operating voltage, and that is what it better get.

Another big deal about transformers is how much current they can handle. Remember, current is how MUCH electricity is moving, while volts are the push behind it. WATTS, or "VA" (volts times amps) is how much power it produces or uses, or how much work can be done. All transformers are rated in VA.

Every relay, every valve, every do-dad that you add to a control circuit adds more LOAD to the circuit and requires more VA of the transformer. A typical low-load (low-power) transformer will supply something on the order of 30 VA at 24 volts AC. That's a little over 1 amp of current. But there *are* some available that will handle much more power.

When ordering or buying a transformer, you must specify what VA rating you want. Some of the larger ones, like 24 vAC 50 VA or 75 VA, may have a circuit breaker built in. Its purpose is to protect the transformer from burning out in the event of an overload.

If your transformer does NOT have a circuit breaker, you should install a fuse in the secondary (output) line to protect it. If your transformer is 24 volts and is rated at 30 VA, then the AMPS part of that "volts times amps" rating is 30/24 = 1.25 amps. So, a 2-amp fuse should protect the transformer. Never fuse at exactly the figure you calculate or you will be changing fuses every five minutes.

Let's take a look at the symbols for some of the more common control devices along with a brief description of each. This is by no means an all-inclusive list. You can find many others online.

Transformer: As mentioned earlier, a transformer is (usually) two coils of wire on a common iron core. The windings are termed primary (input) and secondary (output) and the voltage for each is generally indicated on the diagram. 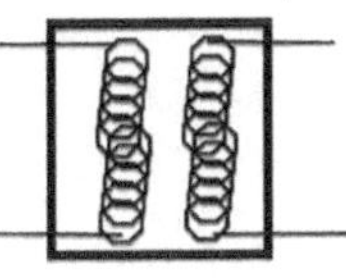

A transformers primary purpose is to "step up" or "step down" the input voltage. Some transformers, called "multitap," have multiple access points to accept or deliver different voltages. The most common is the multitap transformer that will accept different input voltages yet still output the same secondary voltage.

Such as a transformer may be marked "120/208/240" on the primary side, which will accept any of the listed input voltages if it is connected correctly. There is usually a diagram on the case indicating which wires do what. Here is the most common arrangement:

Therefore, if your input voltage is 240, you connect the red and white wires to the line and blue and yellow will give you the 24-volt output. Don't worry about 208 volts. It is a funky animal produced by special industrial three-phase systems, called "closed delta" wiring. Its diagram looks like three coils connected in a triangle. It is NEVER found in a residential situation. Unless you have three-phase power in your house.

White – Common
Black – 120v
Orange – 208v
Red – 240 v
Yellow – 24 v hot
Blue – 24 v common

Switch: —•—•— This is the symbol for a common, manually operated switch. This switch is shown CLOSED, in other words, ON. THIS switch: is OPEN, —•—•— or OFF. Switches in a control diagram will also show any activating mechanism that can cause the switch contacts to reverse, as well as the *normal state* of the contacts. This switch is operated by pressure, —•—•— hence the "cup" attached to the contact "blade." This switch is shown as "Normally Closed" (NC), and because the blade closes the contacts from the bottom, it is known to operate as a "Close On Rise" switch. When the pressure drops below the set point, the switch opens.

Here we see a temperature operated "Normally Open" (NO) Close-on-Rise switch. When the temperature it is sensing RISES, the switch will close. Notice the symbol beneath the blade that indicates it is temperature —•—•— activated. This is that same switch in a NO "Close On Fall" configuration. The contacts as shown in any diagram are always the NORMAL or UNactivated condition.

All the switches we have seen so far are **Single**-Pole because there is only one set of contacts, and Single **Throw** because they only make contact in one direction. Switches may also have multiple contacts as well as two or more positions.

Relays: A relay is a remotely controlled device, usually an electrically operated switch. You shoot a signal, which in most cases is going be 24 vAC to the COIL terminals, which activates an electromagnet that pulls in an actuator that moves the contact(s).

In this example, there are TWO sets of contacts (or POLES) and each pole has two contacts that share a Common input. One contact is Normally Open (NO) and the other is Normally Closed (NC). The diagonal slash indicates a closed contact. To make sure you've got it right, the very top contact here is NO. The next one has a slash connecting the two contacts of that switch and it is 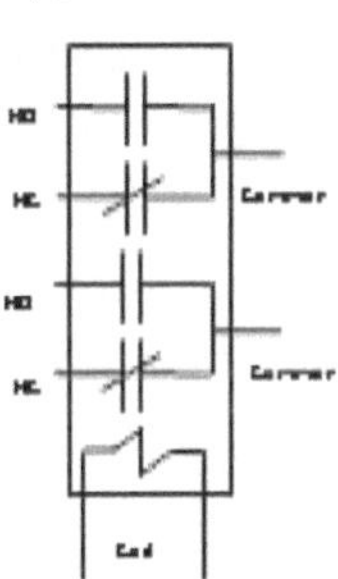 NC. The name of this arrangement is **Double Pole Double Throw**, aka DPDT. If you eliminate the top section of this puppy, you have a SINGLE pole double throw (SPDT) relay. And make note of the symbol for the coil at the bottom because that is probably how the terminals for the coil will be identified on the relay case or any schematic diagram.

Then there is the venerable Single Pole Single Throw, or SPST, which is about the most common relays there is. Energize the coil and the contact closes. Easy peasy, possum's greasy. 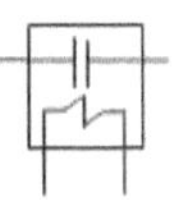

Now let's all gather 'round and gape open mouthed at a special kind of relay called a **Sequencer**. The coil of a sequencer is actually a HEATER. Notice at the bottom, where you would expect to find the operating COIL, the symbol is different. This is the symbol for a heating element. 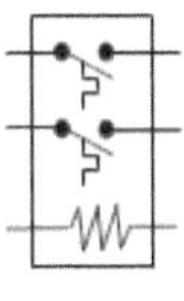

Put 24 vAC on the heater terminals and it starts heating up. Somewhere about thirty seconds later, the temperature operated switches start kicking in. One. At. A. Time. They turn on IN SEQUENCE! Get it? And sequencers come in all sorts of pole count and contact arrangement also. I have seen them stack FIVE switches on one of these puppies!

This type of relay is most often seen turning on the electric heating elements of an electric furnace or the auxiliary heater in a heat pump. This is to avoid throwing a huge load on the fuses feeding the device, which could cause them to blow. Instead, a sequencer puts the load on a little at a time. But sequencers can also be used as simple slow-motion relays.

Ground: I almost forgot the universal symbol for EARTH GROUND. We say it that way in case somebody forgets and refers to the neutral wire as GROUND. This is the ground that GOES to the ground. Rod, that is. In the ground. Outside. If you see this symbol in a schematic diagram, you can pretty much bet that this a point where the wiring connects to the actual metal case of the device.

There are simply *tons* of drawings representing every conceivable type and variation of device known to man. That is a very literal statement, by the way. So we cannot possibly cover them all here. But now you have some idea of how to interpret the symbols.

21

Energy

Well, now that you have some idea of how electricity works and what you can *do* with it, how do you MAKE it? I'm going to assume that you want as much electricity as possible available to you. It's just so darned handy. If so, you need to take advantage of everything you can to make power. A water wheel at the creek, a wind turbine or two, and solar panels. All these things making energy all the time it's available.

To put the problem in its simplest terms, you want to generate electricity at various places, using differing means, and deliver that electricity to where you need it. Right so far? So it should look something like this:

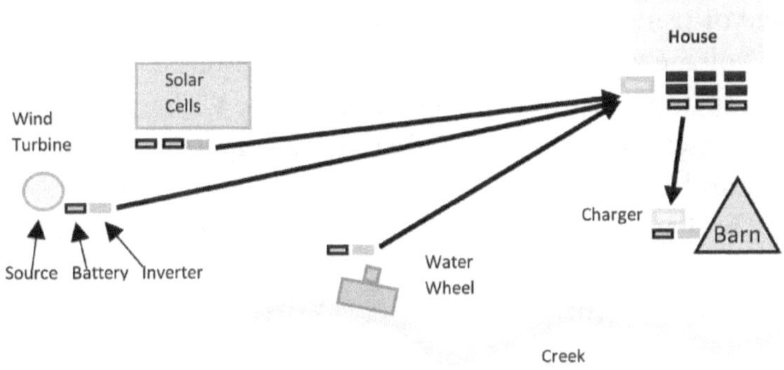

Remember our little chat about how you can send more power through less wire using AC rather than DC? Well, Buck-o, that's exactly what we're gonna do. First, the creek:

If your creek is deep enough and fast enough, you should consider an UNDERshot water wheel. This is a wheel where the water that pushes it flows

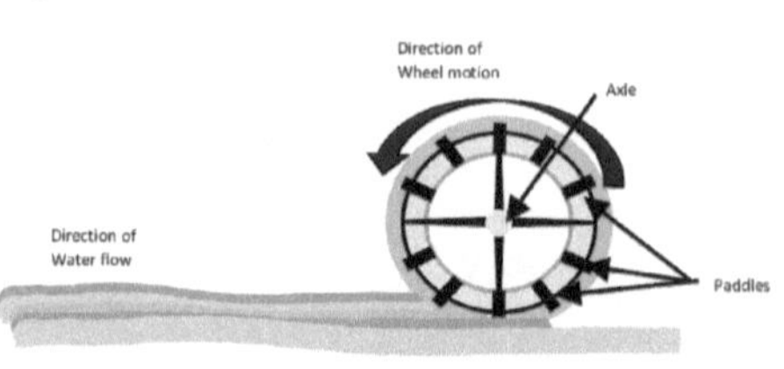

underneath it, propelling the paddles that are actually under the water. An OVERshot waterwheel only works where the inbound water is higher than the top of the wheel and exits at the bottom. Overshot wheels are more efficient due to the weight of the water being actively involved in turning the wheel for a longer time.

The waterwheel axle should extend about a foot past the axle support pillar on the side nearest your house. To this axle, you will attach a V belt pulley that moves a V belt that drives an old truck alternator. This alternator, odd as it seems, outputs 13.5 volts DC. Yeah, that's right, **DC**.

This thing actually *is* an <u>alternator</u>. It makes **AC** power when it's turning. But AC has no place in a car electrical system. So it has internal components that change the AC to DC to be compatible with the car's system.

Well, it *was* designed to charge a battery after all. And that is exactly what we want to do with it. Charge a battery. Or two. The advantage of using a vehicle alternator is that it has a built-in thing called a "voltage regulator" that keeps it from overcharging the battery. Most solar power systems will call this piece a "charge controller."

The waterwheel spins the alternator, which puts out 13–14-volts DC and charges the battery located there at the waterwheel station. The battery then feeds an inverter, probably like a 1,000-watt job.

The inverter will feed that 1,000 watts to the house battery center over a regular piece of house wire. Depending on the distance (look it up in your wire ampacity tables), you might pipe it up over a #14/3 (14-gauge, three wires) UF direct-burial wire. If it is a long haul, you'll have to go up to #12/3. This same arrangement of driver (waterwheel, wind turbine, or solar panel), battery, and inverter is used at every generation system.

ALWAYS keep in mind that the wire ampacity tables are calculated for wire runs of one hundred feet. If you're going up to about 125 feet or so, you can still use the length shown. Past that, you should go up one wire size to be safe.

The pulley system, the alternator, battery, and inverter must all be in a weatherproof enclosure to protect them from the elements. With ventilation for summertime and to prevent the buildup of explosive gases from the battery. No matter where you are, the battery and inverter need to be enclosed and ventilated.

I also recommend that you make the enclosures for your generation systems sealed as tightly as possible, to at least slow the intrusion of insects and rodents. And cover the ventilation areas with screen wire.

See the plan? Generate DC power, charge a battery. Power an inverter from that battery to convert power to AC. Send the AC to the main battery…uhhh…battery, close to the house. At the house, the AC you sent up from each generation point powers a standard battery charger. You have (usually) about 8–10 amps of DC to play with here. You *can* get larger battery chargers if you *need* it. Eight amps at 12 volts is 960 watts. Nine hundred sixty watts divided by 120 volts is about 0.8 amp of AC needed to power the charger. (There's that 10:1 ratio again!) So that one generation point can actually charge several batteries at once. Through several chargers, if needed.

The problem here is that these cheap regular battery chargers do not usually have a voltage regulator built in. So you might need to get a charge controller. Note that *some* chargers DO have a regulator built in. Keep in mind that the purpose of a regulator or charge controller is to keep from overcharging the batteries. That will damage them. Also keep in mind that the electrolyte level in *every* battery must be checked on a regular basis. To top the cells off, use ONLY distilled water. So you might need to build a still for that.

Look at that diagram and you will see that all three generation points are sending AC to the chargers at the main batteries, charging those batteries. Below those black batteries at the house are more inverters. Those are used to send AC to various places around the compound, even other houses! This AC can be used just as it is, like feeding a lighting system and receptacles at the barn. I have *shown* it as powering a battery charger at the barn, charging a battery, and that battery feeding another inverter for use around the barn. This setup has a slight advantage in that if anything happens to power somewhere else, the barn will still have power as long as the battery lasts. And by having many inverters, if one dies, you have spares. You don't lose all power.

At the main battery of batteries, the system is divided into several sections, each set of batteries fed by its own charger and feeding its own inverters. How you divide up the batteries and chargers will depend on how you need to use the power and where. Once you get the power to the main battery of batteries, you can ship it anywhere you like. Like across the field to Fred's house, where he has a battery of batteries along with chargers and inverters to power his own house. I also recommend that you put a lot of thought into how to divide the loads" up among the inverters. This is to allow you to disconnect several of the inverters when those loads are not in use. For instance, you could turn off the one feeding the washing machine when it is not in use. Maybe put the clothes washer and the dishwasher on the same circuit. Just don't try to use them both at the same time. Turn off the inverters feeding the lighting at, say, midnight. Anyone needing to be up and about can use a small flashlight. Think about it.

There *are* inverters out there that can be synched together to make more watts available. Take two 1,000-watt units and synch them up so you can get 2,000 watts out. The big deal is that if you just take two regular inverters and hook the neutrals and grounds and hots together, you will blow them both up. That is because there <u>*will*</u> be a difference in the timing of the hot phases. That timing difference translates into a *voltage* difference between the two units that will back feed one of the inverters and *Bam.*

These "synch-able" inverters have a jack on the back where you connect the two inverters together at their timing circuit, not the power circuit. Plug the synch wire into the two units and one will assume Master status and control the timing circuit of both units. *THEN* you can tie the hots together, etc.

I have a theory that if you cut that synch wire and reverse the two wires <u>inside</u> it, that will reverse the synch timing and will give you 240 vAC between the two hot legs. Grounds can tie together, but neutrals ***DO NOT*** tie together. If you need a neutral with the 240 volts, use only ONE of the inverters to supply the neutral. Or more fireworks. If the HOTS are 180° out of phase with each other, then the NEUTRALS are *also* out of phase with each other.

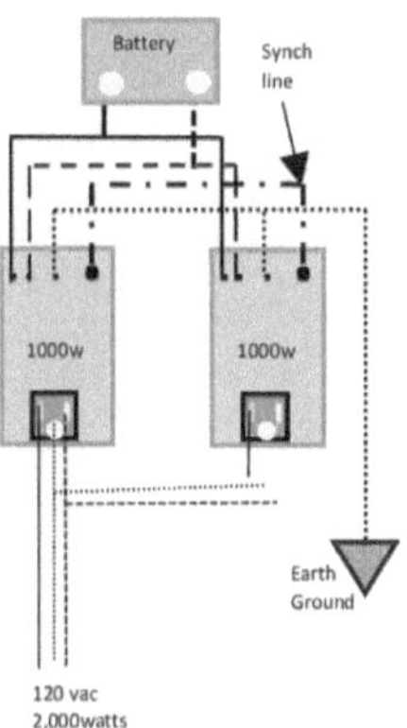

Synching two inverters to get 2,000 watts @ **120v**

It looks like this: Cut the synch wire in the middle. Strip the outer sheath back two inches on each side. Hook red from the left side to black on the right. Left black to right red. I think that it will invert the timing lock and make the two units 180° out of phase. In other words—240 volts. Hook the grounds of both units together and the two HOT wires will give you 240-vAC difference. Use only ONE of the neutral wires if you need a neutral.

WARNING! I have NOT tried this setup! It is only a *theory* that I have, and it has NOT been verified or tested in any way. If you DO try it, be smart. Use a meter to see if the hots read 220–240 volts between them.

>><u>USE AT YOUR OWN RISK!</u><<

Driving The Alternator

This is what the drive setup should look like whether it's a waterwheel or a wind turbine or bicycle. You MUST have some means of tensioning the drive belt from the driver to the alter-

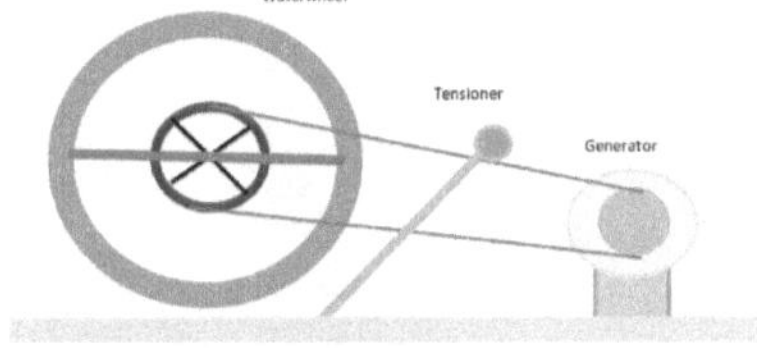

nator. And *please* do not forget that all the 110-volt electrical devices must be grounded to a ground rod driven into the ground AT the source.

22

Heating With Wood

Before I delve into this one, let me remind you that I am not providing all the answers here in this here book here. I am pointing the way. I am reminding you of the things you need to think about, the things you need to research. So, when I mention methane production, I expect _you_ to research the subject thoroughly. There is no other way for you to understand it well enough to decide if that is something you want to do or what questions you need to ask.

As a nation, Americans have traditionally been the greediest people on earth in every way. And energy consumption is no exception. China has finally outstripped us in that regard, though. Due mostly to the fact that they now produce about 80 percent of what WE consume in durable and soft goods.

Still and all, the US uses more than twice the energy per capita of its nearest competitor. When TEOTWAWKI hits, that will come down quite a bit, I am sure. But the adjustment from "Always On" to "Hey, is there enough juice left to charge my MP3?" will be difficult.

Let's look at what your needs will likely be once you get ensconced in your compound, eh? First off is, of course, heat. How will you heat? Most probably with wood, seeing as how it is readily available and quickly renewable.

You will probably use it for cooking also. At least until you get energy production up to a reasonable level and have enough electricity or gas to run a stove.

Wood, with all its drawbacks, is relatively easy to procure and use. Calculating how much you will need is a bit more difficult. The basic unit of measurement for wood is the CORD. A cord is a stack of wood four-by-four-by-eight feet, containing about 128 cubic feet if the wood is split. This is because split wood can be stacked tighter than "round wood," which is what unsplit wood is called.

A cord of round wood will yield about eighty-five cubic feet. The amount of heat in calories and/or BTUs depends upon what kind of wood you have and whether or not it is "seasoned" or allowed to dry about twelve months before use.

As for how much you will use, it depends greatly on the locale. How cold will it be, how long will it last, what is the construction of your home, etc. I will say this…the last year that I heated with wood was in a one-thousand-square-foot, ninety-year-old farmhouse with minor upgrades. We heated with a Baker's Choice wood cook stove, which we also used for…well…cooking.

In southwestern Tennessee, we went through about six cords on a typical winter. So, if your home is better insulated, you can expect to do somewhat better. And don't forget to multiply that by the number of homes you will be heating. And figure in how much you will be cooking also.

Which brings up a good point. You _might_ find it useful to build one _large_ lodge as a communal house for the short term. It depends on how much time you think you have. Maybe build one large one right now, then later make individual units when you have more time.

One idea that I have seen work really well was a cluster of Cob homes built around a central hub also of cob. Each of the outer clusters was its own home for one family or group and everyone shared the community room and kitchen. This way, if you get caught short on time and must go to your BoL sooner than expected, you could do the central area first and everyone camps in there while you build the outlying units. I suggest that if you take this route, you should plan for the other structures as you are building the main one. In other words, go ahead and frame up for the extra doors that will open into the spoke housing units.

I suppose this is as good a time as any to talk about HOW to heat with wood. We already know about things like fireplaces and your standard wood stove or wood fired heater. But there's another kind of wood fueled heater that I have learned about, it's called a ROCKET stove! The design is rather unconventional, but it does a great job.

I first encountered this puppy at a friend's cob house. Snow on the ground and the place a cozy 73° inside. He had the long, horizontal exhaust line running under a window seat made of rock! He said that if the fire went out in the middle of the night, the house was still warm in the morning. Check it out!

Cutting the wood yourself is about the only way to go for your compound. You can fell an average tree of about fourteen to eighteen inches diameter in around thirty minutes with nothing more than an axe. Working it up is a bit more arduous. Cutting off all the limbs and cutting them up into usable pieces takes a bit of time also, but it is necessary.

Use your bow saw for the larger limbs and a hatchet or machete for the smaller ones of about one to two inches diameter. I leave nothing to waste, myself, I even hand-pull the tiny branches off, piling them in a box to be used as kindling later.

It is, in my opinion, easier to drag a whole tree or half tree out of the woods and up to the woodyard before working it up. That way you handle the cut pieces a minimum number of times. And THAT can save your back!

A whole sixty-foot tree will weigh between six thousand and fifteen thousand pounds, depending on variety, age (diameter), and moisture content. You'll need a tractor or a couple of mules or horses to pull it out. Or you can use log rollers to move it more easily. Try a block and tackle with the rollers and you just might move a tree! Keep in mind that wood that is freshly cut contains a *bunch* of moisture. That has two effects. One, it makes the wood weigh 20–50 percent more than seasoned wood. And two, it makes it harder to burn. So try to get some wood cut and stacked right away.

If you don't have either horses OR horsepower, I'll have to backtrack and say work the log up into stove-sized pieces right where she falls. Then you'll need a wheelbarrow or a good cart to haul the wood to the house.

I don't recommend cutting trees real close to where you live. You want the trees around you to protect the housing from the worst ravages of the weather. They'll keep you cooler in summer and warmer in winter.

I also recommend that you build ricks for your wood that have a stone base to keep the wood at least eighteen inches off the ground. If you stack your wood on the ground, you invite termites and rot. Stack the wood so that air can easily circulate between the rows. Cover the wood with a tarp, cover the tarp with branches, to hold them down and for camouflage.

No tarps? No problem. The branches will shed water. You will probably need enough ricking to hold about twenty to forty cords of wood at a time. I do NOT put them right next to each other. They can make an effective barrier against intrusion. Always rotate your wood supply. I use the first-in, first-out inventory method for my wood. The first tree I cut is the first one I burn. Mark the stacks so you don't lose track.

Solar energy is pretty much in vogue these days. And not just in photovoltaic panels either. There are many ways to pull energy from the sun, the easiest being a hydronic (water based) heating systems. A panel with water filled tubes inside, a glass cover to hold in the collected heat. A pump to move the water, and some means of storing that heated water.

I built a solar collector once from an old fourteen-foot satellite dish! Cover the dish with flexible mirror, or even aluminum foil. Reset the axis of the frame so the original motor can make it track straight across the sky. At the focal point of the dish, I used a four-inch concave mirror to focus the sunlight back down through the center of the dish to a heavy iron pipe that held the flowing water that I was heating. Worked great.

If you can heat enough water, you can also use it to heat domestic hot water for washing and bathing by using a heat exchanger, as well as space heat.

Your heat transfer water should never comingle with your domestic hot water. In fact, your transfer water should be a mix of water and ethylene glycol like the antifreeze in your car.

It does two things, it lowers the freezing point and the boiling point of your transfer water. If you're smart, you will combine many different technologies to gather heat and bring them all together to supply all your heating needs, from home heat to domestic hot water to supplying hot air for your clothes dryer.

It CAN be done, amigo! (*HINT:* To use heated air for clothes drying, you need either a coil of small copper tubing, or better yet, a very small (four to eight inches square) condensing coil from a small refrigeration unit. A heater core from a compact car will also work well). All you need is 140° air leaving that coil.

In the last decade or so, another solar energy system has become a contender. It is called "phase change" solar. In this system, the collector panel tubes are filled with Freon. The big deal is that in a hydronic system, you have to bring ALL the water in the collector up to temp before you can pull any usable heat out of it. That can literally take anywhere from hours to days.

In a phase change system, you can start making heat right away, within minutes, because the Freon that is used as the heat collection fluid changes state, from liquid to gas as soon as sunlight hits it (this is the change of phase that gives it the name), and in doing so, it takes up an enormous number of BTUs. The hot, gaseous Freon then goes to a heat exchanger to transfer its heat to a water/glycol mix and that mix is pumped to the storage units. The Freon gives up its heat and changes from gas back to liquid and goes through the cycle again and again.

Now, that was a very simplified explanation of the system, and to tell the truth, unless you are one HOTshot air-conditioning tech or a mechanical engineer, this one might be a little out of your league. But there is a chance that you are one of those, and it is one *great* way to collect and use solar energy.

But still, in the end, all we are doing is heating water. Heat it, store it, use it. Storing the heat is not a huge issue, and there are several approaches to it. I know one guy who went around to home improvement stores and plumbers, collecting old water heaters that had been changed out due to failure.

About 70 percent of the ones he collected did NOT leak! Those are the ones he used for heat storage. The others he cut up to use the steel for other projects. Also keep in mind that since the units are not actively _heating_ water, they are no longer classed as a low pressure boiler (which is what a water heater is, legally); therefore, the internal pressure can never exceed the pressure of your water system. Steve put ten heaters together in some plumbing configuration of his own design and pumped hot water into them for storage.

His system was a little complicated, but I'll try to describe it for you. He had multiple heat sources that would heat the water, and they all pumped it to a central collecting and processing manifold. He had a bunch of remote sensing thermostats like this one: It is typically called by its most popular model number, A19ABC24. But that one has a very limited temperature range and might not work for you.

You can also use a cheap snap-action disc thermostat strapped to the pipe for lots of this stuff.

There are many different thermostats with differing ranges available online from many manufacturers like Johnson Controls or Penn Controls, and can be found at almost any heating and air-conditioning supply house or online. There are also many reliable copycats out there. As long as you understand its concepts, you can work with anything. The biggest issue is the temperature range of activation.

TheA19ABC24 typically has an operating range of -30° to 100°, which is useful for many different parts of the process. You will also need some with different operating specifications such as sensor tube length. The thermostats can be used to open or close valves, turn pumps on and off and things like that. I highly recommend this mechanical type of thermostat as opposed to electronic ones. They will last longer and are not susceptible to EMP, voltage surges, or software failures.

My friend's system was set up so that the inbound hot water was routed first to one storage unit until it was full and up to temp, then a thermostat said, "This one's full! On to number TWO!" until tank #2 was full of hot water and so on and so on. Until all ten water heaters were full of 190° water. Most thermostats of this type have three terminals, called "Common," "Close On Rise," and "Close On Fall." Use them well.

As the names imply, you connect a supply (hot) line to common and your operating terminal would depend on what you want to happen. Or you can connect two <u>input</u> signals to the NO and NC terminals and let the temperature select which one is answered and output to the "Common" terminal.

Another storage version, one that I built early on, was to dig a large pit. Mine was eight feet wide, eight feet deep, and twenty-four feet long, I used ¾" plywood framed up and cross braced. The pit was lined with four layers of 9-mil poly sheet to keep out ground water, then lined with eight inches of polystyrene panel insulation on the bottom and sides and the box built inside that.

The pit was then back-filled with dirt. The box was coated with fiberglass inside. The lid pieces were two thicknesses of ¾" plywood with styrene insulation glued on the top, and the whole thing was fiber-glassed on all sides and edges, and all of it was under about two feet of dirt. You might get by with marine paint on the inside of the box. I used fiberglass.

There were two heat exchanger coils in the tank, one for putting heat IN the tank and one for drawing heat OUT of the tank. These coils were 3/8" copper tubing.

The tank was huge. It was 1,536 cubic feet in volume. There are 7.48 gallons of water in every cubic foot, for a total of 11,489 gallons. Water weighs 8.34 pounds per gallon, so the tank held 95,820 pounds of water. Why are all those figures important? Because now I can calculate how much heat it would hold.

Water is one of those substances that we use as a standard. That to which everything else is compared. Therefore, we say that the specific heat of water is ONE. This means that if you add one BTU of heat to one pound of water, you raise the temperature of that one pound of water one degree Fahrenheit. Got that? So, if you raise the temperature of that TANK of water by one degree, you have added 95,820 BTUs to the tank. Let's take that to its logical conclusion, shall we?

Let's assume I want to keep my house at 70° in the winter. I have the tank water, all 95,820 pounds of it, heated up to 190°. 190 – 90 = 100°. That's the temperature difference that I can use without adding more heat to the storage system. (You need about a 20° temperature difference to actually move heat effectively.) In other words, I can draw the temperature of that tank down to 90° before it is no longer usable as a heat source. So 100° difference times 95,820 pounds of water equals 9,582,000 BTUs of available heat for me.

Now, in reality, there are LOTS of calculations necessary in order to determine how much heat a structure needs, but we can estimate, right? The average house today has a gas furnace of about 75,000-BTU-per-hour capacity. About 95 percent of the time, it will run four or five hours out of twenty-four, coming on for ten minutes at a time, roughly. And at that rate, it keeps the house at 70°, using 75,000 BTUs for every hour of running time. Or roughly 300,000 BTUs per day. And I have 9,582,000 of them.

That means that the heat in that tank would supply 75,000 BTUs per hour for about 127 hours. If I drew heat off at about the same rate as a gas furnace would supply it to my house, four or five hours per day, I could heat my house for almost a whole month off that one tank of water. Without adding any more heat to the tank.

Yeah, it is a bit more complex than that, really. You have heat leaving the tank through the walls and the top all the time, too. But it is slowly. If you want the whole story on how to calculate heat gain and heat loss for a structure OR a holding tank, you will need to get "Manual J" published by SMACNA. That is the **S**heet **M**etal and **A**ir-conditioning **C**ontractors **N**ational **A**ssociation. They literally wrote the book on air-conditioning and heat transfer. Yes. Literally.

It is THE manual that contractors must go by to figure heat gain/ heat loss.

I'm not sure if it now contains calculations for the new ecofriendly methods of home building, such as Cob houses and earth ships, but it is easy to figure out. About the only information you would need to have in order to apply Manual J to these habitats would be the R-value of dirt. Everything else would be the same. And remember that R-value is dependent on the _thickness_ of the material.

Almost any method of heating a structure that you can come up with other than a Plain Jane wood stove is going to involve heating water and storing that heat. That is until you get electricity or gas production up high enough to support a modern forced air system! So let me take a minute to talk about heating water. I have used two methods, and I know of four.

Method 1 was the first one I tried. I had a wood stove inside the house. I tried several versions of heat exchanger tubing inside and outside the flue pipe. Inside the flue, the whole shebang would stop up in just a day. Creosote buildup. That was a mess! Then I tried wrapping the pickup coils around the outside of the flue. The flue stopped up within a week. Seems the water cooled the flue so much that all the creosote precipitated out of the hot gas stream.

Then I built a pickup manifold around the wood stove itself. The water pickup was situated about one inch away from the wood chamber. That way it would not cool the firebox down any, it was just picking up the radiant heat leaving the stove. Of course, the heat picked up by this manifold reduced the amount of heat that was going directly into the house, but it turned out to be a good thing. Now the kitchen was not so dad-gummed hot!

The heated water was pumped outside to the storage tanks. From there, I pumped it around the house and into the various heat exchange modules I had in bedrooms and bathrooms. So the heat got distributed around the house pretty well this way. See the schematic diagram of this system at the end of this chapter.

Method 2 was when I first dug the pit. I built a wood-fired water heater outside. I was spending most of my time outside during the day anyway, so it was nothing for me to walk over to the heater every thirty minutes or so and throw another chunk of pine in the box. This was a brick and mortar affair with two walls.

The inner wall kept the fire and smoke contained to the firebox. Once it got hot enough, the heat started flowing into the water tubing that was between the inner and outer walls. When the exiting water pipe reached 110°, a thermostat turned a pump on. Same as before, the heat was pumped around the house to various rooms and to the storage tank.

This was my favorite method. The heat in the house was not so oppressive in the one room where the stove was. Of course, this was during a time when we had electricity from the grid, I was just experimenting with heating methods. You WILL need electricity to use either of these methods.

Another way to heat water is by using a compost pile and 1½» well pipe. The interior temperature of a compost pile can reach 140–160°F. You can actually use any type of pipe to gather this heat, but everyone I have talked to says well pipe works best. It will not corrode or burn through at those temps.

The fellow who told me about this had built a compost pile eight feet in diameter and twelve feet tall that was raised about four feet off the ground. Hog wire and chicken wire formed the sides and bottom. At the center, he had a hog-wire cage about four feet in diameter going from two feet off the deck up to about six feet. His well pipe was threaded through this to hold the pipe in place. When he finally got the pile filled in with compostable materials, it took a little over a month for it to start making heat. As the compost worked down, the finer particles filtered through the wire at the bottom of the pile and he shoveled it out to make dirt for the garden.

Now let's compare heat throughput real quick. With a wood fired heating system and coils picking up the heat from the firebox, you will be flowing about five to ten gallons per minute through the manifold picking up heat. Ten gallons per minute times eight pounds per gallon (roughly) equals eighty pounds of water per minute flowing. Inbound water was 70° and leaving water temp was 190°, for a 120° rise. 120° × 80 pounds = 960 BTUs per minute, times 60 minutes per hour = 57,600 BTUs per hour going into the storage tank.

Don said the flow rate through his compost pile was about five gallons per HOUR. So it is easy to see that it will not pick up near enough heat for your home. His system was gravity fed also. Hot water flowed out the top pipe, being replaced by cool water coming in the bottom. He was using this system to heat his chicken coop. I only mention this method to demonstrate there's more than one way to heat a cat.

One of my favorite ways to heat a structure is underfloor warm water heating. This is PEX (cross-linked polyethylene) tubing installed on the underside of the subflooring. Usually with reflective sheet metal "cups" under the tubing to reflect as much heat as possible up into the structure and insulation underneath that to hold the heat in.

This system does require an electrical pump in addition to a source of warm water, plus a controlling thermostat just like the one in your house now. Again, I would stick with mechanical-type thermostats instead of electronic ones. Mechanical-type home heating thermostats usually contain a small bulb of mercury on a coil of bimetal spring that tilts the bulb as room temperature changes. Another, snap action type, does not have the mercury bulb, just a pair of mechanical contacts but still on a coil of bimetal.

Another word or two about PEX tubing. It is very versatile, very hardy and very hard to join properly. They have made great strides in making that part easier, but be aware that if your joint leaks, sometimes it can be a real dog to get to it and repair it. So do it right the first time. Be sure to pressure test it before you close it up and make it impossible to access. Some joints have been known to shake loose several years after installation, so be extra careful. Spend the time to do it right.

PEX is freeze proof and heat proof (NOT "flame proof!"), so it is acceptable for use in both hot and cold water systems. In fact, I have seen it in the last few years come out in red and blue sections, so it is easy to keep the lines separate. I would recommend you use it to plumb the entire house even if you will not be putting water in right away. You could embed the PEX inside the cob walls, or the floor, stubbed out for places you will use it.

Now, let's get jiggy with GAS, whadaya say? Gas furnaces, gas stoves, water heaters, and clothes dryers and even electrical generators and LAWN MOWERS can all be run on METHANE gas. Methane is actually the major component of almost all our gaseous fuels. But raw methane can also be produced by septic tanks and compost piles. If the compost pile is enclosed, you can capture the methane and process it and store it. It will be slow. You can also tap into the INLET side of your septic system and capture the methane produced there. Or combine the processes!

I said somewhere else in this book that you can separate your gray water (sinks and tubs) drainage from the black water (toilet) drainage. Number 1, the gray water can be filtered and used for irrigation, and number 2, it reduces the amount of water going into your septic system. Septic systems NEED a certain amount of water to keep them active and viable, but they can be overloaded with excessive amounts of grey water. It floods the leach field and renders it useless until it dries out. This is a really large problem during heavy rains, when the leach field is already overloaded.

Every drain, whether it is a sink, tub, or toilet, has to have a P-trap in the line. In a toilet (water closet), it is built into the base of the unit. These traps prevent those yucky sewer gases from entering the house. And the good news is, it traps those yucky sewer gases inside the system, so you can capture them and use them.

What I did was find a spot a few feet above where my sewage line went into the ground under the house on its way to the septic tank. There, I installed a tee in line with the pipe, with the tee facing upward. ***CAUTION!*** Methane is EXTREMELY flammable stuff! Use extreme caution in all phases of the process, especially where pumps and valves are concerned. Once it is filtered and compressed into a storage tank (usually at about 10 psi), it can be used just like natural gas. It may burn a little more yellow, but you should be able to fix that fairly easily.

On that subject, gas fuels like natural gas usually come <u>to</u> the house at about 100 psi and get regulated down to about 2 psi to enter the house and then at the appliance, there is another regulator to reduce the pressure to about 11" W.C (water column, a means of measuring pressures smaller than 1 psi.) So, if you have yellowing flames, you can slightly decrease the gas pressure or add air by opening the air shutters at the burners. If that doesn't work, you can re-jet the burners. You might want to put a little thought into this process while you have time. Remember, combustion is most efficient at a 14:1 air-to-fuel ratio.

If you and your pack decide to use regular gas appliances at the compound, plan for it now. Get your stoves and dryers and water heaters and whatever together. BE SURE to choose appliances that DO NOT have electronics involved!

Use standing pilot light units only. No "spark ignition" or anything of the sort. They are all prone to failure and the replacement parts are expensive and will be unavailable after The Fall. Be sure to get twenty or fifty thermocouples for each appliance as spares. Those are the most failure prone parts of the whole shootin' match.

Get the standard units, probably at a used appliance shop or thrift store. Then find a reputable appliance technician and tell him what you what to do, burn methane in the units. He will know you need to re-jet. And he should have the tools to do it. You can actually do the conversion yourself if you're handy with tools. You need some M-100 plugs with the appropriate drill bit, and a set of Anderson–Forrester gauging drills with the BTU chart. 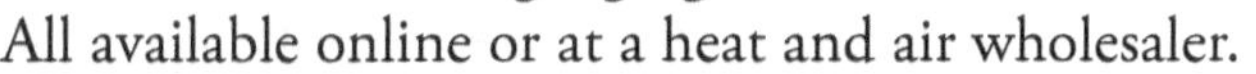 All available online or at a heat and air wholesaler.

First, remove the old main burner jets from the stove or oven or whatever. Drill where the orifice hole is now to install the M-100 plug. Put the plug in. It is a press fit, so one good slam with a hammer should seat it well. Just make sure it seats squarely against the face of the orifice. Next, select the gauging drill size that you have calculated is  needed and drill in the center of the M-100 from the back. TRY to hold the drill perfectly parallel with the shaft of the M-100. You have now re-jetted your orifice. Deburr the drill hole thoroughly.

Selection of the proper gauging drill size can be difficult. I am not certain if the Anderson–Forrester sizing chart includes raw methane, so you might have to do a little digging to get the BTU content of the gas, then compare it to the other standard gases, natural, propane, and butane. If it comes up not exactly like one of those, then find the ratio by which it is off the mark. Use that ratio to adjust your drill size to the next one available.

For instance, if you calculate that you need a 0.037 drill, you will have to use the 0.035 instead, being the next available.

I never did get this far into it, but I can conceive of a need for a way to determine if the gas coming up from your tap point is really methane. Maybe you have drawn it all off or something. At that point, you would probably be drawing regular air. There should be something out there that can tell you that, and then you could adapt it to turn off the pump if methane is no longer available in the stream. Selecting a pump that can pump a flammable gas is important. And it might not be cheap. These are all things you have to think about in your decision-making process.

No discussion of ENERGY would be complete if we did not talk about alternative energy sources, like wood gas or alcohol. Lesson 1 is this: when you burn _any_ solid or liquid fuel, you are _not_ burning the fuel source itself, you are actually burning the _gases_ that the heated fuel source is producing. (Okay, pressurized combustion is a different discussion.)

Light a campfire, look at the flames coming off that wood. The flame is actually about one-fourth inch ABOVE the surface of the wood. That's because the wood is heated by the flame above it and the coals below it. The wood is actually _off-gassing_, meaning the hydrocarbons in the wood are turning from solid to gas. It is the GAS that is burning. Same thing with gasoline, diesel, kerosene, coal, whatever. You burn the _gas_, not the fuel itself. Same thing with candles! Look at the flame above the wick.

There are lots of videos online about how to make wood gas and of people actually running vehicles off it. Wood gas is generated when you "cook" wood in an enclosed container without the presence of oxygen. Any engine that is designed to run on gasoline can be run on alternative fuels like wood gas, alcohol, methane, propane, or hydrogen.

There are adjustments that must be made, precautions that must be taken and maintenance that must be done as prescribed, but it can be done. Wood gas is a *very* "dirty" fuel source. There are simply *lots* of particulates in it. I do not know if it is possible, but were it me, I would try to find some way to filter it before I put it into an engine.

As of right now, it is still illegal for anyone to manufacture alcohol for any reason. Back in the 1970s, during the height of the gasoline crisis, literally hundreds of farmers and other private individuals were jailed for distilling alcohol to run their vehicles. Farmers who grew thousands of acres of corn were thrown in prison for using the corn that they owned to run tractors that they owned. Not cool. But as of right now, it is still illegal. Now, when the end comes, who is going to come around and tell you you're breaking the law? I can't think of anyone, can you?

Making alcohol is what the moonshiners do every day, right? But if you are making it for use in an engine, you do not have to be so particular about how it is done. If you're making alcohol for human consumption you have to be VERY careful about what types of metals the liquid comes in contact with. No lead AT all. Not even in the solder joints of the copper coils. No aluminum! You can use stainless steel and copper. ONLY.

And the copper must be soldered with lead-free solder ONLY. Not even "silver solder" because it contains phosphorus and bronze. But if you're making it to burn in an engine, there are no limits to what you can do.

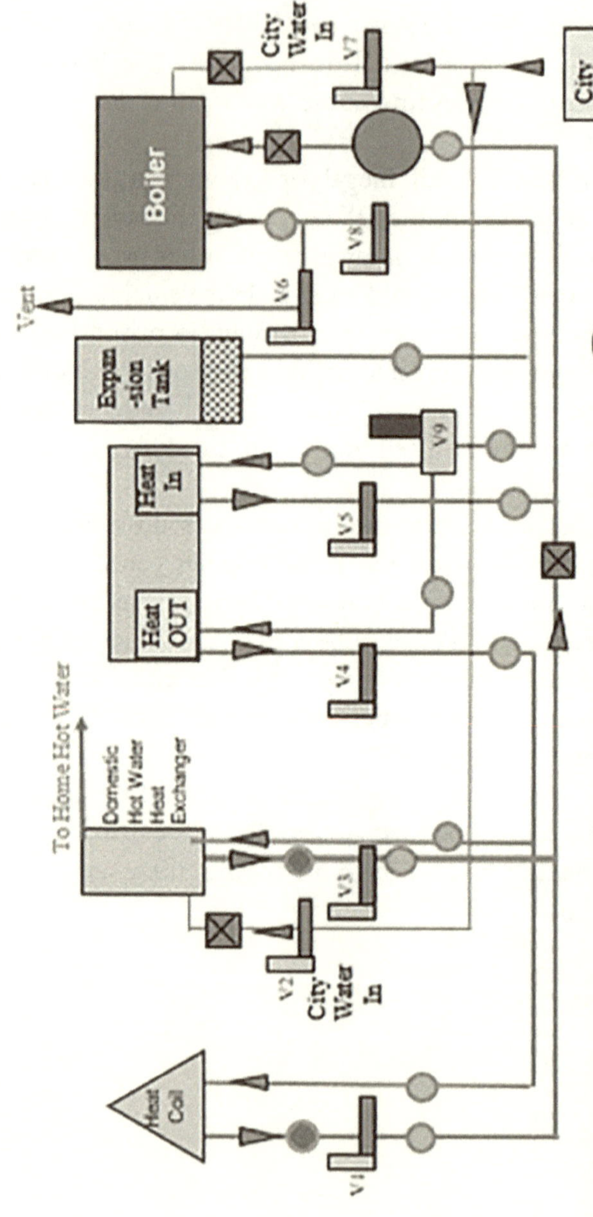

Home Boiler System Piping Schematic
Boiler
City Water In
V7
City Water
Vent
Expan -sion Tank
Heat In
Heat OUT
V6
V8
V9
V5
V4
V3
V2
V1
To Home Hot Water
Domestic Hot Water Heat Exchanger
City Water In
Heat Coil
Pump
V1 – V8 : Solenoid water valves in the RETURN side of each device. Except V2, 6 & 7
V9 : Three-way solenoid valve allows boiler to supply holding tank or demand load
V6 is a VENT valve to drain the boiler in the event of over temp, low water, and shut down
Water temp and flow direction
Check Valve
Balancing Valve
Shut-off valve
Electric Solenoid Valve
Pump

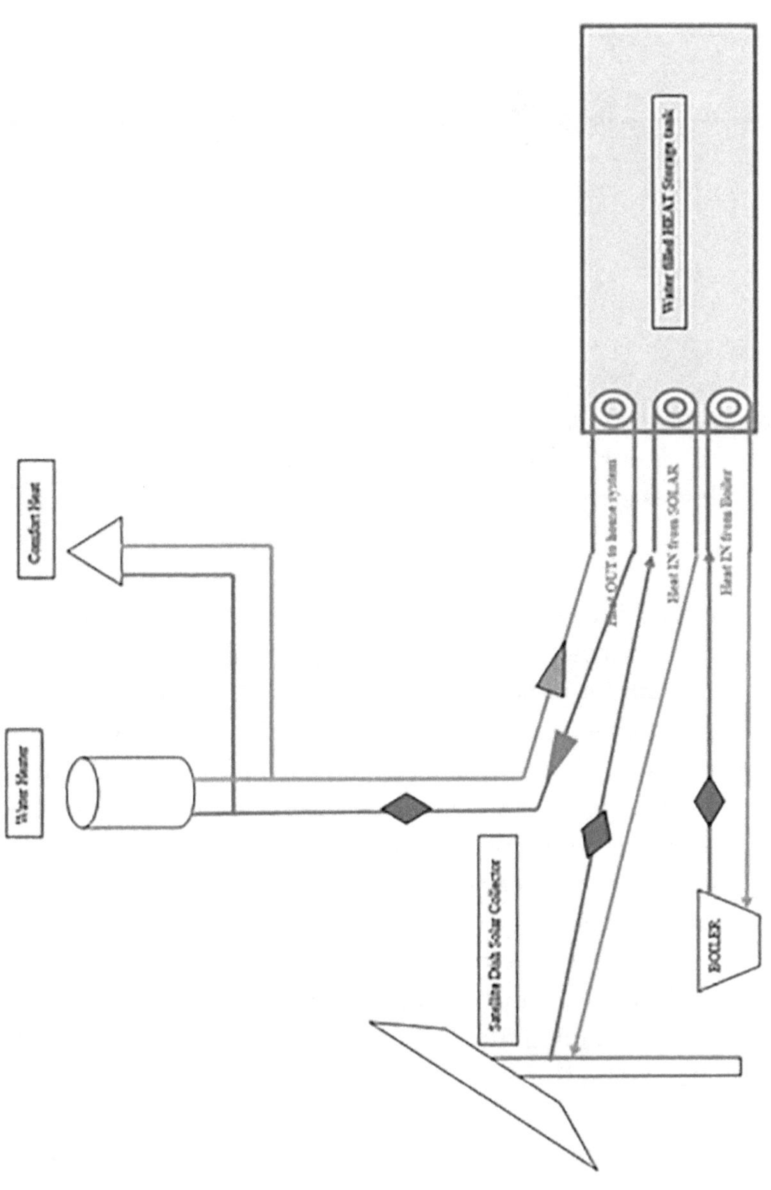

Water filled HEAT Storage tank
Heat OUT to house system
Heat IN from SOLAR
Heat IN from Boiler
Comfort Heat
Water Heater
Satellite Dish Solar Collector
BOILER

23

Fill'er Up

Okay, everything has gone to hell in a handcart. You have made it to your BoL. You have almost everything under control. But you made some choices early on that are coming back to haunt you. Let's check our list.

Heat. You decided to install gas furnaces in your houses because one of your partners worked for a propane company and he said he could steal a bunch of five-hundred-gallon propane tanks and that much would last for decades. It did not happen.

Tractor fuel. Someone forgot to make a backup of the video they downloaded on how to make biofuels. Now your four-wheelers and dirt bikes are dead in the mud. The dump truck you went to such trouble to acquire won't budge.

Supplies. Everyone eventually realizes they left something out of their list. Maybe you didn't get enough shovels? Or your cotton crop failed, and you can't make cloth this year, so you've decided to make a raiding run into the nearest city to clean out an abandoned fabric store. Whatever.

What do you do? What do these problems have in common? Fuel of some sort. Even your need for cloth comes down to fuel. How do I get gasoline to run the truck to go a hundred miles to get it? Okay. It's not that hard. Not many people know this, so…listen up. Or…read on…

The gasoline and diesel tanks at all those convenience stores, gas stations, and truck stops are underground. Under the driveway and parking lot. Ever see a tanker truck delivering gas to a store? With those huge hoses running from the truck to the holes in the concrete? That's it. That's where they are!

There's GOOD news, too! Those tanks have some pretty good caps on the inlet connections. Plus, the tanks are underground, where the temp is always 55°. Keeps the evaporation down, doncha know. You just need a 12-volt DC fuel pump (get yourself several of those right away) and maybe thirty-five to forty feet of ½" i.d. fuel line. Cut ten feet off. This ten feet goes from the pump outlet to whatever tank you are going to fill up. Take the other piece and hook one end to the pump inlet. Put a strainer on the other end and a weight to hold it down in the tank so it won't float. I would put a float switch on the tank I'm pumping into to shut off the pump, just in case. To make it super cool, add a check valve at the bottom of the draw line and a priming tee and valve at the pump end. Then you can prime the pump with gasoline from a can before you start drawing from the tank. That will be MUCH less harmful to your pump. Running a pump dry ain't good for the baby.

Each station will have at least three tanks in the ground—regular, mid-grade, and high-test. If there is a diesel pump, that means there will be four tanks. One cap per tank. You should be able to tell which one is diesel by sniffing. As for gasoline, it doesn't matter which grade you pick, it'll all burn. Aaannnd, you ain't payin' for it anyway, sssooo…

Speaking of burn, remember we spoke earlier about gasoline going bad over time? So the plan was to put STA-BIL fuel stabilizer in the tank? Gasoline goes bad because it evaporates quickly, and that evaporation takes the good stuff out and leaves the bad stuff behind.

Now here's the punch line…inside those underground tanks with the tight, gasketed lids on them, there just ain't a whole lotta shaking going on. That gasoline should be good for years to come.

So just pop a cap, drop the hose, and turn on your pump. You'll probably be pumping about three gallons a minute. So, if you're filling a 250-gallon tank, you'll be there an hour and a half. Bring some friends. With guns. Spread them out into the woodwork with their radios. Like any other family outing, all eyes watching, all heads on a swivel. No BS. And if a firefight breaks out, for the love of Mike, don't hide behind the tank you're filling. And lead the opposition on a route that will draw their fire away from the tank. You _might_ want to consider some shielding around that tank to prevent damage.

There is also another way, if you're smart. And brave. Inside the bottom door of each pump at the filling station is the actual Pump. That thing that drags the gas out of the ground tanks.

There are three pipes coming from the tanks to a selector valve that is electrically operated. When you push the button on the face of the panel, that valve switches to connect the dispensing pump to the correct tank.

Now, I do NOT have a diagram of how to wire up a Wayne or a Gilbarco dispenser, but you might be able to find one somewhere. Maybe bribe a guy who works on them. You see them every once in a while, at a station, working on the dispenser. This is NOT the guy from the state, in a state-emblemed truck, drawing gas out into a large can. THAT guy is checking the accuracy and flow rate of the dispensers. He might take offense at the question. He might call the cops.

To get into the dispenser, you will need to either have a key or pick the lock or bust the lock. Maybe drill it out, I don't know, I haven't tried it. Yet. But you gotta get into the dispenser. Maybe into both the top and bottom. But I would try to do it in such a way that I can put it back together in some manner that looks okay. Like it's not been tampered with.

Once inside the dispenser, look for a wiring diagram pasted inside, Look especially for the nomenclature plate on the pump and the plate for the selector valve. They are electric also. You MIGHT need both 240 for the pump and 120 for the valve. Be prepared. And remember that a generator will be noisy. If you have been successful with synching two invertors to make 240, you are golden. Ninety-five percent of those pumps use single-phase power, not three-phase. Which is good.

I don't want anyone knowing that I was there. They may keep a watch on the place and force you to get THEM some gas when you come back for a fill-up. Not that this is such a bad idea in itself, but the whole thing is just fraught with danger, in my eyes. They may want to follow you home to meet the fam. That's why I will try for a damage-free entry and exit. So now you have an idea of how to score gasoline.

Propane is a little harder. You'll need one of those propane delivery trucks. You'll need fuel for the propane truck, whichever type it needs. It might even run off the propane in its humpback tank. You'll need to jump that truck off, more than likely. You will also need to power the pump at the depot in order to fill the truck. That must be done with a generator, because the pumps are usually powered by 240 vAC and more watts than most inverters can supply. CHECK THE NAME PLATE ON THE PUMP. It might even be three-phase. In which case you need a single phase to three phase convertor. Easy enough to wire up, but make sure you have a shut-off switch that is constantly manned. You can find videos on the internet about how to fill a propane truck.

24

Grow Your Own

Food. I love it. I'm addicted to it. I admit it. Personally, I don't want to do without it. So I guess I'll have to grow my own. How about you?

Growing your vegetables is just half the problem, pal. Vegetables have a notoriously short shelf life. They must be *preserved* in order for you to eat them later. And vegetables are only the tip of the iceberg, Goldberg. Think of things you use every day in preparing your food. Or just EATING your food! I don't know about YOU, but I don't *ever* sit down to a table without a salt and pepper shaker!

Did you ever <u>once</u> think about where that stuff comes from? Well, Buck-o, if you want to continue to have it available, you better start thinking about it now, because you have only two choices. You can stockpile enough salt and pepper to last fifty years for a hundred people or you can figure out how to produce it. Okay, salt has to be mined, yes. And it can be found in many places. You will need to know how to find it, get it out of the ground, and process it. Not necessarily *iodize* it, but at least make it usable.

And speaking of iodizing salt, <u>IODINE</u> is an absolutely *necessary* nutrient in our lives. How do you get iodine? How do you take it? Can you make it? THINK, boy! What else in your life is there that the body needs that you cannot pick from a tree or grow from a seed or dig from the ground? NOW is the time to figure these things out. You know. Look it up. (Hint: Iodine is available in several vegetables.)

Throwing some seed into the ground is not all it takes to feed your family. What happens if you run out of beans tomorrow? Well, tomorrow you would just run down to the store and buy more beans, probably. After The Fall, if you run out of beans, Jack-O, you are OUT of beans. How do you avoid that? You plan. You and all your confederates, you plan. You sit down at the table and you figure out menus. Plan menus for a month for everybody. How do you dry beans for storage? SOMEone is doing it. They sell them to us.

Calculate how much each person at your table will eat. At every meal. How many ounces of beans, potatoes, and corn? NOW you begin to get an idea of how much you must grow to supply this demand. How many eggs will you all eat per week? How many chickens will you need to lay that many eggs? How many MORE chickens will you need to put a chicken in every pot? Three times per week.

How will you incubate and hatch eggs? Let me give you one or two tips here. Keep your roosters separated from the hens. When you want fertilized eggs, put one or two hens in with the rooster, and leave them there for a week. Remove the eggs they lay daily and keep them separate from the other eggs produced. Then follow whatever procedures you find for incubating and hatching. Next time you put girls in with the boys, use different girls.

When you take the girls out, keep them isolated from the other girls for a week and discard those eggs, or try to hatch them. I'm just not fond of fertilized eggs, but I don't think there's anything inherently wrong with them. Not. Sure. Get all the fertilized eggs out of the food stream. Unless you like them.

Each vegetable has its requirements for growth, how much sunlight it needs daily, what temperature range it can flourish in. How much rainfall? When temperatures or available hours of sunlight fall outside their range, they are ripe and must be harvested. Usually, any crop will mature in about ninety days, more or less.

Those things have been proven and charted long before now by wiser men than I. Use their wisdom. Plan your planting. Plan when to prepare the ground and how to do it best for which crops. How to tell when to harvest and how to do it.

Don't forget the BEES! Besides the fact that honey is just yummy, almost all plants need bees to pollinate them. So, in your BoL setup, you should put up a beehive or four and take some lessons on apiculture from an apiarist. Learning how to take care of bees from someone who does it is the best way.

You can extend growing seasons for certain crops by using greenhouses. But beware of buying cheap ones if that is your intent. They tend to fold up at the first good wind. But you can try and tie them off to withstand the wind. Tie from the top to an anchor about ten feet from the base. With that in mind, I will tell you of an idea, a dream that I have always held to. I got really close to making it happen once, but events came along and destroyed it for me. But I give it to you freely.

Remember how I talked about under floor warm water heat? Do you have any idea why I like it so much? It is because of air stratification. If you have a wood stove heating your house, the hottest air is always at the ceiling, the coldest at the floor. But if you use under floor heat, the warmest air is AT the floor! The air layers literally flip over! The coldest air is now at the ceiling! This is not urban myth, it is science. Remember, I have done this stuff for over forty years. (And I have the second highest score in state history on the contractor's exam!)

Let's take that concept into the realm of vegetable farming, shall we? One of the biggest deals in growing your own vegetables is ground temperature. It's why you cannot raise certain crops at certain times of year. Like green peas do not like hot weather! So let's take some of this warm water we are producing and use it to heat the ground where we plant those summer vegetables like potatoes and corn. That will help. Some.

But let's take it a step further and put a wall of polyethylene sheeting around that crop, to hold the warm air in so that the entire plant is warmed. I wanted to set the thermostats on the system so that the return water was maintained at 65°; therefore the ground temp at the roots would also be 65°. That might need to change a little, depending on the crop. Research it.

Now, if you tie the last paragraph in with the ones before it, what do you get? You get temperature inversion in your garden! A system where the warmest air is surrounding the plants. I do not recommend that you <u>count</u> on this to grow *all* your crops until you have experimented with it, adjusted the operating parameters and verified that it all works. But I believe that it will work. You might even consider putting a sheet of poly over the top to keep wind from sucking your warm air out. You would need to put some one- or two-inch holes in the top sheet to allow rain to enter.

So do you remember the little story about the chickens a few paragraphs back? Good. Because the same thing applies to…Well… everything. You're going to eat meat, sure. Beef, venison, maybe some sheep. And goats? Goats are cool. Goats can keep your grass cut and the underbrush cleaned back. They have some awesome milk, not much meat, but it's tasty. Goats don't need much. A little shelter, a little water, a heavy rock and twenty feet of chain to hold them in place while they eat. Not rope. Chain. They eat rope. Cushion the chain where it wraps around the goat, please. They will appreciate it EVER so much!

Rabbits. You can raise rabbits in a pen, but a hutch is safer. Bunnies are pretty easy prey in the open. So are chickens. There are lots of things flying around up there that like your little livestock. When I was a kid, we used to take turns sitting on the back porch and shooting the crows, vultures, and hawks that loved to dive bomb the barn for lunch. But you? You don't really have the ammunition to waste, do you? So you need to either protect your little buddies or find another way to reduce the predator population. And there are some. You just got to find them.

Oh! Corn! I almost forgot about the CORN! You need to grow a *lot* of corn, sport. Corn has many, many uses. It's a great food, you can use it to make alcohol for consumption OR fuel, AND you can grind it for meal! Don't forget it also makes great feed for the livestock. ANYthing can eat corn. But it does take a bunch of it, pal. And that's not the whole story either. You can use the stalks and husks and cobs for all sorts of things.

My great-grandpa used corn cobs in the outhouse to…, well, he also used them to heat his cabin. Point is, you need corn. The pigs can eat what's left. Corn will feed your livestock and fuel your truck, if it's a gas burner, that is. Just one more thing to put on your "I have GOT to learn this" list. Along with how to STORE corn for animal feed *and* for human consumption.

You also need wheat. Wheat makes bread, bread makes sandwiches. Wheat also makes beer. What else do you need? You've got beer and a sandwich. Yeah, it will make cereals, too. What more could you want?

Oh. On the subject of beer, you also need to grow barley and hops. Yeast is needed, but you can get brewer's yeast from a brew shop and then grow your own. But be sure to keep some of the yeast secure somewhere. Read up on storage techniques for yeast.

The one thing I am sure of is that you canNOT put it all in one place, in case something happens to it. You have to have a viable yeast culture somewhere safe. As long as there is a *little*, you can rebuild your stock. Just something to think about. Like a glass jar with a good, tight lid? And remember that there is a difference between brewer's yeast and baker's yeast, and you will need both. If you want your wife happy.

Oats? Oat YEAH! Oats can make some awesome cereals! And beer. And animal feed. And beer. See where I'm headed with this line of thinking? Trying to get YOU thinking about foods you take for granted every day. In lots of forms. Do you ever think about the fact that there will be no loaf bread? You canNOT store it. Bread, that is. Wheat you can store. The FLOUR that you MAKE from wheat you can store. BEER you can store! So work on that idea. Figure out how to make oatmeal, dude! And cornflakes. And beer.

Speaking of baking bread, what are you going to do about baking powder or baking soda? In addition to the salt and pepper. Mustard? Mayo? Ketchup? Man, the list is ENDLESS! Guess what. MOST of this stuff you CAN produce yourself. SOMEbody made it first. From scratch, right? All you need are instructions. Here's another thought…If it turns out to be next to impossible to make something small, like baking soda, a five-gallon bucket just might last fifty years. Consider it. The amount of difficulty of making it should be compared to the amount you would need on hand to last three or four generations. It's just math.

Growing your own herbs for seasoning is just TOO easy, but you will need some heritage seeds to start it up. Just like you MUST have heritage seeds for all the food crops you intend to grow. What are heritage seeds, you say? Simple. These are seeds that will leave a heritage. Seeds where the crop they produce will actually produce more seeds. Which is getting rarer these days.

I'm not sure if you're aware of it, but SomeCompany has rigged the farming game so that every farmer _has_ to buy seeds from THEM. Because they have engineered the seed for higher yield, greater resistance to rot and RoundUp®, and then the ~~bastards~~ fine gentlemen there PATENTED the seeds.

Ohhh yeah. They also engineered the seeds to _not produce seeds_. So, each and every year, the farmers have to buy more seed from SomeCompany. Want to or not. If they want to grow anything, they have to buy seed from SomeCompany. A few decades ago, farmers would keep a portion of every crop to use as seed for the next crop. Not anymore. So stock up on heritage seeds. Now. For every conceivable crop. 'Cause, you know what? If YOU don't grow that particular item, you can barter those seeds or that crop to someone who will use them.

Of course you _have_ thought about fruits and have probably already planted twenty or forty fruit trees around the property. And nut trees. Don't forget nut trees. Did you consider oranges? Lemons? Limes? Bananas? Pineapple? Avocado? Agave? (Can't make tequila without agave!) Did you know that SOME trees have to have a male/female pair planted within a certain distance of each other or they will not produce? It's true!

Likewise, with certain of the berry family. So be sure you read up on these things very thoroughly, because you absolutely want blueberries, blackberries, strawberries, raspberries, and grapes of several varieties.

Be sure to look into growing things needed to produce your own beer and wine and liquor. Maybe even tea and coffee. I firmly believe it can all be done. The issue is that we have never before had the NEED to grow our own coffee. It was always available for purchase. That will end. But if you have the time, the space, the money, and the will, you could backstock these things. Just how much will you need?

Speaking of fruits, what about bananas and pineapples? Did you know that you cannot grow a banana tree <u>from</u> a banana? At least not the kind of banana you are used to buying at the grocery store. Those bananas are all of a variety called "Cavendish," which is the name of the British guy who first found bananas and worked with them to produce what he thought of as the perfect fruit. After generations of breeding certain characteristics into the fruit, it now has no seeds and propagates by spreading out "suckers" at its base that grow into trees. But you CAN buy the trees. You can also grow bananas from seed, just not the Cavendish. It takes some research to get it right. I love bananas.

Sugar. What on EARTH are you gonna do about sugar? Well, you could stockpile four hundred thousand pounds. Or you could learn what to grow and how to process it to get the sugar. The most used plant is the sugarcane. Grow it, cut it, grind it, boil it, dry it, grind it; you have Turbinado. It ain't white, but it IS sugar. And it IS good!

Go to a Mountain Fair somewhere in the hills of Georgia, Tennessee, North Carolina, Arkansas, whatever. Just about anywhere in the Deep South. You can see the whole process being done as a demonstration of how it was done in the old days.

Your next choice is sugar BEETS. The further north you are, the better they look. Cane grows best in really warm areas, while beets can do well in cooler areas. They are about 20 percent sugar! And they supply about 20 percent of the world's sugar supply.

Just be certain that you make a list of everything you eat, everything you use in cooking or preserving food or life in general. Even the utensils and pots and pans. There will be no more. You have to bring it with you. Make the lists, hang them on the wall where everyone can see it and edit it. Go through your pantry, shelves, drawers, whatever. Look at everything.

Go through the grocery store with your list. Maybe you don't like the…whatever…right now, but someone might want it later. So, put it on the list and try to deal with it. Every family in the pack has a copy of the master list, and at every pack meeting, we merge the lists into a new master, print it out, and distribute it. Buy several utensils for the compound every trip to the store.

Silverware, knives, shears, canning jars with lids and rings, coasters, trivets, spoon rests, mixing bowls, plates, cups, glasses, some means for sharpening knives, and specialized tools needed for harvesting or processing certain crops. Boys and girls, there is a lot of thinking to do to get this list complete.

Fish. I forgot to talk about fish. There are loads of things you can do with fish and most of them are legal. (Except in the seven southern states.) And there are several ways to go about it. At one place we had a pond. About a half acre. We stocked it with two hundred minnows and two hundred blue gill and let those do their thing for about four months. Then we added fifty tilapia and bass. Or one hundred. It's your thing, you do the math. Then we just went fishing for supper.

Another thing you can do with fish is a little thing called aquaculture. Fish go in trough tanks about two feet off the floor. About three feet above that are tanks growing vegetables in a liquid nutrient solution. The solution from the top tanks flows down into the bottom tank.

The fish (usually tilapia) live on what comes down into their world. They then excrete into the water that is pumped into the top tank to fertilize the plants. Fascinating stuff, really. And your list of things to research just _keeps_ growing, doesn't it? See why I did not decide to include all the particulars of how to do everything? There just ain't enough space, ace. Get lots of material on aquaculture. And materials FOR it.

Coffee. What would we do without our morning shot of joe? I don't know about you, but that is a major issue for me. I have had coffee every morning for over sixty years. Unfortunately, coffee is one of those things that we here in the states must import. It just does not like our climate. There are rumors of people actually growing coffee in the US, and some of those trees actually bear fruit, allegedly. Special techniques like hoop houses or greenhouses, planting the coffee trees underneath avocado trees, lots of stuff. Look it up.

There are also alternatives to coffee. You can substitute yaupon holly (*Ilex vomitoria*). Then there is *Camellia sinensis* black tea. It ain't coffee, but it ain't bad.

You also need—yes, I said *NEED*—citrus fruit like lemons, limes, oranges, and grapefruit. Stuff you cannot stock up on. It's the whole "vitamin C" thing. Citrus prevents scurvy. Lemons and limes *can* be grown in higher latitudes, although maybe with some adjustments.

There are stories about people who just threw the seeds from their lemons into an outdoor planter over the years. The plants that survived had the genes to survive colder weather. Then there are varieties specifically grown for this climate, such as the Meyer Lemon.

Okay. Back to the research books.

Frankly, I believe you could grow chocolate (cocoa) in a greenhouse in Ohio. It just takes a little ingenuity and some knowledge and a lot of work. Like what are all the factors that the plant needs? They were listed earlier. Hours of sunlight per day, month, and season is really important. If I wanted to grow tropical plants this high up, I would make a spreadsheet about the locale where it grows well, showing daily temperature, rainfall, and sunlight. Then try to duplicate those conditions in a greenhouse. Actually, you need to include everything in this spreadsheet.

Uuuh…I almost forgot to mention vanilla! That's going to be something that everybody wants. There's hardly anything baked that doesn't use vanilla. Where do we get vanilla? Everybody I ask says "vanilla beans, dummy." Yeah, right, but where do we get vanilla *beans*? Trees? Bushes? Vanilla *fish*?

Nope, an *ORCHID*. That's rich. But true. A flower grows one of our favorite flavorings. Check it out. Grow it. TONS of people will be willing to barter for vanilla. You'll be rich. Look up **Vanilla planifolia** *and* **Vanilla pompona.** The two main versions of the vanilla orchid vine.

And while we're in the discussion about growing things, I want to share with you another of my dreams that I never got to check out. That would be continuous production farming. Today's farmer, in order to maximize his land usage, grows crops that are better suited for summer and then crops that do better in winter, such as "winter wheat."

Think back to my heated greenhouse idea. Heated underground at the roots. Or aquaponics even. Here's the theory: Rather than plant your entire crop at one time and have to preserve and store the product, why not plant what you need NOW? Right? Let's say one cornstalk produces three ears. It takes ninety days to mature. Your tribe, given the availability, could consume sixty ears per week. Times three months (or twelve weeks the average maturation time for corn [*Zea mays*]) equals 720 ears or 240 plants.

Two hundred forty plants every ninety days will keep you all in corn. All year long. But what if you planted twenty corn plants today? Then twenty more <u>next week</u>, and twenty more *the week after that*? At the end of ninety days, your first twenty plants are ready for harvest. The sixty ears they produced will feed you for a week. Next week, the second crop of twenty plants reach maturity, and there's your sixty ears for *that* week. And so on and so on. So here you have twelve plantings of twenty plants each instead of five acres of corn that you have to harvest, process, and store.

What YOU need to do is figure out exactly what elements of the corn cycle need to change over time to ensure its proper growth and productivity. The biggest factor, I am sure, is sunlight hours per day. Many plants (if not most) know when to ripen their fruit by how the days are shortening. And sometimes by the temperature changes.

Chart these factors and control them for each weekly crop and you should be able to grow corn year-round. And I figure you can do that with almost any crop. **DO NOT BET YOUR FARM ON THIS WORKING!** Get your crops growing normally first. THEN you can experiment.

Medical

I guess you have figured out by now that there will be no doctors, no dentists, and no medicine when it all comes tumbling down. So what do you do if Maggie breaks a leg or Johnny gets shot with an arrow? You're going to have to work it out, pal.

I talked a bit about stockpiling medicines earlier. There, I was speaking mainly about those maintenance medicines that you and yours currently take to enhance your health. Like blood pressure regulators, blood sugar moderators. But what about antibiotics? Antifungals? If you can, get those in your stockpile too. Anything you can gather will be of use, I'm sure.

Especially supplies. Things like gloves and surgical equipment like hemostats, suture kits, and scalpels. Some things, even gloves, can be cleaned and reused over and over. I have managed to accumulate about four cases of surgical gloves over the years. Gauze will be very hard to come by. Both in roll (Kerlix) and pad (2 × 2, 4 × 4) form. Tape may or may not work, folks. The adhesive has a tendency to dry out and become brittle. Doesn't seem to matter which tape you talk about. (But you might be able to get it to last by nitro packing it.) Gloves also tend to deteriorate and could probably also benefit from Nitro-Pak.

You will need surgical tools. There are several kits available on Amazon that include many different useful items. Some of the stuff you need is a little harder to come by. Like suture packs. These are needles with pre-attached suture material. I know that surgeons have thirteen dozen different types of sutures and each one has a particular purpose, but it is hard to go wrong with two-aught and four-aught Vicryl. Let's not forget dentist tools, too. If would be very nice indeed if you could get hold of injectable anesthetics like lidocaine or Novocain.

Then we've got the problem of skills. What do you DO with this stuff? I joined the local volunteer fire department. They offered all sorts of classes for free. Like Emergency Medical Responder, which is a basic life support class. Kinda like really advanced first aid. So that was a large part of my training. Then I talk to doctors, EMTs, paramedics, I watch videos on surgery, I practice stitches on pig skins. Download some videos.

Plaster of Paris has been used for a hundred years to hold broken bones in place, but there are other ways. In the emergency medical service, we have a moldable, formable splint that we use to immobilize broken limbs, called a SAM splint. It can be used and reused long term if you care for it well, and you can buy these online. I would definitely recommend you get a dozen of these. If you decide to stock plaster of Paris, don't forget to also stock up on cotton and gauze for cushioning and also a cast saw to take the thing off.

I think that one key factor to keep in mind here is that you, or whomever gets designated as the doctor, is *going* to be afraid to do the things that are needed, simply because it is not their original role in life, it is not what they trained for, not what they expected. But *someone* has to put that shoulder back in place. Set that broken leg. THEY know, and the patient will know, this is going to hurt. Who wants to hurt someone they love? You have to be dispassionate, disconnected, and detached in order to do these things.

Spending some time researching and archiving all the medical knowledge you can gather will be worthwhile if you do not have a medical professional in your klatch. I described in an earlier chapter how to go about roping a medical professional. But you <u>can</u> do the job if you have to. Collect the skills, and practice on stand-ins.

You should get a copy of *Grey's Anatomy*. Both hard copy and electronic would be good. And do the same for the most current PDR—Physician's Desk Reference. The PDR lists every drug we've got. What it does, how it does it, side effects, interactions, everything you could possibility want to know. And then some.

If you can manage it, get some nursing books on emergency care, like setting bones and joints, stopping bleeding (HINT: AFRIN NASAL SPRAY will stop most bleeding in seconds.) If you look hard enough, you might even find some reference books on stocking a small clinic, or surgical textbooks.

Here's another little tip for you. Immediately after The Fall, druggies will be raiding every pharmacy within reach. THEY will be looking for pain pills. The mess that they leave behind will be pure gold for you, because YOU want the GOOD stuff—the antibiotics, antifungals, anticholesterol drugs, blood pressure controllers, anesthetics, and all that stuff. Do your homework. Figure out what you might need.

Make a list that contains both the brand and generic names of the drugs you are looking for. Most drugs are stocked in the pharmacies in alphabetical order by their generic names. If I were leading a raiding party on a pharmacy, I would probably hand everybody a large garbage bag and just tell them to pick up everything they can find. Sort it out later. Of course, any raid should begin with good reconnaissance.

No how-to guide about TEOTWAWKI would be complete without mentioning alternative medicine methodologies. Like herbal remedies, homeopathic medicines and even spiritual healing modalities. I have personally seen and participated in some amazing healings that were accomplished purely by spiritual means. Especially study up on herbal healing and herbal medicines.

26

Motors, Motors Everywhere

Motors. They drive everything in our modern world, but without fuel, they are useless. The good news is that fuel is not that hard to get or make. If you know where and how. The workhorse of the world of motors is, of course, the diesel engine. A symphony of simplicity, the diesel engine can burn any liquid that has a flash point higher than 126°F. For comparison, gasoline has a flash point of -45°F.

Gasoline engines must have a high-voltage spark to ignite the fuel/air mixture, but a diesel engine does it a bit different. As the piston moves downward, the intake valve opens, and air is drawn into the cylinder. The intake valve closes, and the piston then travels upward, compressing the air that is trapped in the cylinder.

This raises the temperature of that air. Greatly. Just before the piston reaches top dead center (TDC), the diesel fuel is injected under high pressure into the cylinder. The superheated air ignites the fuel, creating the explosion that drives the piston down. As pointed out above, diesel engines can use almost any liquid fuel other than gasoline or alcohol. They don't do too well with gaseous fuels either.

The good news about diesel engines is that you can make bio-diesel fuel on your farm. You can also process just about any used oil and burn it in a diesel engine. After The Fall, you can break into restaurants and take their old fry oil. Then filter it and process it per the instructions you download off the Internet. While you still HAVE Internet, that is.

A gasoline engine, on the other hand, *can* burn alcohol and does quite well with gaseous fuels like propane, butane, methane (natural gas), wood gas, or even pure hydrogen. There are always some drawbacks to running any engine on a fuel other than the one it was originally designed for.

In the case of the gasoline engine, alcohol burns hotter than the gasoline and that can burn the valves and valve seats. Hydrogen is even worse in this regard. But propane, butane, and methane work quite well as alternative fuels.

You can order an internal combustion engine to be fitted for propane or methane (natural gas) fuel straight from the factory, and there are also aftermarket conversion kits available as well. I know several people who had gensets that were designed for propane or methane, so they could run the generator on the same fuel that heated their homes in the event of a power outage.

You can do the same thing yourself and save some bank. Factory built systems of this type have some model specific alterations to facilitate the use of these fuels, but you *can* take a standard gasoline engine and run it on these gases. Books and videos on the conversion process are available.

My own venture into the world of alternative fuels and gasoline engines was with my generator, a 20,000-watt genhead pushed by a 25-hp Honda engine. Almost all small engines are carbureted, meaning the liquid fuel is drawn into the air steam that is going to the intake manifold by means of a venturi. The amount of fuel is determined mostly by the quantity of air flowing past the venturi.

The volume of air drawn into the engine is primarily a function of the position of the throttle plate inside the carburetor throat. This makes it very easy to set up a feed system to introduce the proper amount of gaseous fuel into the air stream.

I may have oversimplified the method somewhat, but it worked. I drilled a hole in the 1½» rubber connecting hose between the air filter and the carburetor throat and glued a piece of ¼" i.d. rubber hose into it. That hose fed to a screw adjustable petcock that was attached to the appliance regulator feed from the propane system. It took a little tinkering between the petcock and the regulator pressure output, but within an hour after hooking it up and getting the engine to at least crank, I had it purring like a…Honda.

The same setup—minus the pressure regulator—should work equally well for methane, hydrogen, or wood gas. Okay. Rethink. With or without a pressure regulator depends on the pressure of the gas that you want to put into the engine. A pressure regulator for a gas appliance should reduce the pressure to about 11" WC, which is equal to a little less than ½ psi. So, if your input pressure coming to the engine is greater than 1 psi, you probably need a regulator. Don't forget to include either a manual stopcock or an electric solenoid valve to shut the gas fuel off when the unit is not running.

Methane is *the* major component of natural gas as used in our homes, factories and certain vehicles. Natural gas is typically found in pockets covering a petroleum deposit underground. It is also produced by rotting vegetation, or decaying waste matter of almost any type. Like the stuff found inside a septic tank or sewer system. Once I came to that realization, it was just a quick turn-around to make my generator run on the methane I could collect from the sewer system of the small town I lived in.

I crawled under the house and located the 4" PVC sewer drain leaving the house and running toward the street. I cut the line and inserted a sanitary tee (not a standard tee, there's a difference) into the line, with the leg pointing upward. I added an extra six-inch piece of 4" PVC and reduced that down to ¾" PVC.

Then I piped that gas out to the generator through the ¾" PVC and tied the gas into the generator. Make sure this piping is assembled GAS TIGHT. That means use the purple cleaner at each side of each joint. Apply the glue liberally and be sure to TWIST the joint in one continuous motion and in one direction until it becomes too hard to turn. This spreads the melting plastic around in such a manner that it is BOUND to be gas tight.

Since methane is lighter than air, I was not too concerned about losing the methane lock into the motor, but I did experience that issue twice. I had no chance to determine the reason the motor had suddenly sucked in air instead of methane before I had to dismantle the rig to move out of state. So I have not solved that.

My initial inclination was to build a tower of 4" PVC ten feet tall, feed the methane in about a foot from the bottom, and draw the methane out of the top. That should trap the air at the bottom of the column. If you do this, be sure to put a bleed valve at the bottom of the column to occasionally release any air or water trapped down there.

While we're talking about internal combustion engines, let me clue you in on another trick I used to make heat and domestic hot water. I got curious about the heat coming off the exhaust of the generator, so I measured the temp of the exhaust gas. I was surprised to find the exhaust was 600°F. In addition to that, the cooling air blown over the cylinder heads was leaving the generator enclosure at 150°F. So, with the water heating system I had in play, I added the generator into the circuit. First, return (cool) water went into the cooling air stream between 30° and 70°F, leaving there at 90°F before going into the pickup coil in the exhaust air stream, where it left at 195°F.

And on that note, a quick note. About water flow and heat exchange. What happens to water at 212°? Steam. Steam happens. And when water turns to steam, it expands 1,600 times. That's right. One thousand six hundred times increase. One gallon of water becomes 1,600 gallons of steam. Real quick. I bet your entire piping system will not hold *twenty* gallons in the piping.

So what happens to your piping system if it cannot contain the steam? Rupture. Rupture happens. It blows up. I was using CPVC pipe for the hot water system when my pump decided to fail one night. I heard a blast like a shotgun outside the window and I jumped up to investigate. The ½" CPVC pipe was now thirteen inches in diameter. Except where it was strapped to the wall. Three places in a fifteen-foot run were still one-half inch. The rest of the pipe was over a foot in diameter.

To prevent future blow-outs of this sort, I set up a thermostat on the pipe. No matter what happens, whether it is a mechanical pump failure, power outage, or anything else that makes the system lose water or hit a critical temperature, a shutoff solenoid kills the water feed to this part of the system, the water exit from the unit, and a dump valve opens up to release the water that is IN there, to prevent explosive flashover into steam. And it turns on an alarm light. And ahead of all of that safety valving, you want a manual shutoff, so you can dismantle everything for repair. And another manual shut off on the outlet side for the same reason.

So the way to hopefully keep all this from happening is quite simple. Don't let the water get to 212°. How, you say? My water is going into a 600° airstream! Easy as pie, Fry. Move the water *faster* through the pickup coil. Heat transfer depends on several factors: The temperature difference encountered, the surface area of contact and how long the two substances are in contact. So, if you have a very large temperature difference, keep the contact time low or reduce the contact surface area. Push that water through there quickly! About the only way to do that is ramp the pump speed up. Push the water faster. Or use smaller diameter tubing.

In other words, you need either a gate valve or a ball valve to adjust how much water goes in other places of the system. You have to put balancing valves all over the system anyway. Anywhere you're heating or using water.

Adjusting these valves correctly lets you balance water distribution all over the place and minimize pump strain. I also used safety thermostats that would shut the water flow through this part of the system off if the outlet temp got over 190°F, as described above. At every part of the hot water system, you need this "balancing valve" to adjust the rate of flow through the device.

Run the pump speed up to max and fire up the system, heat some wa-wa. Anything you use to heat water, make it heat water. Anything that uses hot water, make it use hot water. Using a thermometer, go around adjusting the balancing valves to achieve maximum throughput along with proper temperatures.

So even though fuel for our motors will be difficult to come by after The Fall, it CAN be done. But given that, I hope you also noticed that one of my recommendations is that you procure tack and trace and implements to farm using horse and mule, and also to take lessons in the old methods of working and husbanding the animals.

So get busy and do your homework. Learn about alternative fuels and how to produce them, like how to filter and process used oils for use as biodiesel. I'm pretty sure that the methods would be different from used vegetable oil from a restaurant to using used engine oil from junk cars found abandoned after The Fall.

But I will say one more thing. If I had it to do over and had the bux, I would stockpile ten or twenty generators and use them to supply all my electrical needs as well as heat water for domestic use and home heating. Just run the things 24-7. With appropriate muffling, of course. That's easy enough. Pipe the exhaust into a large pipe with many small holes. Read up on it.

Be sure to properly prepare the generators for long-term storage. Each one might last ten years if properly maintained.

Hope for the best, prepare for the worst.

27

Water, Water Everywhere

Water. The elixir of life. The universal solvent. Without which…we die. And not only us, but our crops and our livestock, our fish. Oh, wait, they're IN water. Right.

I remember a time when the freshest, best water you could get was from the creek running at the back of our property. Or from a cold mountain stream. Not anymore. It is really not safe to put too much trust in an open water source anymore. Unless you know exactly what is upstream from you.

If you're on the top portion of a hill or mountain, okay. You're probably good to go. But if your creek is at the bottom of a valley, watch out. Animals will die and fall in that creek upstream of you. You drink that water and then…well…YOU die and fall in the creek. Someone two miles upstream has cattle that drink from the stream. And urinate in it. And defecate in it. And have hoof and mouth in it. *yuck*

But even if you are certain that the source is fairly safe and uncontaminated, you should be sure to have a prefilter sock on the foot valve ahead of your intake at the creek. Then pump the water up to the compound and filter and treat it thoroughly before giving to the livestock or crops.

A swimming pool sand filter is a good start. And you WILL want a filter with that kind of flow-through capacity to handle the total load. Perhaps a second sand filter filled with diatomaceous earth (DE) and a third one using charcoal to decon the water that will be used for human consumption. After all, we are talking about your life here, guys. And if you are going to go this route, be sure to stock up on filter sand, DE, and charcoal. (Instant light charcoal is not good for this. Another one of those "You Die" things. In fact, you should get <u>food grade</u> charcoal.) And that stuff will be hard to come by after *The Fall*. Heck, it's hard to find, NOW!

You canNOT filter too much. If you would like to treat it further before you consume it or cook with it, you can distill and condense it. Just be sure to use metals and joining methods that will not poison you. Or you can do what we do. A high-quality home filter. Something that traps down to the micron level. That filter will get all the bacteria and almost all the viruses that may be present. I use the Berkey filter.

Everything I drink except soda pop goes through that Berkey first, including the water for tea and coffee, AND the water that we put in the countertop icemaker we use. I swear, I could *not* do without that ice, and those little rascals do not use much power. Well worth the hundred bucks. I have three at my compound, two for backup. And two spare pumps and control boards. I need more of each.

If you do decide to use a good countertop filter system like Berkey (and I cannot recommend Berkey high enough, folks!), be sure to get a supply of filter elements that will last you for decades. We've been on one set of filters for two years now, but we disassemble it and clean it regularly. Including scrubbing the filter elements as described by Berkey. Even if we triple filtered as I described above, I would still Berkey the water that I drink. JIC.

So that covers open source water. But the safest water you will find will come from a well. Honestly. Talk about your SAND filter! After traveling through five hundred feet of Mother Earth, how bad could it be? I mean, **I** grew up on well water. It sure tasted better than any city water I've drank. But I would still put it through a high-quality filter system before using it to drink. I do realize that I was raised on a farm where ALL our water came from a hand-dug well where you drew the water up in a bucket! I survived. But that was nearly seventy years ago, and things are not the same anymore.

Underground water is not that hard to find, Buck-o. I know most people will say it's stupid, or it's a myth, or maybe it's from the devil, but it works. I'm talking about water witching, or divination. It's not just for witches anymore. (LOL) Anyone can do it. Trust me. You can get a good book on it and make a pair of divination rods and before you know it you have found your water supply. I use 1/8" brass rods twenty-four inches long. Bend one end to a 90° angle about six inches from the end.

Hold the short ends in your fists loosely. I ASK the rods several questions before I start.

1. Show me a YES response. (Note which way the rods react.)
2. Show me a NO response. (Again, note the response.)
3. Will you work for _me_?
4. Is there any malevolence associated with you? (Meaning the energy controlling the rods. Note the response. If the rods answer YES. Get new rods and start over.)
5. Will you give me truthful responses in my search for water? (If NO, move twenty feet and start over.)

Think what you will, do what you will. This method works. I pass it on to you to use or not.

There ARE other methods of locating water that don't involve the spirit world. But any way you look at it, any way it goes, find the water. The water from the well should be fine for livestock and agriculture straight from the ground. But I would still filter it for human consumption.

Digging a well is damned hard work, mostly because it must be so big. To hand dig a well, it must be about six feet in diameter, and anywhere from ten to fifty feet deep. Depending on how deep the water table is. WHICH, by the way, just might be something the local county agent can help you with. Or you could ask your divination rods. "Is the top of the water deeper than ten feet here? Less than thirty feet here?"

If hand digging a well, be sure to go as deep as possible, even after you hit water. You want a reservoir down there for sediment and debris. The flow <u>through</u> the well may not be high enough to answer all instant demands. A reservoir can help mediate this.

If you use a dug well, be sure to build a wall around it to keep critters and kids out, with a removable top. Include a rat ledge around the well. That's an edge sloping down and outward at about 45°. It is usually steel, but whatever it is, you must make it out of something that a rat cannot cling to and clamber over. That's why sheet metal is best. Make it too high or wide for a rat to bypass it. And nothing above the well mouth that a rat can clamber to and then drop into the well. Takes a bit of thought.

If possible, it is best to line the walls of a dug well, usually with brick or rock. This keeps the walls from caving in unexpectedly. You always want to know when to expect a wall to cave in on you, right? You can get water from a dug well using a surface mounted pump with a dip pipe and foot valve/strainer on the bottom of the pipe.

This system requires you to _prime_ the pump before it can draw water up. This means fill the pump and the well dip pipe with water. The foot valve will have a check valve included. This keeps the prime water from running out the foot valve. Once primed, the pump can suck the water up the pipe and discharge it into the system under pressure. The foot valve also needs a strainer sock over it to keep sediment out of the pump. This sock might need to be changed occasionally.

I prefer to pump the water from the well to the house(s) and then through a sand filter and on to an elevated storage tank. This keeps sediments out of the storage tank. This type of system will require level sensing valves or devices in the storage tank to shut the pump off when the tank is full. Try to set things up so that the pump does not run again until the tank is down to like one quarter capacity. Saves power.

You can also get a power driven two-man boring machine that digs a hole about six to eight inches diameter. It usually comes with a thirty-six inch long auger. Digging deeper than that requires some ingenuity. Making extension pipes that fit the power head and the auger. Constructing a lifting rig to pull the auger and pipe up. But you can do it.

Of course, the best situation would be to have enough auger that bolts together so that it keeps feeding the dirt back up to the top. This is actually a BORED well, and it must be lined with pipe, and you have to use a submersible pump with a foot valve and strainer along with a bladder pressure tank and pressure switch. This system uses a good bit of electricity. But if you plan for it, it can be done, bud. It can.

Now, if your habitat just happens to be downhill of a good stream, you could just build a partial coffer dam and divert some of the water into pipes and then downhill to the filter system and storage tanks. It is possible that this system could provide enough "head" to free-flow the water through a sand filter on its way down to the compound.

So what do you do with the water once you've got it? You need to store it in a tank. Let the height of the tank supply the pressure to the water system. The tank should ideally be stainless steel. In lieu of that, a food grade poly tank. One of those in a steel wire cage.

Beware. I bought one once that had been used to transport grape flavoring for manufacturing. I *never* got the grape taste out of it. The water was at least usable, but the coffee tasted a bit weird. OH! Don't forget to do something about keeping your tank and associated plumbing from freezing. And NEVER **_EVER_** use a tank that has been used to hold petroleum or non-food products of any sort. You canNOT wash it out enough to get rid of the chemicals.

Anyway, get a tank and put the water in there. You'll need some means of controlling the water inlet to the tank. You don't want to overflow it and waste the water. You can use a float-type valve installed near the top of the tank. The pump pumps water up to the float valve. If the tank level is low, the valve lets water in until the water level raises the float and the water flow shuts off. Then the pump needs a way to sense that the valve has closed, and the pressure is building up. A simple pressure switch, then, can shut off the pump.

The drawback to this system is that anytime someone uses water, the level will drop in the tank, letting the float valve open pretty soon.

The pressure on the pump line drops, the pressure switch turns the pump on and it adds a gallon or ten to the tank. Not very efficient.

One easy work around on this problem is to lengthen the rod between the float and the actual valve. With one of those CarBoy tanks (plastic tank in a wire cage), you'll have about two and one-half to three feet from one side to the other. So just get length of rod— brass or stainless—and make the float rod reach almost across the tank. Remember that it will hang down at about a 22° angle before the valve opens. In a 250-gallon CarBoy, that should let you use down to maybe 50 gallons before the pump comes on.

A level sensing magnetic switch would be a better choice if you can manage it. That way, you could use down to say, one-fourth or one-eighth tank before the pump is turned on by a relay. This will use less juice.

For the most part, you can pipe domestic cold water through ½" or ¾" PVC pipe. But outside, you need to bury the pipe _below the frost line_ or use heat tape and insulate it to prevent freezing where it is exposed.

Below the frost line means eighteen inches deep in North Georgia and thirty-six inches deep in New Hampshire, so check with the local building authority to find out what it is in your BoL location. It's just a harmless question that tells you a lot about the climate in the area and gives nothing away about your location or intent.

For the compound, you will be supplying four or more families, so you need a lot of water. I should think that two 250-gallon tanks should suffice. This gives enough reserve to allow your pumping system from the creek or well to catch up, because I am sure that there will be times when your demand will outstrip your supply. Especially if you are using a ram pump to move water from a creek to the house.

Keep in mind that if you are using a bored well with in well pump, and a pressure tank, you cannot use a storage tank. The entire system is under pressure from the pressure tank.

If you have two 250-gallon tanks plumbed in parallel, that would mean the compound households could use 250–400 total gallons before the pump comes on and puts it back in the tanks. Water is so vital to existence that you should really do your homework thoroughly on this one. If the tanks have a large bore connection, like 1½» pipe, you need put a float valve on only one tank and the other will fill through the crossover pipe.

IF you use a ram pump to get water from a creek into a tank, the best bet is to just let the tank(s) fill and then spill the overflow BACK to the creek through something like 1¼» well pipe that is cheap and easy to install. You could even tee-off at certain points to provide the possibility of irrigation water for certain crops or animals. Maybe feed an auxiliary tank at the barn! Just _don't_ valve off a ram pump.

Well, shame on me. I forgot to talk about how to get water from a creek that is _below_ the level of the house. First off, there is the ram pump.

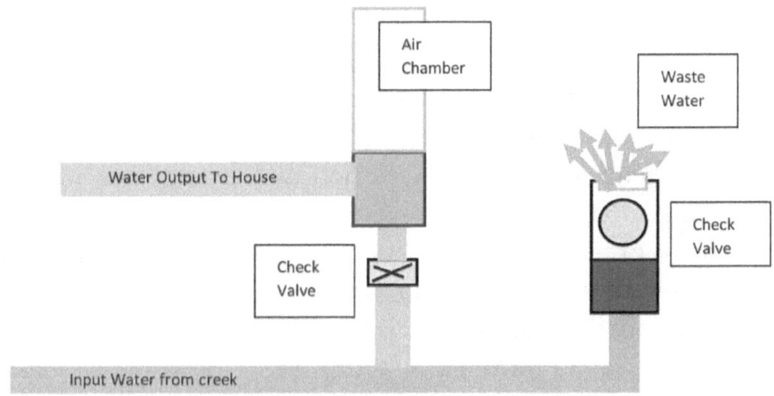

It is inefficient, but who cares, it's free water, it uses no energy and it works 24-7 without a coffee break. Simple to build, easy to maintain. You just need a few feet of head from the stream to power it. You can let the wastewater run right back into the stream.

The ram pump works because of the air chamber. The sizing of the air chamber is key. Water rushes in from the stream. The increase of pressure forces the wastewater valve (on right) closed. This forces the water to exit through the water drive check valve on the left. Water going up will force some into the delivery pipe and some into the air chamber, compressing the air in the chamber. When the pressure in the air chamber equals the pressure of the water in the delivery pipe, the drive valve closes, letting the waste valve open and spill.

28

Supplies

Wow. This might just be the toughest chapter of the book. For both of us. There is SO much that the title covers, and the list changes with every different person who is planning for the end. But let's give it a try. Don't forget that everything I list here is just a suggestion.

If you intend to take this suggestion, you better stock up for a fifty-year run. OR MORE. Feel free to pick and choose from these lists. Also, this list is by no means intended to be all-inclusive. I'll bet a dollar against a doughnut hole in multiples of a dozen that as soon as I turn this loose to the publisher, I'll think of a hundred things I left out of this list. So put on your thinking cap and add to it. You will want *multiples* of everything here. Some types will need more redundancy than others. Think about what will wear and what will break and need replacing. Think fifty years or longer.

Tools

Hammers

Curved claw	Framing	2# Sledge	12# Sledge
Ball Pein	Rubber	Soft-face brick	Dead blow
Tack	Tinner's	Rubber mallet	Flat Pein

Hand Saws

Crosscut	Rip cut	Back	Bow
Hack	Two-man	Coping	Compass
Keyhole	Scroll		

Other Saws

Seven-and-a-half-inch electric circular saw with rip, crosscut and ply-wood blades and metal and stone cut off blades (*LOTS* of blades!)
Table saw?
Radial arm saw?

Chain saw—minimum 18" bar   with spare bars and chains
Extensible pruning saw   Loping shear
Pruning shears

Other Tools

You will need a collection of regular mechanics tools, like:
Sockets and ratchets, in drive sizes ¼", 3/8", and ½"
Regular and deep well sockets, standard and metric
Combination wrenches, standard and metric
Specialty sockets like 1½» and others
Screwdrivers, Philips, Flat, Torx, Allen, Star, and Security
Allen wrench assortment—standard and metric
Scrapers and putty knives
Wire brushes, wire wheels for drills,
Crow bars, wrecking bars, and pry bars of various sizes
Pinch bars
Nail pullers and wonder bars
Vise grip plier assortment—two each min
Regular slip joint pliers six inches, ten inches

Channel lock plier assortment from four to fourteen inches at least
I would even want pipe wrenches in six, ten, fourteen, eighteen,
twenty-four inches
Crescent wrench assortment, four to fourteen inches
Twelve-volt test light
Needle nose pliers
Diagonal wire cutters of various sizes
Tin snips, left, right, and straight
Hand tongs for bending sheet metal
Fencing pliers

Digging And Ground Work

Shovel	Spade	Mattock	Pick axe
Paddle hoe	Warren hoe	Onion hoe	
Scuffle (loop) hoe	Heart hoe		
Garden (or BOW) rake		Lawn rake	Leaf rake
Berry rake		Post hole digger	
Axe, single bit			Axe, double bit
Hatchet			Axe, Bush
Sling blade			Scythe
Sickle			Machete

Ladders

Four foot, six foot, ten foot and fourteen foot aluminum step
Twenty foot and forty foot aluminum extension
A-Frame twenty feet, thirty feet
Same in wood or fiberglass

Gloves:

Leather palm work

Grip enhancing (gorilla grip)

Chemical resistant

SAFETY GLASSES

Jersey (hundreds of pairs!)

Rubber kitchen

Surgical (THOUSANDS)

Drills and Accessories

Wood chisels from 1/8" to 1½"

Cold chisels from ¼" to ¾"

Brace and bit drill with bit sets

Twist drill bits—get sets of at least sixteen-piece assortments

Long twist drill bits 18" long by ¼", 3/8", and ½" diameter

Wood paddle bits assortment 3/16" to 1½"

Corded 3/8" VSR drill

Corded ½" Impact drill

Cordless 3/8" VSR drills with spare batteries

Hex Shank Screwdriver bits for drills—Phillips, flat, Torx, Allen, square bit

Brick Chisels 1", 2"

Planting auger

Corded ½" drill

Consumable Supplies

Electrical tape

Teflon tape

Spray paints

Paint brushes

Stains and lacquers

Duct tape

Wood glue

Thread lock compound

Paint thinners

Masking tape

Thread sealant

Interior paint

Exterior paint   Paint brushes

Sand paper in various grits from 80 to 600

Gasket material   Plumbing solder

Electronics solder   Silver solder (6 or 5 percent)

Glues—wood, super, rubber cement, contact cement

Wire—16-ga lamp cord—5,000' minimum

#14/2 WG Romex—several thousand feet

#12/2 WG Romex—several thousand feet

#10/2 WG Romex same

#4,6,8—1,000'ea

#12 THHN 4,000 to 8,000 feet

Fuses for cars, trucks, equipment

Ten-, 12-, 14-, and 16-ga primary wire (for auto and equipment wiring)

NOTE: Lengths for wire are suggestions only. If you plan well enough, you will know to within probably one hundred feet exactly how much of each type you will need.

NOTE: The adhesive on tapes will decay and dry over time, rendering the tape useless. I suspect, but have not tried, the Nitro-Pak routine with tape. Put the tape in a zip lock or plastic ammo box and preserve it as described in a previous chapter. If you open the container to take some out, be sure to repack it with nitrogen.

Hardware

Nails, common 16d, 12d, 8d, 4d, finish

Nails, CC Sinker   16d, 12d, 8d

Screws, grabber   1½", 2", 2½", 3", 4"

Lag bolts, screws and eyes

Assortments of bolts from #10 to ½" with nuts, flat washers, and lock washers

Worm clamps up to four inches   Grommet repair kit

Lock, gate

Hinges, door

Hinges, gate

Spring assortments

Felt paper for roofing

Roofing nails, roofing screws

Ropes nylon from ¼" to ½"

Chains, proof, 3/16" to ½" 2–50' lengths each

Split bolts to connect large wire—several dozen assorted

O-ring assortments

Hinges, "T"

Lock, door

Snap ring assortments

Metal for roofing

Wire nuts all sizes

Ropes, hemp, 3/8" to ¾"

Equipment

Seed spreader   Wagons, carts, hand trucks

Pulleys, ropes, clinches

Food grade polypropylene tanks for water

Polypropylene tanks for fuels

Nitrogen tanks, regulator, hoses

For the nitrogen tanks, you can get larger 125 cubic feet versions

Small gauge 110-volt wire welder

Oxyacetylene welding kit with spare tanks

Fire extinguishers—10#, 25# ABC Type

Garden hose, 5/8" × 25', 50', 100'

Pulleys, block, and tackle   Come-along

Ratchet straps, bungee straps   Inline water filters

Tack, trace, harness, and saddles for horses and mules

Shoes, nails, and farrier tools for horses and mules

Generators   Generator heads

Truck alternators

Deep cycle marine batteries—preferably dry charge with acid separate

Battery chargers 8–10 amps, 100–150 amps

Air compressor, 5 hp 50 gal, and 2-gal pancake

V belts, tires, tubes, hoses, spark plugs, fuel filters, oil filters, air filters
for all equipment

Reasonable spare parts for each piece of equipment, including ignition coils, spark plugs, pulleys, woodruff keys, clips and pins

Electronics/Electrical

Handheld radios   Handheld GPS Scanners
Base and mobile radios with antennae
Voltmeters   Oscilloscope
Soldering equipment for electronics
Hand tools for electronics
Television   VCR   DVD/BluRay player
Satellite dish and receiver
HD antenna and set top box
Junction boxes and covers
Electrical device boxes (switch)
Receptacles, switches

Pipe And Others

PVC, schedule 40–¾", 1", 2", 4"   PEX–½"
ABS well pipe, 1¼"
PVC electrical conduit ¾", 1", 2"
Hose bibs–¾" FPT × MGH
Couplings, elbows, adapters for above
Plumbing check valves
Rolled soft copper tubing (RST) ¼", 3/8", ½", 5/8", ¾" with couplings, tees, reducers, adapters to pipe thread

Petroleum Products And Others

Motor oil in various weight Two-cycle oil
Chainsaw bar oil
Wheel Bearing Grease, 1# can 90 Wt Axle Grease
WD 40 Axle Grease in cartridge gun
Fuel treatments Oil treatments
Various penetrating lubricants
Thread lock compound
RectorSeal pipe thread sealant
Teflon tape pipe thread sealant Antifreeze

Crops

Agave Asparagus Barley
Beans, lima, pinto, Great Northern, soy, green (several varieties)
Beet Broccoli Carrots
Celery Chard Chilis
Corn Cotton Flax
Hemp Kale
Lettuce—several varieties
Honey dew melon, watermelon, cantaloupe
Mustard Oats
Onion—white, yellow, red, sweet, green, scallion
Parsnip Peanuts
Peas, green, black-eyed, etc.
Peppers bell—red, green, yellow, orange, chili

Potato, Idaho white, sweet, red, yellow
Rice Turnip Wheat
Rutabaga Rye Strawberry Sugar Beet

Sugar Cane   Sunflower   Tomato

HERBS

Basil   Bay laurel   Caraway
Catnip   Chives   Cilantro
Dill   Fennel   Garlic
Lavender   Marjoram (sweet)   Mint
Oregano   Rosemary   Sage
Sorrel   Taragon   Thyme

Vanilla planifolia, flower. It's actually an ORCHID. But it can be done. This is where you get vanilla beans

Trees And Bushes

Almond   Apple   Apricot
Banana   Blackberry   Blueberry
cherry   Cocoa   Coffee
Fig   Hazelnut   Peach
Pear   Pecan   Lemon
Lime   Nectarine   Orange
pineapple   Plum   Raspberry
Walnut

Canning And Preserving Supplies

Glass jars, ½ pt, pint, quart with rings and lids
—four lids and rings for each jar minimum
Jar lifters   Cooling racks   Gelatin
Pressure cookers   Magnetic lid lifter Canning funnel cornstarch
Pectin

Animals

Chickens	Rabbits	Ducks	Beef cattle
Goats	Horses	Mules	Pigs
Donkey	Sheep	Turkey	Fish

Medical

Alcohol (hundreds of gallons)	Hydrogen peroxide
Triple antibiotic cream	Cortisone cream
Rolled gauze (Kerlix)	Gauze pads (2 × 2 and 4 × 4)
Antibiotics	Paper tape
Surgical tape	Splints, reusable
Casting materials	Super glue
Surgical tools	Suture supplies
Dental kit	Band-Aids

Household Goods

Zip lock bags	Aluminum foil	Utensils
Parchment paper	Knives	
Cooking oil	Yeast, baker's	Yeast, brewer's
Wax paper	Pots and pans	Toilet paper
Spices, flavorings, and herbs		Sheets
Laundry soap	Bath soap	Towels
Face cloths	Hand towels	Kitchen towels
Blankets pillows	Cleaning supplies	Brushes
Toothbrushes	Toothpaste	Denture supplies
Razors	Shaving cream	Hair grooming
Reusable ice packs	Heating pads	Sewing supplies
Sewing patterns	Sanitary supplies	Cloth for sewing

| Scissors | Toys for kids | Coloring books/crayons |
| Cloth diapers | Diaper pins | Diaper pail |

Random Info To Research

HOW TO MAKE: vinegar, mayo, mustard, ketchup, other condiments, cider, butter, beer, wine, soap, Portland cement

STOCK UP ON: toilet paper, soap for bathing, laundry and dishes, salt, pepper, baking soda, and powder

LEARN HOW TO: shoe horses, work and care for draft animals, general blacksmithing, build without nails, tan leather, make leather products like tack and trace for draught animals.

Find, identify, mine, and process various substances like salt and ores, tan and preserve animal skins, make leather, spin yarn, weave cloth

GAME SUPPLIES: balls, nets, gloves, bats, helmets

Board games   Card games

Fishing rods, reels and tackle

Grinders for meat, sausage stuffers

You can use electric but also have hand crank versions JIC

Hand crank ice cream maker. If you have a refrigerator and a countertop ice maker, you have ice cream

Guns And Metal

My purpose here, like elsewhere, is to make you think about the subject a little and then get to researching and thinking.

The ability to make your own gunpowder could well be very handy down the road. It is nothing more than charcoal, sulfur and saltpeter, or potassium nitrate, which is found in nature as NITRE. What you need to know is how to identify the materials, where to find them, how to treat them and turn them into usable materials and also the recipe for gunpowder.

As for metals, you want info on how to find, identify, and purify the ores that make iron, tin, and copper. Maybe coal, too. You need that to make coke for a hot forge fire. You will need to know how to smelt and purify metals that you mine. What do you need to do this?

More Items You Need To Stock Up On

Measuring utensils—measuring cups—mixing bowls—cooking utensils—mixers—blenders—food processors—sewing machines with spare parts and oil—juicers—blenders—hand soap—laundry soap—dish soap—starch—bleach—washboards—corn starch—flour—corn meal—cooking pots and pans—printer paper—printer ink—rechargeable batteries—filters and filter media for water, fuel, air

Don't forget hobby items and games. Down time will be important.

29

Barter

Well, when it all comes down, we will all pull through. But there will be no more money. No way to keep score. No set prices for anything. How do I buy that nice bay from farmer Jones? I know! I'll BARTER with him!

Well, you're going to be very lucky if you just have enough stuff stockpiled on your property to keep you and yours happy and healthy for the next thirty years. What are you going to barter WITH?

Try to think of anything you might be willing to trade for goods or services later. Particularly things that will very hard to come by after The Fall. The simplest of things can be valuable. Like cigarette lighters, book matches, strike anywhere matches. Light bulbs? Cigarettes? Tobacco? Cigarette papers? Vanilla extract that you grew and processed?

There will likely be some exchange between "neighbors" once things settle down some, but it will not be of the sort we know now. The big difference is the fact that under our current economy, things have a definite value, that value having been agreed upon before time. A chicken dressed and ready to cook is worth about $2 per pound right now. But if there is no government, there is no valid monetary unit of exchange and therefore no agreed upon price for goods and services.

Every transaction, therefore, must be negotiated on its own merits, on a case-by-case basis. The value of the items exchanged *on both sides* of the equation are variables that each party must decide upon. Some of the things that you can pretty much count on having value will be gemstones and precious metals like gold and silver. The reason for this is portability.

Sure, you might be able to trade a wagon for four bushels of barley, but how many people will be carrying four bushels of barley around in their pocket? Enter the exchange rate. This much silver is equal to that much barley. Or one wagon.

That is the main reason that I am a proponent of precious metals collecting. I am particularly fond of silver. I have a fairly large collection of Pre-1964 US coins, because they are 90 percent silver. Admittedly, there are other ways of holding silver in today's market. I suppose I just find these esthetically more pleasing than a bar of silver, and I also believe that they will only rise in value, <u>not</u> because of their silver content but also because of their rarity.

Bars of silver are not that rare. Whatever the rhyme or reason, I think bars will be an impractical means of exchange, and difficult to break down into smaller pieces. So I will stick with silver coins of whatever type, even if they are commemorative strikings. As long as they are high silver content. When things return to normal in fifty years, silver will still be silver. Currently you can still buy sheets of one-gram gold pieces. That could work.

With that said about gems and metals, I guarantee that if YOU are growing COFFEE, you are going to VERY popular! Same with LOTS of things on my lists, like vanilla orchids. You will be blown away by how many people will want vanilla beans or, better yet, processed vanilla essence. It is VERY popular in baking, you know.

30

Drone, Drone On The Range

The first few drafts of this book somehow overlooked this vital subject. "I don't KNOW _why_, Miss Scarlett, I just _dropped_ the baby." Thanks, Butterfly McQueen, for one of the most memorable and useful movie lines ever.

By now, almost the entire world knows about drones. Drones of all sizes, types, and functions. "Drone" actually means a mindless worker that does their job tirelessly, endlessly, and repeatedly. Think of worker bees. They are called drones. Or hamburger flippers in a fast food joint. Mind-numbing endless repetition of the same task day in and day out. Drones.

A drone can be anything from a palm sized (or _smaller!_) "quadcopter" with four or more fans providing lift and direction, all the way up to the military's predator drones, pilotless airplanes capable of flying hundreds of miles and either providing intelligence or delivering payloads, such as gunfire or bombs. But somewhere in between those two extremes are some very useful little devices. Actually, ALL of them can be used in some fashion, for some purpose. Even if it is only for distraction.

For instance: If you have a band of miscreants on your trail in the woods while you are bugging out, let a few of your teenagers fall behind, uphill, upwind (if possible) and ten to twenty yards off the trail, with two or four small drones. They can place the drones on the edge of the trail and wait for the enemy to get there. Suddenly, the drones pop up, flying all around the troop. Falling, climbing, ducking behind them, flying at them. Can't you see the chaos! It will look like the Three Stooges as they try to swat them away, bat them down with their rifles or shoot them down. And as soon as it starts, you just mow them down with withering fire from the bushes.

If one of them decides to shoot back, your pilot sends a drone straight at his face. If your pilot is good, he might even develop a control program that can command three or four drones at a time, sending them flying about like a swarm of midges, circling and darting about one central point (where the prey is located) without any further intervention.

That would be an excellent use for the smaller drones. For other things, you might want some bigger units. And consider that almost all drones have some kind of video capability. The smaller ones usually record onto a memory card, but some have streaming video available. THAT is what you really want. A drone about twelve to eighteen inches square with a flight time of maybe thirty to sixty minutes, a range of a half mile or more and streaming video that works on either its own individual screen on the controller or maybe transmits to a cell phone. I prefer the former.

Keep in mind your cell phone might not be working where or when you need it most. A control mounted screen would be best. This type of unit might set you back several hundred clams, but it would be a worthwhile investment, as you will soon see. I would also like to recommend that you get one that has infrared or night vision capabilities also. Never can tell when THAT might come in handy!

Now let's look briefly at some of the other things we have discussed previously and apply the use of drones to those scenarios. First, the BoL selection process. You've chosen an area, got your maps and set up camp. Hopefully you brought along a folding camp table. So now you set up you drone command post. Map laid out, remote control set up, coffee at hand. Mark the spot on your map where you are now, check it against the drone's GPS settings for continuity and accuracy. Then you can plan out the drone's route against the map. SOME drones might even have a programmable flight mode where you can tell it to go to 36.48° × 132.324° then head out at 27° for 1,575 feet.

That gets it to the creek. See how this works? Or you could manually control the craft and easily explore the terrain around you. If you're good, if you're smart, figure out a way to share the controller screen to your laptop so your buddies can easily see what you are looking at. Using drones to explore your potential BoL terrain also lets you more easily plan those entry choke points and booby trap locations I wrote about. MUCH easier to do with an aerial view. Then you can go check out the spots that were *really* interesting.

Having a drone at this point can also be handy for several other reasons. If you followed my suggestions and set up perimeter sensors to alert you to the presence of incoming personnel, the drone can be used to investigate. Before you commit to any action. In fact, let's say your camp is located a quarter mile from the road.

I would consider sending a drone out toward the road and parking it in a tall tree. Let it sit there, looking at the entrance to the property from forty feet up. Saves battery, no fan noise to alert the incomers, lots of advantages. Just keep an eye on time or on a battery meter if your system has one. Don't let it run down or you'll have to climb a tree to get your $500 toy back! Another reason to have several!

Now, let's take a look at how to use a drone in a drive-out bug-out situation. IF you followed the advice I gave earlier, you already have some clue about where trouble might find you along the road to your BoL. Those places are marked on the map. Stop your convoy one hill or a quarter mile before that trouble spot. Send a drone to check it out before you blunder into an ambush.

One word of caution here, and this is good advice for ANY scenario where you are spying on potential adversaries: Keep the craft flying as high as practical or possible. Why? Because the higher it is, the less likely it is that its fan noise can be heard on the ground! And that can save your bacon! Use the drone anytime you feel uneasy, like you see a bridge you must cross that has several cars blocking off the middle of the span. Send a drone, send it high.

Next, a quick look at your trail hike. Doesn't matter if this is the TRIAL run or the TRAIL run (LOL), the reasons are the same for using the drone. Whether it is a leisurely jaunt through the woods just checking out cache points and marking your map for that just-in-case-we-have-to-walk thing or if you really ARE bugging out on foot. The process is the same. You WILL be stopping several times per day for rest, food, and toilet breaks. Take these opportunities to launch a medium size drone to scout the area. Particularly up-trail (ahead) and down-trail (behind) you. But if you have the time, also check the sides of the trails, or maybe even over the top of that ridge to your left.

When you stop for the night, set your drone in a safe place AWAY from your campsite, some place where it can get airborne easily, like by just lifting straight up. This way, if something disturbs your sleep or alerts your sentry, the drone can go check it out. Especially if it has night vision or infrared.

Just a reminder: Be on the alert for danger signs the wildlife might share with you. When you first enter the woods, you are a stranger. Everybody in the trees and burrows stops and gets quiet, trying to figure out who you are and why you're there. After a while, it becomes apparent to them that you are not a significant threat, and they will resume their normal life, the chatter will pick back up. From THAT point on, if you hear everything suddenly go quiet, you can be assured that the forest has detected a NEW threat and YOU should be on alert.

Charging the drone could be a challenge on the trail. In the car, not so much, but on the trail, you need some means of charging a high-capacity high-drain battery on the run. It could also come in handy to be able to charge cell phones and walkie-talkies as well.

There are many "survival radios" out there that have a crank-style generator in them, and some offer USB ports for charging your phones. AND drones. It would take a little work and some ingenuity, but that CAN be adapted to other uses. You could also consider carrying one or two small batteries for charging purposes. The kind used on small motorcycles, like dirt bikes. They are small, usually about two-by-five inches and weigh maybe 5#. But they can carry a pretty good amount of electricity for you. Look back to the chapter on POWER if you need a refresher on how to figure out how much you need and how much you can carry. Also, these batteries are

SPILLPROOF! No acid will leak out to ruin your pack or clothing. You might think in terms of a solar panel charging system, also. A little ingenuity will rig a system to carry it on your back while walking so it can recharge the motorcycle battery.

31

Get Used To It

This section is some leftover notes about a few miscellaneous things. But I don't want to throw them out.

There are many, many things that we take for granted in our current day-to-day life. Items that we will NOT have available after TSHTF. The kinds of items that are SO innocuous and ubiquitous that we never even notice them until we run out and don't have a spare handy. Things like paper towels and toilet paper, aluminum foil, zipper storage bags. Basically, anything we would typically term as a "consumable," meaning the act of using it consumes it and it must be replaced. SOME—definitely not ALL—of these things can, with a little forethought and care, be recycled and reused, IF they are recovered from the previous usage without damage. I mean, I don't know about YOU, but I am NOT going to recycle my toilet paper.

Let's take zipper storage bags first, they're definitely easy to recover, recycle, and reuse. It's just a matter of making sure they don't get punctured or torn and then wash and dry them thoroughly. My hardest part of that was always being impatient to open a bag I just took out of the freezer. Just ripping it open usually results in a torn, and now useless, Ziploc® bag.

The issue is that any moisture that was ON the zipper when you closed the bag is now frozen IN the zipper and holding it tightly closed. If the item is something I want to use right away, I grab the closure end and slowly move my fingers from one end to the other, letting the warmth of my fingers melt the frozen moisture enough to enable it to turn loose. Then unzip it, remove the contents, annnd Bob's your uncle.

From there, it's just a matter of thoroughly washing the bag and letting it dry. Personally, I find it best to wash the outside with soap and warm water, then carefully turn the bag inside out so I can really get the inside clean. Don't tear the corners! Rinse well and let it dry overnight before turning it right-side out and replacing it in storage.

Aluminum foil is a bit more tricky, but it is doable. The hardest part is un-crimping it from whatever you had it wrapped around. Once you get it loose, use a SOFT hot water spray to remove loose particles and liquid greases, then gently wipe it down with a hot water and soap cloth, and rinse. Once I get it pretty well dry, I put it on a cutting pad and smooth it out as much as possible. Let it air-dry and place in storage for another use. I have managed to get as many as ten uses from a single piece. I believe you can do better if you plan at it and work at it. But you will probably want to stockpile as much as possible. And THEN, use it *sparingly*.

So what you see here is that with a little thought, you can manage to get a lot of extra life out of almost anything. You *will* need to. I would also recommend that you try to stockpile as much as possible of those durable consumables. NOT paper goods.

I was raised in an era when we did not _have_ paper towels. In fact, I was probably six or seven years old before I ever saw toilet paper! Seriously! We lived in one of those areas where a nighttime trip to the bathroom involved shoes and a small kerosene lantern. No kidding! A two-holer outhouse and you wiped your bum with newspaper or catalog pages.

WE did not HAVE paper towels back then! My grandma used cloth towels for everything, and they took meticulous care of those things. Kitchen cloths were rinsed and hung on a rack to dry immediately after each use. They will stay usable for days at a time before they need to be washed.

As for toilet paper? About the ONLY substitute for that little item is a bidet. That's a French innovation that washes your backside for cleaning. Then you can dry with a cloth that is then washed. Simple, but a lot of people will find it distasteful until they get acclimated to the idea. There's plenty of info out there about bidets and how to use them. There are also personal portable versions that are _very_ handy. With that, you do not need a pressurized water system. They can even be used on the trail or at camp.

Water is also something that can be recovered, recycled, and reused. Your _need_ to do this will, of course, depend in large part upon the availability and dependability of your fresh water supply. Judicious water usage and control can get you through some tough spots of drought, if they don't last too long, and it will at least stretch your available water longer in those times.

Be sure to have a water rationing plan ready to go at all times and have everyone trained in its use and implementation. This will be especially difficult if you set up a pressurized water delivery system that is close to what you had before the End. Everyone will still be used to using water like it is an inexhaustible supply. That is a hard habit to break. But the sad truth is that even your water supply is fragile and apt to dry up at any time. So plan to survive through it. Most of these occurrences can be expected to return to normal pretty soon. But plan.

Sewage, of course, will get recycled through your septic system. If you have followed my suggestions and have a separate drain system for your grey water, then you are in good shape to recover at least 50 percent of your water. Recycled gray water can be used for many things like watering crops, washing equipment, animals, stalls, etc.

I'm not real sure I would want to bath in it, and I certainly won't cook with it or wash my dishes in it without some serious filtration and treatment. Which is to say that water CAN be totally recycled if you put enough effort into the job.

Even for watering crops and washing hands, I would want my gray water to at _least_ be thoroughly filtered. Recall that when I was talking about water systems, I described how to filter and treat the water you draw from a creek or well. For MY money, I would have two filtration systems. One would be dedicated to treating the gray water. IF POSSIBLE, the gray water should first go to a baffled sedimentation tank.

That will let the water slow down enough for those invisible particles to settle out. After that, you can pump the water through a sand filter. At this point, it is fit for most uses, but it is definitely not potable yet. To get it clean enough for all uses, it needs to go through the filter system and then a germicidal treatment. Probably the most logical type of germicide for you is going to be a UV light system. They are readily available and very effective, but you WILL need electricity to operate it. And be sure to observe the operating instructions, especially flow rate.

The UV has to impinge on the water for a certain amount of time in order to do its job. This time varies with the wattage if the unit. Flow rate, in gallons per minute (GPM), can only be controlled by pump speed or a valve. All of this is discussed in the instructions.

Things You WILL Be Giving Up

Internet—radio—television—newspapers—deliveries—consumable goods—fuels—electricity—fuel gas (propane/natural gas)—replacement parts for anything—tires—oils and greases—staple foods like flour and meal—batteries—paper products—building supplies—community ties—city water and sewer—church/religious affiliations—emergency services like police, fire/rescue and ambulance—medical services

32

The Final Word

Well, all good things must come to an end, yes? And this book is no exception. I truly hope that you have enjoyed reading this book as much as I enjoyed writing it. Nineteen times. My objective was to share as much of the life experiences and knowledge that I have gained in sixty-eight years as I possibly could. The rest is up to you. If this book has gotten you thinking more critically about your situation now and in the possible future, then I have done my job.

But to recap a few high points, please allow me to remind you of a few things:

Start choosing your tribe as soon as possible. Try to gather an assortment of skillsets that complement each other and benefit both your tribe and possibly the surrounding community as well. If you are past your prime, as am I, you should definitely shoot for people who are much younger. Put *your* years of experience to use leading, teaching, and directing the group.

But if you are a sixty- to seventy-year-old physician and wish to embark on this journey, go for it, Doc. Be sure to choose someone for your pack that you can train to take your place within five years and who will then be capable of passing the skill on. Gather your textbooks and teach. Please don't spend too much time on how to name the multitude of ligaments and muscles. How much can the name actually affect treatment, anyway? Okay, in a few cases, it can. But think back to med school and remember how much you hated that part of the training, okay?

No matter who you are, what you do, or how old you are, there are still certain things you absolutely must do. One is to keep your mouth shut. Don't tell anyone about your plans unless you are sure they will fit in and want to join your clan.

Two is to start getting ready RIGHT now. Even before you put your pack together, discuss this with your spouse and then the kids. Only if you have the entire family four-square behind you can you hope to pull this off. Start training everyone to keep quiet about it. Train to shoot. Train to observe. Train to fight. And most important, train to act and think like a team.

Three, start gathering information. NOW. Get everyone to devote <u>at least</u> one hour a day to research for the project. Preferably more. That could result in twenty to forty man-hours *per* day of research getting done when it is spread around the whole tribe. Remember that warning to never store anything on a thumb drive? Well, if you're working at your office on research, you're going to have to put it on a thumb drive to get it home.

Many companies these days have keyloggers following each employee's computer usage. You might get fired if your boss does this. Unless you know how to turn it off. *Wink, wink.* If Johnny is working on his laptop, it has to go on a thumb drive so it can be transferred to the main computer. Point is, I *would* use a thumb drive for a quick transfer. What choice do you have?

That bit got me to thinking back to the early '90s. I was programming one of the first point of sale systems. HUGE project. Six people working on individual parts of the system, and they all had to come together daily for a trial run. Intra-office computer system communication was still in its infancy. Getting computers to talk to each other was a mess. So everyone would save their work to a floppy disk and physically walk it to the head guy (me) for integration. We called it "Sneaker Net" since we couldn't get the Ethernet to work half the time.

Your time might best be spent putting together the lists, at this stage. Walk through hardware stores taking notes. You and Mom walk through the grocery taking notes. Look online for oddball catalogs, off-grid living websites, alternative healing methods. Where to get training in things you do not know, like how to work horses. Or medicine.

Make spreadsheets to track the websites you visit and what they offer. Have a file to hold your login and password for each site. Like an Excel spreadsheet. Set up a blind email account to register all these places with. Try to NOT leave an electronic trail that would lead to your physical address. Maybe use a forwarding service for things you buy online. It ships to them. They ship it to you. You _can_ overthink this part, so try to not.

Start gathering what you can right away, even if it is just one shovel. The sooner you start, the larger the time span you can spread the financial load over.

Assemble your bug-out bags _right_ now. And get your guns as soon as possible. You want to be going to the shooting range at least once a week. Lots of indoor ranges have family nights and date nights and all sorts of special gatherings. One of the best things you can do to improve your shooting is to compete in a bracket match. I used to shoot in one every week. But keep in mind that **target proficiency does NOT equal COMBAT proficiency!** The whole world changes when you are being shot at.

Understand that things will change drastically. You canNOT store enough toilet paper to last fifty years. Think about bidets or sink-type sprayers for washing your backside. Or get used to wiping with cloth and then washing it. Things are gonna change. You cannot avoid it.

Make new friends, go new places, feel people out, and see how they feel about the government, the world economy, Disneyland's latest ride, The End Of The World As We Know It, whatever. Change your life up a bit. Get out of your comfort zone. Turn off the TV. Throw away your paper. Don't be afraid to talk to folks once you feel them out a bit.

But most of all, practice. Everybody. All. The. Time. Practice. Practice radio skills, silent communication, tracking, and evading. Being silent without being bored.

Learn. Grow. Move.

Check out www.ldsavow.com for some great survival stuff. This is the Mormon Church. I mention it NOT because I follow their doctrine. I do not. I have my OWN beliefs, thank you. I mention them because they have done one of the best jobs of assembling and preparing information for the *end time*.

There are _hundreds_ of other prepper sites to see also. Be careful, be choosy about what you believe and what you do. Remember that you are looking mostly for HOW to do things. I have pretty much given you WHAT you need to look for. Not that there's nothing more to see or discuss, but I do believe this book has pretty much covered it all.

In the immortal words of Leslie Nielson:

Good luck. We're all counting on you.
Thomas Moore

About the Author

Tom has spent his 68 years learning, building, and doing. He has been a computer programmer, mechanical and electrical engineer & contractor, corporate management specialist, systems analyst, inventor, a world class multi-instrument rock musician and an A-1 rated audio & recording engineer.

These days Tom spends his spare time immersed in science fiction movies and books, dabbling in small engineering projects and making useful little nonsensical things with his 3D printer. Occasionally he will still climb onto a stage somewhere with some old friends and whip out some rocking Texas/Chicago style Blues. He lives in Tennessee as loyal servant to two cats and a German Sheppard/Irish Wolf Hound mix.

www.ingramcontent.com/pod-product-compliance
Lightning Source LLC
Chambersburg PA
CBHW051040250726
48656CB00001B/69